"...that I may be in after years an ornament to Society and the delight of my dear parents."

Maggie N. Vaulx
January 27th, 1862

Maggie

The Civil War Journals of Margaret N. Vaulx

Ross E. Hudgins

Ideas into Books: WESTVIEW®
Kingston Springs, Tennessee

Maggie: The Civil War Journals of Margaret N. Vaulx

© 2011 Ross E. Hudgins
All rights reserved, including the right to reproduction in whole or in part in any form.

ISBN 978-1-935271-76-5 Perfect Bound
ISBN 978-1-935271-77-2 Case Laminate

Third Edition with Index, March 2018

All sketches by Pepper Mayfield.

The author gratefully acknowledges assistance and resources from the Tennessee State Library and Archives, Nashville.

Printed in the United States of America on acid free paper.

IDEAS INTO BOOKS: WESTVIEW®
P.O. Box 605
Kingston Springs, TN 37082
www.publishedbywestview.com

This book is dedicated to:

My wonderful wife, Marsha.
Her help and support was a must and deeply appreciated.

The memory of my grandfather, Earl W. Marshall.
He rescued the journals; without him this book would not be with us.

My dear friend Catharine.
Prior to this, she "never had a book dedicated to her," but she does now.

Thanks to:

George and Pepper Mayfield, along with their group, the Southern Sons & Daughters. Pepper's sketches helped Maggie's story come alive.

My children; Rosha, Stacy, Joseph, Brayton and Katie.
For over thirty-five years, Maggie's journals were stored in the bottom of our grandfather clock. The kids, thinking the old clock to be haunted, would not go near it. I never told them that old clocks make noise.

Rick, Rosha and Kayla Spencer, whose support has been invaluable.

Key to Fonts used in Maggie: The Civil War Journals of Margaret N. Vaulx

Maggie's Journal Entries

Text Composed by the Author

Quotations from Barnes' Brief History of the United States

Transcription of Newspaper and Magazine Articles

Photo Captions

Footnotes

Table of Contents

PROLOGUE ix
INTRODUCTION xi
Chapter One - Volume One 1
Chapter Two - Summer, 1861 19
Chapter Three - School, 1861 29
Chapter Four - The Panic 35
Chapter Five - Ensconced at Aunt Jane's 45
Chapter Six - Ensconced at Hedge Lawn 73
Chapter Seven - Stones River 109
Chapter Eight - Home at Last 133
Chapter Nine - Volume Two 153
Chapter Ten - Homesick at South Side Institute, 1863 159
Chapter Eleven - Summer, 1864 189
Chapter Twelve - Hood's Assault on Tennessee 209
Chapter Thirteen - The Battle for Nashville 221
Chapter Fourteen - Nashville, the Aftermath 233
Chapter Fifteen - The War's End 241
Chapter Sixteen - Lincoln 253
Chapter Seventeen - The Homecoming 257
Chapter Eighteen - Volumes Five and Six 277
EPILOGUE 279
APPENDIX ONE: Maggie's Notes 283
APPENDIX TWO: The Jackson Building 295
APPENDIX THREE: Index 299
BIBLIOGRAPHY 309
ABOUT THE AUTHOR 311

Prologue

In 1862, a 17-year-old girl growing up in what is now the Berry Hill area off Franklin Pike in Nashville, Tennessee, during a time of great national strife wrote the following words, *"that I may be in after years an ornament to society and the delight of my dear parents."* Margaret Nichol Vaulx came of age during the American Civil War and has left us writing which is that very ornament which she so prophetically spoke of. Margaret, hereafter known as Maggie, was indeed the delight of her dear parents and of future Vaulx generations. Maggie's journals have been described as both national and state treasures, and as one Belmont University journalism instructor said,[1] "she can be compared to a Civil War Anne Frank." Even though Maggie identified her journals as private, I believe that she would approve of them being read, studied, and pondered over by all who confess to love God, family, and innocence of youth.

The aim of this historical narrative is to allow Maggie's writings show the reader what effects the Civil War had on the lives of citizens of her day. To better illustrate Maggie's realization of the times, a brief history of the war is provided beginning with the secession of seven Southern states and ending just after the unfortunate assassination of President Abraham Lincoln. This account covers mostly the Western theater of the war. The source of this history is researched from the 1885 edition of A. S. Barnes' *A Brief History of the United States*. To aid the reader, guide notes have been provided after Barnes and just prior to Maggie's actual entries. Words in brackets are either added or edited for clarification. The guide notes, footnotes, pictures, and sketches are not part of the original manuscripts.

I have often been asked the same three questions regarding my relationship to these journals. In response to question number one, I am not related to Maggie or any other member of the family, although over the past years, I have had some contact with her living descendants. As to the second question, how I got the books; in 1961, my grandfather, Earl W. Marshall, was getting ready to tear down an old barn. Before the barn could be removed, the contents had to be taken out including several crates of old books, which were tossed aside. Their final fate would have most definitely been eventual decay. Being a lover of

---

[1] Stephan Foust, Belmont University New Century Journalism Instructor.

anything looking old, I opened the crates and found assorted volumes of mostly nonfiction books.[2] There were copies of the official records of the War of Rebellion, books on the life and times of Andrew Jackson, United States history books including Barnes' *A Brief History of the United States*,[3] and most importantly, four of the journals of Maggie N. Vaulx. These immediately caught my eye, and after some quick negotiations with my grandfather, I went into the barn-tearing-down business for the wage of two crates of old books. A great deal for my grandfather; but for me, a treasure which I have held on to for almost fifty years.

The third thing people want to know is how the books got in the barn. In the late 1940's, my grandfather was the last building superintendent of the Jackson Building in downtown Nashville. According to the Nashville City Directory, the building housed business offices and also rented rooms as private residences. There were at least 39 apartments. There is no way of knowing how many of the residents of either the apartments or the offices might have known of Maggie, which one had ownership of the journals at the time the building was razed, how the journals might have come into their possession, or why the journals were left behind when the building was condemned. What we do know is that they were abandoned in the Jackson Building sometime between May and August of 1949 after the decision had been made by the owners to sell. The building had to be vacated in time for the wrecking ball, so the local papers ran stories, and occupants were notified of the decision in order to give them time to remove all personal or business property which they still had in the building.[4] My grandfather told me that when the time to do so had expired, everything left behind became his responsibility to discard. He loaded up everything that looked interesting, and the old barn in Fairview became a storage area until we tore it down. These amazing books, which originally belonged to Maggie one hundred and fifty years ago, were eventually abandoned in the Jackson Building almost ninety years later, only to be rescued for the first time in 1950 by my grandfather, and then eleven years later, for the second time, by me.

I have had great joy in putting this book together. I know that it will provide equal enjoyment for you, its reader.

Ross E. Hudgins
Fairview, Tennessee

---

[2] These books are believed to have been owned by Maggie. See the March 13, 1862 journal entry.
[3] Barnes, *A Brief History of the United States* by Joel Dorman Steel, P.H.D, F.G.S and Esther Baker Steele, Lit.D., published by the American Book Company, New York, NY, copyright 1885, is used throughout this work as Civil War source reference.
[4] These two newspaper articles can be found in Appendix Two.

Introduction

The American Civil War grew from strife and division as old as the union itself. Slavery, the state of one person being owned by another, had been debated from the very time that Thomas Jefferson penned the words, "We hold these truths to be self-evident, that all men are created equal, that they are endowed by their Creator with certain unalienable rights, that among these are life, liberty and the pursuit of happiness." To some, slavery cut into that hallowed American document as a two-edged sword. To others, slavery was a necessary way of life which had to be protected at all means. These two prevailing thoughts would arise again and again until they would culminate in the union being threatened with severance. Slavery, the underlying cause, led to the question of states' rights. Does a state have the right to dissolve its union if it feels freedoms outlined in the Federal Constitution are being violated? Over the years the nation's problems grew and as states were added to the federal union, the question of slavery would often raise its ugly head. Due to the commerce of the day, with the Northern states being industrialized while the Southern states remained mostly an agricultural society, the need for Slavery would naturally become a concern. The 1860 Presidential election of Abraham Lincoln caused the Southern states to feel their way of life was threatened. This fear along with the prevailing thoughts of states' rights resulted in eleven southern states seceding from the federal union. It started with South Carolina and ended with Tennessee in June 1861. The stage had been set and dark clouds of war would blanket the nation for the next four years. On February 4, 1861, the congress of the Confederacy met in Montgomery, Alabama and elected Jefferson Davis as the first president of the Confederate States of America. His inauguration took place in February 1861 with Lincoln's following in March. One nation was now divided over issues and sadly bent on war.

Both sides of the conflict had plans to win the war. The Southern leaders recognized that they were outnumbered in terms of population. Their economy was agricultural with very little industrial ability, and they knew that the fighting would be largely on their soil. They hoped this would lead to personal patriotism from both military and citizens alike. They planned on obtaining some quick and decisive victories which would prompt the Northern people to quickly lose hope and sue for peace. They needed outside aid from Europe, and they envisioned that success on the battlefields would gain them worldwide recognition and support from other nations.

In turn, the Northern leaders merely hoped to survive the opening months of the war until their industrial strength could make a difference. They felt that once it did, the South would not be able to keep up with supplies and men. On May 3, 1861, General Winfield Scott proposed his Anaconda Plan, which called for the Federals taking control of the Mississippi River in conjunction with a coastal blockade of Southern ports. This blockade would limit the export of valuable crops of rice, tobacco, and cotton and stop foreign imports from entering. The plan also called for a divide-and-conquer strategy. The port of New Orleans and other major points along the Mississippi, Tennessee, and Cumberland rivers needed to be taken. These included the cities of Vicksburg and Memphis and the Confederate Fort Henry on the Tennessee River and Fort Donelson on the Cumberland.[5] With federal control of the vital western rivers, the Union Army could be kept supplied from the American Midwest. With the Tennessee and Cumberland rivers secure, Nashville could be conquered and occupied. From Nashville, the South would be cut into sections from Nashville, to Murfreesboro, to Chattanooga, to Atlanta and then to Savannah. The end result; the Confederacy divided. Nashville had to be taken. Nashville had to be held. Nashville had to be occupied, and occupied it was. Nashville was surrendered on February 23, 1862 and never went back into Rebel hands. Nashville, along with Washington D. C. and Richmond, Virginia, became one of the most fortified cities in the country. A newspaper writer[6] coined the phrase "The Great Panic" to describe the time during which Nashville was surrendered — and those were the very days that Maggie found herself a part of.

---

[5] In May 1861, Tennessee Governor Isham G. Harris had Fort Henry on the Tennessee River and Fort Donelson on the Cumberland River constructed to protect against invasion from the north.
[6] John Miller McKee, a Nashville Union and American newspaper editor.

Margaret Nichol Vaulx

Maggie Vaulx, young and energetic.
A daughter of pioneers, settlers and military men.
Educated in some of Nashville's finest schools.
Skilled in pen, voice, piano, religiosity, and family caring.

Chapter One
Volume One

"Will I ever be enabled to write a perfect account of myself?"

Home, 1861

The journal entries begin on April 26, 1861, two weeks after hostilities erupt. In introduction, Maggie gives the following as the purpose of her journal: *"May this be the means of bringing me nearer to my Saviour and make me delighted to do his holy will."* The following excerpts are the entries as found in the original journal manuscript.

Friday, April 26th 1861. – Mount Alban

I again take my pen to commence a journal! I hope by writing down the different states of my heart, I may be enable to judge after my progress to Him. Yet, I fear that snares compass me in this small undertaking. Let me then to ask my Heavenly Father to make me faithful in the performances of my duty; teach me to search the depths of my sinfulness and be not afraid to discover its extent. Let me never write anything concerning myself that is inconsistent with the strictest truth. May this be the means in bringing me nearer to my Saviour and make me delight to do his holy will. If I have backslidings, why should I not pray and try to conquer the evil in my heart? I have a friend on high who knows my vileness and will forgive and help me too. May I henceforth live near to Him, and may every thorn that pricks make me look up to that beautiful city where is a tree of life without a thorn, and a morning without a cloud!

Mount Alban

Far away from Maggie's peaceful life at her childhood home Mount Alban,[7] events were unfolding which were destined to shatter her young life and change

---

[7] George Washington Campbell served as a U.S. senator, secretary of the treasury, ambassador to Russia, and U.S. district court judge of Tennessee. The home was built by Campbell around 1820 and became Mount Alban when Joseph Vaulx purchased it 1847.

her forever. Maggie was about to learn what Thomas Paine must have meant by writing the immortal words, "These are the times which try men's souls."[8]

Throughout the 1860 Presidential election campaign, the Southern leaders had threatened to secede if Lincoln were elected. They now declared that it was time to leave a government which had fallen into the hands of their avowed enemies. This act of secession was not a sudden movement on their part. The sectional difference between the North and the South had its source in the difference of climate, which greatly modified the character and habits of the people; also, while the agricultural pursuits and staple products of the South made slave labor profitable, the mechanical pursuits and the more varied products of the North made it unprofitable. These antagonisms, settled first by the Missouri Compromise of 1820,[9] reopened by the tariff of 1828,[10] bursting forth in the nullification of 1832,[11] pacified by Henry Clay's compromise tariff,[12] increased through the annexation of Texas[13] and the consequent war with Mexico, irritated by the Wilmot Proviso,[14] lulled for a time by the compromise of 1850,[15] awakened anew by the "squatter sovereignty"[16] policy of 1853, roused to fury by the agitation in Kansas, spread broadcast by the Dred Scott decision,[17] the attempted execution of the Fugitive Slave Law[18] and the John Brown[19] raid, had now reached a boiling point where war was the only remedy. The election of Lincoln was

---

[8] Thomas Paine's Revolutionary War pamphlet, *The American Crisis*, 1776.
[9] When the admission of Missouri as a state was proposed, a violent debate arose throughout the country as to whether it should be free or slave.
[10] The Tariff of 1828 (known by South Carolina as the Tariff of Abominations) was a protective measure passed to protect American interest. It was lauded in the North but censured in the South.
[11] South Carolina passed a nullification ordinance declaring the 1828 tariff law "null and void," and threatened that the State would secede from the Union if force should be employed to collect any revenue at Charleston.
[12] Henry Clay's celebrated "Compromise Bill" was a measure agreed upon which offered a gradual reduction of the 1828 tariff. It was adopted by the Senate and accepted by both sides, and temporary peace was restored.
[13] Texas was admitted to the Union as a slave state in 1845.
[14] This bill would forbid slavery in any new territory acquired by the federal government.
[15] This solution to California's application for admission to the Union as a Free State brought slavery again to a focus.
[16] This doctrine called for the right of the inhabitants of new territory to decide for themselves whether a new state should come into the Union free or slave.
[17] The Supreme Court declared in 1857 that slaveowners might take their slaves into any state in the Union without forfeiting authority over them.
[18] This 1850 law intensified the already heated controversy, and the subject of slavery now absorbed all others. The provision which commanded every good citizen to aid in the arrest of fugitives was especially obnoxious to the North. Disturbances arose whenever attempts were made to restore runaways to their masters.
[19] In 1859 Abolitionist John Brown seized the United States Arsenal at Harper's Ferry and proclaimed freedom to the slaves in the vicinity. The military was sent in, captured Brown, and hanged him for treason.

the pivot on which the result turned. The cause ran back through thirty years of controversy to the difference in climate, in livelihood, and in the habit of life and thought. Strange to say, each section misunderstood the other. The Southern people believed the North to be so engrossed in money-making and so enfeebled by luxury that it could send to the field only mercenary soldiers, who would easily be beaten by the patriotic Southerners. They said, "Cotton is King;" and believed that England and France were so dependent upon them for that staple, that their republic would be recognized and defended by those European powers. On the other hand, the Northern people did not believe that the South would dare fight for slavery when it had 4,000,000 slaves exposed to the chances of war. They thought it to be all rant, and hence paid little heed to the threat of secession or of war. Both sides sadly learned their mistake, only too late.

Since the time of John C. Calhoun, many in the South had been firm believers in the doctrine of State rights, which taught that a State could leave the Union whenever it pleased. In December of 1860 South Carolina led off, and soon after Mississippi, Florida, Alabama, Georgia, Louisiana, and Texas passed ordinances of secession. In February 1861 delegates from the Confederate States of America chose Jefferson Davis, of Mississippi, as President, and Alexander H. Stephens, of Georgia, Vice-President. United States forts, arsenals, customhouses, and ships were seized by the States in which they were situated. President James Buchanan did nothing to prevent the catastrophe. General Scott urged action, but the regular army was small, and the troops were widely scattered. The navy had been sent to distant ports. The Cabinet largely sympathized with the secessionists. Numerous unsuccessful efforts were made to affect a compromise. It was the general expectation that there would be no war, and the cry, "No coercion," was general. Yet affairs steadily drifted on toward war.

Jefferson Davis

All eyes were now turned on Fort Sumter. Here Major Robert Anderson kept the United States flag flying in Charleston harbor. He had been stationed in Fort Moultrie, but fearing an attack, had crossed over on December 26, 1860 to Fort Sumter, a stronger position. The South Carolinians, looking upon this as a hostile act, took possession of the remaining forts, commenced erecting batteries, and prepared to reduce Fort Sumter. Major Anderson was compelled by his instructions to remain a quiet spectator of these preparations. The Star of the West, an unarmed steamer, bearing troops and supplies to the fort, was fired upon and driven back. The Southern leaders declared that any attempt to relieve Fort

Sumter would be a declaration of war. The government seemed paralyzed with fear. All now waited for the new President.[20]

Great uneasiness prevailed across the South when Abraham Lincoln, a young, tall and lean Illinois congressman won the 1860 Presidential election. Rumors quickly arose of a plan to assassinate President Lincoln impelled him to come to Washington in secret. He was inaugurated March 4, 1861, surrounded by troops under the command of General Winfield Scott.

The condition of the country was now engulfed in an air of uncertainty. Southern officers in the army and navy of the United States were resigning and joining the Southern Confederate cause. There was still a strong sentiment in the South. Many prominent men in both sections hoped that war might be avoided. The Federal authorities feared to act unless they should give rise to civil strife. In contrast to the Federal actions, the new Confederate government was gathering troops, money and supplies and rapidly preparing for the possibility of war.

Abraham Lincoln

Sitting in the midst of Charleston harbor was Fort Sumter still under the command of Major Anderson. Upon finding that supplies were to be sent to the fort, Confederate General Peter G. T. Beauregard who had command of the Confederate troops at Charleston called for the surrender of the fort. Upon Major Anderson's refusal of surrender, on April 12, 1861 gunfire was opened from all rebel forts and batteries. The Civil War began with that bombardment and after thirty four hours, the fort was forced to capitulate. The union barracks were set on fire by the shells and the worn out garrison surrendered the fort on April 14, 1861.

The effect of the surrender of Fort Sumter was immediate. It unified the North and the South toward their causes. The spirit of war swept across the country like wild fire. President Lincoln called for 75,000 troops, with 300,000 volunteering. The military enthusiasm in the South was equally ardent. Within days Virginia, Arkansas, North Carolina, and Tennessee joined the original seceding states of the infant Confederacy. The Confederate capitol was relocated from Montgomery, Alabama to Richmond, Virginia with President Jefferson Davis and his cabinet. Virginia troops seized the United States arsenal at Harper's Ferry and the Navy yard near Norfolk. Troops from the south was rapidly pushed into Virginia and threatened Washington city. The sixth Massachusetts Regiment, hurrying to the defense of the national capital, was attacked in the streets of Baltimore and several men were killed. These were the first recorded

---

[20] Barnes, *A Brief History of the United States*, Epoch IV, pages 185-200.

deaths in the civil war. The date was April 19, 1861, the 86th anniversary of the Revolutionary War battles of Lexington and Concord.[21]

For much of the first year, the diary functions mostly as a religious journal. Maggie constantly examines her life and her relationship with God. Maggie laments one of her weaknesses to be her temper. It is a constant failing and she often writes of her disappointment in trying to control it. Her daily activities include prayer, school studies, church activity, and relationships with her family, friends, and neighbors. Contained within the inside back cover of her first volume, Maggie has a list of important dates. She lists April 26, 1861 as the beginning of her religious life.

Saturday, April 27th 1863.

I rose very early this morning and prepared all my lessons for Monday. I read a chapter in the Bible and poured forth my earnest prayers, for divine aid to execute my work of bringing myself nearer to my Saviour. During the last few months one of my school-mates, Lizzie Rains was called to her long prepared home on High. In her life and in her sickness she gave the most satisfactory evidence of a full preparation in the "freedom of the skies." It only remains for me to cherish fondly her memory and prepare to meet her in that bright and beautiful world above where:

> "Sin is known no more,
> Nor tears nor wants, nor cares.
> The good and happy beings dwell
> And all are holy there!"

Sunday, April 28th 1861.

The Sabbath has come. The scene is bright and calm, and all nature seems to praise Him, to whom it owes its being. Strange that my heart should be so out of tune, so little in unison with this sweet and universal concert! I am still trying to become one of God's children, though I feel at times as if I were too great a sinner to become a Christian. Why should I feel so? Because imperfect in everything, I am imperfect in my repentance. But did not my Saviour say, "Come unto me all ye that labor and are heavy laden and I will give you rest."

---

[21] Barnes, *A Brief History of the United States*, Epoch IV, pages 215-217.

Monday, April 29th 1861.

Went to school to-day and knew all my lessons. I am still trying to fight the "good fight of faith" and hope to come out victorious. I want to examine myself yet I fear to do it. There are so many things to be disentangled. One sin I am constantly falling into is my temper. Even my blessed mother who deserves so much of my affection; her tender heart has been sorrowing with grief, and I have filled her with sorrow instead of gladness. This pains me much and I can scarcely write for tears![22] Oh! my Heavenly Father when shall I faithfully perform my duty towards her? I love her better than anyone else in the world, and hope at some future day to become her joy and comfort. May she never find me engrossed in the sinful pleasures of this world; which are as fleeting as the morning dew or the passing cloud; but may she see [in] me the passion of that pure delight, that holy joy which flew from the humbly believing on a crucified Saviour. May I from this time forward never let a frown be seen to darken my brow, or angry words fall from my lips; when she bid me do what is for my own good.

Tuesday, 30th.

I rose quite late this morning and had therefore little time to pray. Nothing has occurred worthy of recording in this book. Once or twice I find myself falling into the most violent fits of passions at the most trifling things, things I would only let go unregarded by, would save me many hours of bitter remorse.

Wednesday, May 1st.

I had a holiday to-day and I spent it in visiting my dear friends with mother. I am not satisfied with the state of my mind; for when I kneel in prayer it is constantly wavering. Oh! my God when shall I be wise? Not until I can cease thinking of the fleeting pleasures of this world, and set my heart on those that are everlasting. Ah how unlike the children of God are the thoughts that occupy my heart! It is the beginning of a new month, and may I begin to draw nearer to my Saviour and live more truly happier than I have otherwise done.

Thursday, May 2nd.

I rose very early this morning and thanked my heavenly Father for his manifold blessing to me. I do not think I am lively enough in secret prayers and therefore I do not feel at peace. I

---

[22] The original manuscript has ink smears in this area. I believe it to be the result of falling tears.

think far too much of earthly things, and eternal ones dwindle from my view. But God is showing me that all is vanity here below and I must not look for happiness in this world but I must turn my attention to those realms of eternal rest and peace.

Friday, May 3rd.

I have very little to put down in this book as each day is the same. Last night I made a resolution not to fall into any passions, or speak a disrespectful word to my mother or any one, and as the day is drawing to a close, I can look back upon the expired time and conscience tells me I have acted according to my resolutions. May it ever be so is the fervent prayer of my soul!

Saturday, May 4th.

Spent a very pleasant day with my beloved friend Mollie Berry,[23] and was very much surprised on returning home, to find a cousin of mine (Dr. Armstrong) here, on his way to Richmond Virginia. I had not seen him for several years and was over-joyed to see him. Another week has fled and I have been strangely tossed in spirit. Now that it has passed; but oh, how much sin there has been in all parts of conduct. Oh! may He lead me out of temptation, and "create a new heart, and renew a right spirit within me".

Sabbath, May 5th.

I am again compelled to remain at home from church on account of the inclemency of the weather. But I think I have made proper use of my time. I am now reading the "Life of Mary Lundie Duncan." Whilst reading of her life I often wish that like her I may become one of that happy few, who make Jesus their all. Oh! may I be enabled like her to go to Jesus, bear his reproach and esteem, nothing dear compared with his love. Oh, I feel that I do not love God enough. I feel that I am very backward in laying down my burden at the foot of my Redeemer's cross. But I do wish to become one of the lowly children of Christ; and I will still continue to endeavor to become one.

Monday, May 6th 1861.

Oh! what an unhappy day I have spent! I have fallen into angry passions at my mother. Oh! could my hands become useless as I write this act. No wonder I have given away to

---

[23] Mollie J. Berry, daughter of Nashville wholesale druggist William W. Berry, owner of the Elm Wood estate.

angry passions; for when I kneeled in prayer my mind wandered and I uttered solemn things on a thoughtless tongue!

Tuesday, May 7th 1861.

I arose very early this morning. Have been unwell to-day with a wretched cold. Tonight I was reading my Bible when my sweet little sister came and said to me "Sister I am going to commence reading my Bible and praying." Oh! what a joyful resolution that was to me. Oh! how thankful I am to see that she is awakened to a sense of her sin! May she too go to Jesus, bearing his reproach, esteeming nothing dear compared with his love. May I behave more wisely to her and by my example win her to her and my Saviour.

Wednesday, May 8th 1861.

I have not much time to write in my diary as I have been very busy with my studies and in showing my little sister her composition and her other duties. I am anxious that she should make great progress in all her studies and be first in her class; and I will endeavor to do all in my power to advance her.

Thursday, May 9th 1861.

I arose very early this morning and read two Psalms and said my prayers. Went to school and knew all my lessons; and I hope and think that I can now say that it is knowledge of Jesus Christ which gives me such an interest in all my pursuits. It is his approbation which encourages me in prosecuting all my studies. The earth seems so far in my eyes because he enode [to make clear]; and in looking forward to the glories of a happy eternity. Still I am often unhappy. I feel with the apostle Paul[24] that when I wish to do good evil is always present with me. My old sin of temper is an enemy hard to be subdued, and one which needs constantly to be guarded against. Oh! it is humbling to find that, however much one may long and strive to be holy, there is something in the heart, which keeps the soul cleaving to the dust. Sins which dishonor God, and give away the Holy Spirit! Yet, in the midst of sins and backslidings, the language of my heart is, Oh! for a closer walk with God! ["Mabel Gant"]

---

[24] Rom. 7:21

Friday, May 10th.

I have been sick all day and therefore have not gone to school; but I have tried to pass the day profitably, reading my Bible, and praying for more grace.

Saturday, May 11th.

I have been very busy all day, studying my lessons, mending my clothes, and cleaning out my drawers, &c.[25] I read my Bible this morning but my mind wandered. I hope the work is God's, so it cannot fail; but how very long I am [before] becoming completely his. I will not cease to beg him to make me so. I ought to pray more to Him, for divine aid, to enable me to surmount the many difficulties which are constantly appearing in my path.

Sabbath evening, May 12th/61.

Did not go to church to-day again on account of the bad weather. I began to get the shorter Catechism and to memorize a hymn every Sunday and hope to keep it up. I am very much puzzled about the state of my feelings. May God direct me, and forgive me. I want to be all his now. I don't think I pray to him enough to direct my faltering footsteps. He says "Return and I will heal your backslidings." May I do so this very day, and pray more for "growing grace." May I love him more, not only in name but in deed and in truth. Oh! that I could live as seeing Him, who is invisible. Why should I write this wish, and yet not pray more earnestly that it should be realized? Help me my King. Leave me not to wander in the dark without a guide to point my way: but guard my soul from my foe, while I am a pilgrim [here]; and in my departing hour may I see heaven opened, and expire with the dying prayer of the first martyr on my lips, "Lord Jesus, receive my spirit!"[26]

Monday, May 13th 1861.

I rose early this morning and poured forth my earnest prayer thanking my Heavenly Father for his un-measurable blessings to me during the past night. Oh! that I could serve my God; more faithfully! When I wish to do good, evil is always present with me. Oh! how long will this complaint be mine. I earnestly hope when vacation comes I will have more time to give my whole mind and soul to my Saviour.

---

[25] This is Latin for *et cetera* used in 19th century formal or literary work. The usage of *&c* can be found in Harriet Beecher Stowe's novel, *Uncle Tom's Cabin*.
[26] Acts 7:59

Tuesday, May 14th 1861.

I have not much time to write in my diary as I have been exceedingly busy ever since I returned from school, and I can only say I do not enjoy the sweet communion with my God as I did last week. O my Heavenly Father recall the poor wanderer, strengthen tottering footsteps, lest he should fall. Pluck out the evil which is constantly rising in my heart.

Thursday, May 16th 1861.

Went to school to-day and recited all my lessons well. Oh! how miserable I am today, and have been so for the past week. I have not had the same sweet communion with my God as I formerly did. Oh! when shall I be able to write down my actions as free from all evil? Words fail to tell of the unhappy hours I spend thinking over all my past sins, and wondering if Jesus will ever forgive them. Oh! could I feel a sense of my sins forgiven. What a happy creature I would be.

Friday, May 17th 1861.

I am still the miserable creature I have been all week. I have given away to angry passions, and have spoken cross words to my companions and little sisters. Oh! what a miserable child of wrath I am! No wonder I have been so wretched! This morning whilst I knelt in prayer my mind was constantly wandering and I even – oh! my Father, dare I to confess? I <u>even</u> stopped to say an unkind word to my sister.

Saturday, May 18th.

Nothing has occurred to-day that deserves to be recorded in this book. I still find myself wandering from that "narrow but pleasant path that [leads] to Jesus and to eternal life."[27]

Sunday, May 19th 1861.

Have employed this day profitably in getting my Catechism, hymns, &c. It has been raining all day, and I am therefore compelled to remain at home from church.

Monday, May 20th 1861.

I arose this morning, and studied my lessons for to-day. I have been trying to seek God. "My best desires are faint and few." I have to mourn for "half heartedness." This was my

---

[27] Matt. 7:14

complaint when I first began this book; and it is so still. But amidst all my backslidings, I want to be one of the lowly children of God. I want to be called his own. He says, "return and I will heal your backslidings." May I return to Him immediately; and as when Daniel confessed, Gabriel flew swiftly to him with a messenger of mercy,[28] may my Father pardon me, and let me feel myself pardoned.

Tuesday, May 21st.

I am not satisfied with my feeling to-day; and I will never be so unless I pray more earnestly to God to help me to root the evil from my heart. I am always making resolutions, which are no sooner made than they are broken. When I think of Christ who groaned for me on Cavalry, he is my only hope for he can wash away my sins in his blood, which was shed for sins. May I love Him more not only in name, but in deed and truth.

Wednesday 22nd 1861.

I rose very early this morning, and poured forth my earnest prayer to God thanking Him for his many blessing to me during the past night, and earnestly supplicating his mercy during the day. I am still striving to surmount the difficulties, and temptations which I am daily called upon to encounter.

Thursday, May 23rd 1861.

I have had no time scarcely to write in my diary as I have been very busy all evening since my return from school, preparing my tasks, and waiting upon and reading to my little sick sister. My state of mind is still the same. Ever wandering from the path of true righteousness.

Friday, May 24th.

Was up early this morning as I had several things to attend to before going to school. At times I feel very buoyant in spirit, but this is no proof of nearness to God; for while I am reading His holy Word all kind of foolish thoughts have flitted through my mind. My days this week have been idly spent, for I have not sought God to direct my footsteps; and no wonder I have been wrong in all my occupations. O! God whom I have so often forgotten, look down upon me a poor

---

[28] Dan. 9:21

sinful creature, pity and help me. I am thine save me. Do what thou wilt with me; but do not let me forget thee any more. Leave me not to perish, O my God!

Saturday, May 25th 1861.

I did not rise early this morning on account of being up so much during the past night waiting upon my sister, who is still sick; and needs much care and attention; which I am ever ready and willing to give. To-morrow is the beginning of a new week, and may I when it is finished look back upon those fleeting days, and say that my days have been employed in drawing myself nearer to the fold of Jesus Christ.

Sunday, May 26th.

It is very warm and sultry today; and it is on that account I did not go to church. It is a month to day since I commenced my diary. On looking back upon the expired time, I find many things that which causes me much regret. Still amidst all my mis-givings, I find Jesus Christ my only relief; and may I when religion is [dispel] and this vile heart is negligent of His blessings, then may I think of his dying love, of his various admonitions, then may I gladly make the most painful sacrifices so that I may escape the never dying worm,[29] and become a partaker in his righteousness, and an heir of his kingdom.

Monday, May 27th.

I arose very early this morning, and attended to my regular duties. I do not think there is anything of importance to record; once or twice to-day I find myself straying from the strict path of truth! I think I am too fond of hearing myself talk;[30] and in my eagerness to talk, I let things unconsciously fall from my lips which are contrary to truth! I will endeavor to correct the growing evil!

Tuesday, May 28th.

I did not go to school on account of not being well. In reviewing the past day I feel satisfied with my mind; because I acted according to my resolutions of the preceding day. I have so many things to attend to that I have scarcely time to write in my diary; so if I do not write

---

[29] Mark 9:44
[30] Prov. 10:19

in it daily, it is not because I am growing weary of this important duty; but because there are other things that need my attention, and which occupy me until night.

Wednesday, May 29th.
I am again compelled to remain at home, on account of having a very sore neck. The day has passed away without one thing to be regretted. I hope I will be enabled to look back upon every day, and say there is nothing which I have done or said that is contrary to a Christian's character. Pa went to camp.[31]

Thursday, May 30th.
Cheatham to see Brother Joe.[32]

Friday, May 31st.
Went to school today after an absence of 3 days. Nothing of importance has occurred to-day worthy of being mentioned; but once or twice I find myself indulging in things which I ought not to and therefore I am not all at ease.

Saturday, June 1st 1861.
It is the beginning of a new month, and I firmly resolve to devote my fleeting years to my Creator. The day has passed away, oh! that could I say on looking back upon the passed day, there is nothing that I have said or done that makes me regret! It is otherwise.

Sunday, June 2nd.
I have retired several times to-day to offer up my prayers to God; asking him to draw me nearer to the fold of Christ; and make me one of his humble followers here-below. It is my desire to press forward. Oh! that I could praise my Redeemer more than I do! If I had a thousand hearts and a thousand tongues, they all should be employed in praising and adoring my Redeemer. Oh! that I could leave the world and all its sins! When my mind is taken up

---

[31] The Rock City Guards was a Nashville military unit headquartered at the Market House and camped across the Cumberland River in Edgefield.

[32] The Provisional Army of Tennessee was activated on May 9, 1861 by Governor Isham Harris. Harris chose Benjamin Franklin Cheatham, a Nashville native and veteran of the Mexican War, to head up the important post of quartermaster general. Joseph Vaulx, Jr., having both commercial business and military background, was sought out by Cheatham to help organize the department.

with the thoughts of eternity, then I want to be gone to that world where neither sin nor sorrow shall wound:

> "Where they who meet shall never part,
> Where grace achieves its plans;
> And God, inviting every heart;
> Dwells face to face to man".

I want more grace to subdue all the passions within; and bring them with sweet and humble subjection to the holy will of God.

Monday, June 3rd 1861.

I arose early this morning and poured forth my prayers to the most High. One thing still bothers me; and that is I do not pray enough. I know I rise and pray and pray before I retire to rest, but I do not think this is sufficient. O my heavenly Father, let prayer, as it is be my [largest] privilege, be my dear delight. While I am pursuing my pilgrimage to eternity, may I retire <u>daily</u> and <u>often</u> in the day to hold sweet communion with thee O Lord! To then may I flee all my heart; and show thyself the hearer of my prayers.

Tuesday, June 4th.

Nothing has occurred to-day that I think deserves to be recorded. I want to draw neigh to God; but I still find it difficult. I am sick of myself and of my way ward heart. Help me oh my Father, and save one miserable creature who is ransomed by the blood of thy Son.

Joseph Vaulx Sr.

The school which Maggie attends is the South Side Institute[33]. Music is an important part of her life. She is occupied with regular piano and singing lessons. It is recorded that Joseph Vaulx, her father is a constant source of encouragement to her. She often writes of wanting to please him in her progress.

---

[33] South Side Institute, a private school owned and operated by Mrs. Emma Holcombe. The 1860 Nashville City Directory lists it as a Young Ladies School located at 19 South Summer Street.

Wednesday, June 5th.

I went to school to day and was not quite perfect in my duties. Our school will be out in a few days, and I am glad on some accounts; and sorry on others. It may be that close dear friends and teachers whom I love so well may be called during that time to their endless home with Jesus. This is what pains me. If they are called away, oh let me prepare to meet them in those regions of bliss. Then may we join in that triumphant strains. "O death where is thy sting! Oh grave where thy victory is! Thanks be to God, who giveth us the victory through our Lord Jesus Christ."[34]

Thursday, June 6th. [There is a date given, but no journal entry.]

Friday, June 7th.

I spent a wretched day to-day. I do not care to record it. O! that I could blot it out from my memory! Forget that such a day has ever passed. On reviewing it, I find everything has gone wrong.

Saturday, June 8th 1861.

I am again puzzled about my state of mind. May God direct me? I have a weight at heart, when I view it all [lightens]. I am alone very often and may I use those moments in praying to God to pluck the evil from my heart, and make me entirely his.

Sunday, June 9th.

My days are passed so much alike that I do not think it is worthwhile to record each day unless something of importance has occurred. Have retried to day as last Sunday to offer up my silent prayers to God to help me to endeavor to become a child of His.

Monday, June 10th 1861.

I am far from feeling tranquil in spirit and in mind. I think I am falling in to my old habit of straying from the narrow but pleasant path what leads to life everlasting! I will, however still endeavour to become one of the children, of Jesus, and may he lead me by His sweet and gentle influence, though I should not know whither I am going. But I do not think I pray

---

[34] 1 Cor. 15:55-57.

enough to conquer the many evils in my heart! I ought to consider prayer my chief delight, and I earnestly hope at some future day to do so!

Tuesday, June 11th. [There is a date given, but no journal entry.]

Wednesday, June 12th 1861.

I had no time to write in my diary as I was compelled to go to the city to attend the "Commencement" of our school (South Side Institute). Even now I am in a hurry as I have to hasten to town to attend also the Soirée Musicals of the Institute.

Thursday, June 13th.

I am now again spending my days in the country and I am glad to escape the many nuisances of the city. When I am in the city my mind is drawn from the quiet reflection that I so love to enjoy and when I retire to offer up my silent petitions to the Throne of Grace, my mind wanders, and I hastily utter "solemn sounds on a thoughtless tongue."

Friday, June 14th.

Went to town this morning to take a music lesson, and returned home and spent the latter part of the day with Mollie Berry.

Saturday, June 15th.

The week has passed and on reviewing it, I find myself wrong in everything. This week is very unlike last, during that time I was in a very tranquil spirit, but this week just the reverse.

Sunday, June 16th.

As I am writing I can distinctly hear the church bell pealing forth,[35] and how I long to be there to join the group that are now assembling to hear the blessed Word of God. It is one of the many privileges I am now denied of attending church regularly on account of, living so far in the country.

---

[35] There were several churches with bells in Nashville. Given the context, I believe these church bells to be of the First Presbyterian Church, three and one half miles away in downtown Nashville.

Monday, June 17th.

I am yet the poor wanderer from the fold of Christ! Will I ever be enabled to write a perfect account of myself? I do not think I seek God enough in many of my occupations and no wonder, I have been wrong in everything.

Tuesday, June 18th. [There is a date given, but no journal entry.]

Thursday, June 20th. [There is a date given, but no journal entry.]

Chapter Two
Summer, 1861

"I am often sad, because my only brother has gone to fight the battles of the sunny South; and perhaps I will never see him again."

Friday, June 21st.
Two days have fled and I have not had time to write in my journal but there is nothing to write in it of any importance, but I do not like to fail to perform this duty for I fear that I will neglect it all to-gather, if I delay writing in it as often as I possibly can.

Monday, June 24.
I spent my Sabbath in the city, and employed it in going to church and in other devotional exercises in which I do delight. I have not been lively in secret prayer and therefore I am now far from feeling peaceful in my mind. I must endeavor to steal a portion of time to devote it in offering up my prayers to God in the solitude of my own chamber.

Thursday, June 27th.
I did not write in my diary yesterday on account of being compelled to entertain a friend at a very late hour. I have been very busy all day serving, practicing and in consequence I felt weary both in body and mind, and do not feel inclined to write much in this book.

Friday, June 28th.
I am far from happy to-day. I am again allowing myself to fall into angry passions and I let words fall from my lips which ought to cause me much regret, could I feel the evil of them aright.

Sunday, June 30th.
Another month has fled, and I can only look back upon the expired time with feelings of regret. Each month I make resolutions, to walk in the narrow but pleasant path that leads to life everlasting, and when I close it only finds me straying more and more from it. "O! most

merciful Father lead me to the rock that is higher than I! Lead me to the atoning blood, which washes all sin away. Lead me to Christ crucified! Forgive for his dear sake the past and oh give me strength for the future."

Monday, July 1st 1861.

I arose early this morning and found to my disappointment it pouring down rain, as I did not feel much inclined to sally out and contend with the wind and rain to take my music lesson. This is the way with our nature all ways discontented with things which happen in this life; not stopping to reflect and ask ourselves is it not for our own good. I know it is in the case for our crops have suffered for the want of rain, here I was this morning grumbling on account of it raining, because it prevented my doing something which I had so long set my heart upon.

Thursday, July 4th 1861.

I was prevented from writing in my diary yesterday on account of my friend spending the day with us, and being too late to do so when she went away. Carried some fruit to a poor girl, who is dying of consumption,[36] and I never felt so sorry for any one in my life. Best if she is prepared to go to Jesus (which I hope she is) why should I wish her to remain in this world of sin and sorrow.

Friday, July 5th 1861.

Went to the city this morning to take my music lesson and returned home immediately as I had various things to look after. I am unhappy to-day, and have been so for the last few days.

Sunday, July 7th 1861.

I rose early this morning and poured forth my prayers to God earnestly asking him to give me grace to surmount the numerous difficulties that are constantly besetting me. Went to church to-day for the first time in two weeks. Mr. Bardwell preached a very good sermon, but the text I could not understand where to find it.

Monday, July 8th. [There is a date given but no journal entry.]

---

[36] **Consumption,** pulmonary tuberculosis, or TB is a contagious bacterial infection that mainly involves the lungs but may spread to other organs.

Wednesday, July 10th 1861.

I arose early this morning and performed my usual duties. After breakfast, I practiced two hours, and then employed myself in various other ways. At times I feel so happy and at others I am perfectly miserable. I wish I had a friend to whom I could confide all my most secret thoughts, and who would try to become one of the lowly children of Christ; and like me endeavor to surmount all the difficulties of this world. Oh! God unite with me in faith every friend. I fondly love, may they too go to Jesus, bearing his reproach and esteeming nothing dear compared with his love, and thus prepare us all to join in those triumphant strains. Oh death where is thy sting! Oh grave where is thy victory?

Thursday, 11th 1861.

I arose early this morning and had an hour of quiet to offer up my morning prayers to God. I have just finished reading a work, of great interest, and I hope will prove a great assistance to me in drawing myself nearer to God.

The July 12, 1861 journal entry identifies the family's military association. Maggie records that her brother, who she identifies as having the rank of captain with Company A, is a member of the First Tennessee Infantry Regiment and has been ordered to duty. *The Official Records of the War of Rebellion* and *Confederate Veteran* magazines will further identify him as Major Joseph Vaulx, Jr., later a staff officer with Major General Frank Cheatham. It can be noted that he was a graduate of the Western Military Institute of Georgetown, Kentucky and was also one of the original members of the unit known as the Rock City Guards. The Institute moved to Nashville in 1855 and formed up with the Nashville University under the direction of General Bushrod Johnson. One of the most noted Nashville graduates was Private Sam Davis, the boy hero of the Confederacy.

Friday, July 12th 1861.

Went to the city today and on arriving there found the 1st Tenn. Regiment was ordered off the day before. My brother is the Captain of A company, and was of course among those who went to fight the enemies of the South. Oh! How sad I felt when I found he had gone, without my bidding him perhaps a last goodbye! Save and deliver him O' Lord from the hands of our enemies that he being armed with thy defence may be preserved evermore from all perils to glorify thee who art the only giver of victory through thy Son Jesus Christ, our Lord, Amen!

Saturday, 13th 1861.

Been very busy all day waiting upon mother who is quite sick with chills. Nothing gives me more pain than to see her prostrate on a bed of sickness; we all miss her so much when she is taken from us for a time.

July 16th (Tuesday)

I rose early this morning as we expected some visitors to breakfast with us. I have not been happy to-day. When I become so much engrossed in conversations, I forget myself entirely, and often let imprudent things fall from my lips when upon reflecting always causes me regret. I do not think though that I am as much addicted to this fault as I once was, and sincerely hope to overcome it entirely.

July 17th. [There is a date given but no journal entry.]

Thursday, July 18th.

Another day has fled, and on looking back on the expired time, I find myself wrong in everything. My <u>temper</u> needs guarding against constantly. At times I find myself falling into fits of passions; not I am thankful to say at my mother or father, but to my little sisters. I ought to endeavour and set by an example for them to follow. Enable me, oh Lord to act according to my resolutions!

Friday, July 19th.

I arose very late this morning on account of being up late last night, as the children begged me so hard to read them a tale. I have not given away to my temper; still there are many things that must be corrected. I am now reading Persuasive to Early Piety, a very interesting little work, which entreats me to devote my few but fleeting years to God. She gives me many examples of young persons, one who gave her early youth to God; but not finding the holy peace at once, which He promises to give to his believers, she felt tempted to give up trying; she still persevered and at length obtained the peace she desired. As I was reading it I was struck with the like temptations I am daily called on to encounter; and at the same time inwardly hoping to surmount them all and press more eagerly forward to those sweet bodies of bliss.

Saturday, July 20th 1861.

Was up early this morning and cleaned and arranged all my wardrobe, dresser &c. I want to acquire the habit of rising earlier, and cleaning and fixing my own room. When I rise late I feel so inert, that I am not in the notion to do anything, but if I rise early it is just the contrary. I intend following my resolution, and I will when I have an hour to appreciate one of my greatest delights – <u>prayer</u>.

Sunday, July 21st 1861.

I went to church this morning: and upon returning home I immediately retired to my room and earnestly poured forth my prayers to God to enable me to profit by the sermon I had heard. The text was 5th chap 2nd Corinthians and 1st verse. "For we know that if our earthly house of this tabernacle were dissolved, we have a building of God, an house not made with hands, eternal in the heavens."

Monday, July 22nd 1861.

I did not rise early this morning, and therefore was hurried in my devotions. Once or twice to-day, I have given away to evil passions, but I must not despond for I hope to overcome it entirely by perseverance.

Tuesday, July 23rd.

I have not much time to write in my diary. Took a long ride up the road, and enjoyed it exceedingly. The country looked so beautiful, having just been refreshed by a heavy rain.

Wednesday, July 24th 1861.

I arose early this morning. Queeny and Annie Humphreys,[37] Terry Martin, and Les Trimble spent the day with me, and I endeavored to make them enjoy themselves as much as it was in my powers. There are many things to be corrected in my conduct.

Friday, July 26th 1861.

I arose early this morning. I have been unhappy all day, and I cannot tell why. Spent a delightful day yesterday with Mollie Berry; but on returning home and reviewing the past day, I found myself saying very imprudent things. Let me correct the evil.

---

[37] Sisters Queeny and Annie Humphrey, nieces of Gen. Gideon Pillow were residents of Columbia, TN, in Maury County.

Saturday, July 27th 1861. Nothing to record.

Sunday, July 28th 1861.

I rose early this morning and had a full hour to devote to my religious exercises. Went to church this morning and heard an excellent sermon, thanking God for the victory [1st Battle of Bull Run][38] we gained last Sunday. The text was very appropriate being the 15th chap of II Chronicles 2nd verse. "The Lord is with you, while you be with him: and if you seek him he will be a friend of you, but if you forsake him he will forsake you."

Jackson's Stand at Bull Run[39]

Monday, July 29th 1861.

I do not feel at peace to-day. I can't tell why but all day I felt so unhappy. I do not think I am as ardent in my devotions as I was last week, and perhaps this is the cause of my

---

[38] The First Battle of Bull Run was fought on July 21, 1861, near Manassas, Virginia. (Barnes, *A Brief History of the United States*, Epoch V, page 219.)

[39] During the First Battle of Bull Run, Confederate General Barnard Bee observed General Thomas J. Jackson in action. His remark, "There stands Jackson like a stone wall," was the basis for Jackson's famous nickname, Stonewall. General Bee would later perish in the same battle.

unhappiness. O! what an happy creature I would be [if] I could look back upon every day that I record in this book and find myself becoming more and more like a child of God! Why should I wish to become like them, and then not make an endeavor to gain my point?

Wednesday, July 31st.
It is very warm today and I therefore do not feel much inclined to write in the book.

Thursday, Aug 1st 1861.
I arose quite early this morning and went in town to see my teacher Mrs. Holcombe; and enjoyed my visit exceedingly. I am not happy to-day and have not been for some days past.

In the following entry, Maggie is reading a soldier's journal that has been published in the newspaper. She is impressed with his steadfast endurance of hardships. This article must have had a great effect on Maggie, because she later records the making of socks, quilts, and other items which soldiers can use to improve their life. Maggie's increasing fervor for the Southern cause borders on the black market and against marshal law.

Saturday, August 3rd 1861.
I rose early this morning and read a chapter in my Bible, and then set to work and cleaned and fixed my wardrobe, drawers &c. before breakfast. Started cleaning my room but did not do much due to it being very warm. I was reading in the newspaper to-day and came across a journal kept by a young soldier who related all the hardships he had to endure but bore them with great fortitude.

Sunday, Aug 4th 1861.
Up early this morning, and had an hour of privacy to devote to my devotional exercises. Went to church this morning and returned home very much edified by the sermon I had just heard. Have retired several times to-day to offer up my heartfelt prayers to the Most High. I always feel so happy when I arise from my knees after sending up my silent petitions to Heaven, to enable me to become more and more like a child of God.

Monday, Aug 5th 1861.
I was up betimes this morning, and however because I had my inclination to do so; but it was so very warm I could not sleep. Have had company to-day and I therefore have not retired as

is my word to offer up my prayers to the Most High. I will here after endeavour to steal a portion of time to devote to this duty, no matter how much I am engaged.

Tuesday, Aug 6th 1861.
I arose early this morning and performed my usual duties. Have retired to-day to offer up prayers to God. I always feel so calm, and happy after performing this duty. Have given away to angry passions to-day, and I therefore do not feel very comfortable.

Wednesday, Aug 7th 1861.
I didn't rise very early this morning. Been unhappy all day because I have let my temper get the whip hand of me.

Thursday, July 8th 1861.
I am very far from feeling happy to-day; because I have said and done many things that are very, very wrong. I have not retired to-day to pray and that is the reason why I am all wrong. I rise in the morning fully determined to record a perfect account of myself; but night closes with all my resolutions broken.

Friday, Aug. 9th. Nothing to day.

Sunday, Aug 11th.
I have been prevented from writing in my journal for the last few days on account of being absent from home. I did not go to church on account of having heavy rain for the past few days, but I have employed the days reading my Bible and prayer. Have not done or said anything that is amiss and I therefore do not feel at all unhappy.

Monday, Aug 12th.
I arose early this morning and had an hour after performing my devotions to read to my little sister. I feel very comfortable because I have not given away to angry passions, and hope to be enabled to record such an account of myself every day.

Tuesday, Aug 13th 1861.
What a different account I am compelled to write from yesterday! Today I allowed myself to fall into a passion at the most trifling things; and on that account have spent a wretched

day. I intend commencing a course of history which I hope I will be enabled to keep up. A complete <u>failure</u>.

Wednesday, Aug 14th. [There is a date given, but no journal entry.]

Friday, Aug 16th 1861.
Circumstances, over which I had no control, have prevented me from writing in my journal for the past two days. Have not been happy because this morning when I arose to perform my duties, my [mind] wandered and all kinds of foolish things passed through my mind, when at prayer and I uttered "solemn sounds on a thoughtless tongue."

Saturday, Aug 17th 1861.
Was up early this morning. I have been quite happy to-day. Have been busily employed in various ways and felt very tired and I do not therefore write as much as I would like.

Sunday, Aug 18th/61.
Went to church this morning and heard an excellent [sermon] from Dr. Sion. "For I know that my Redeemer liveth, and that he shall stand at the latter day upon earth." Retired to my room on arriving from church and spent some time praying for more grace to subdue the many evils within. I am often sad, because my only brother has gone to fight the battles of the sunny South; and perhaps I will never see him again. If it should be so may the blessed Jesus be near and dear to him in his last hours. Do I pray enough for that absent brother? My heart condemns me!

Sunday, Aug 25th 1861.
A week has gone and so many things have happened that I have been prevented from writing in [my] journal. A sad accident has happened during that time. Late Friday evening (23rd), Charlie Percy was riding on horseback down in the meadow when the horse threw him and broke his arm very badly. He is staying with us and will probably be several weeks before he can return to the city.

Tuesday, Aug. 27th/61.
It has been raining all day to-day. I have been busily employed sewing on my quilt, which I intend selling and sending the money to the soldiers.

Wednesday, Aug 28th/61.

I arose early this morning and had an hour to devote to my exercises. Aunt Jane [Brown] and Ellen Percy came out and spent the day with us to-day and returned home in the cab. Charlie's arm is rapidly improving and I hope to see him ere long recover his usual health and spirits.

Sunday, September 1st 1861.

Was up early this morning and went to church. Brought Grandma[40] out with us to see Charlie. She returned with Dr. Martin. Have been perfectly miserable to day. Can I ever gain that holy joy and that settled peace which I so long for? I have been doing and let me not utter solemn sounds on thoughtless tongue.

---

[40] Great-grandmother Eleanor Ryburn Nichol (1781-1864), wife of Josiah Nichol (1770-1833). Both are buried in Nashville's Old City cemetery.

Chapter Three
School, 1861

"...that I may be in after years an ornament to society and the delight of my dear parents."

Monday, September 2nd 61.
Started to school to-day with the full determination of improving myself in every one of my studies.

September 3rd/61.
I arose early this morning all fixed for school. Took a music lesson from Aunt Sarah Nichol. Nothing more worthy of recording.

Friday, Sep. 6th/61.
Went to the city to day to take my lesson but did not go to school as there is nothing doing. I do not feel at all happy to day. I don't know why but all day I have felt miserable. I have retired to offer up my prayers but still feel sad.

Saturday, Sep. 7th/61.
This morning I rose after spending a sleepless and unhappy night. Have been busy all day mending my clothes, practicing, &c.

Monday, September 9th/61.
Was up early and started to school in good earnest. Returned home and started part of my task for tomorrow and hope to know them perfectly. We are now studying Wilson's Outline of History, Dagg's Moral Science, English Synonyms, French, Latin, Philosophy, Chemistry and many others.

Tuesday, Sep 10th /61. [Date given, but no journal entry.]

Saturday, Sep 21st/61.

I arose very late this morning and set to work to study my lessons for Monday. I have so many things to attend to that I have not as much time to devote to this duty as I have hither done. I get up in the morning and have time to get through my duties before the bell rings for breakfast. I then go immediately to school and return at 1:30 o'clock, and then prepare my lessons, practice my music and by that time [it] is night. I feel so tired that I immediately perform the most important of all duties, and am soon sound asleep.

Sunday, Sep 22nd /61. [There is a date given, but no journal entry.]

Sunday, Oct 7th 1861.

The weather prevented me from attending church this morning; but I endeavored to spend the day profitably in "meditation, prayer and praise."

Friday, November 29th (1861)

I again take time to write in my journal. Have been prevented from doing so for a long time on account of the many duties I have now to attend to; but I am sorry to say in endeavoring to take a high stand in my class, I have left undone all those duties which are of so much more importance than worldly gain! Oh! God lead me in the right, heal my many backslidings, and give grace and strength for the future.

November 30th 1861.

Arose early this morning and practiced nearly two hours; I then assisted Sissie in many of her duties, and prepared my own tasks for Monday. Have given away to my old enemy temper, and at times I feel as if I will give up trying to subdue it; but I will still hope and persevere and think by asking God to assist me in subduing it I will at length stand victorious in the contest.

Maggie closes the year 1861 without writing in her journals for the longest period of time since her first entry. The entire month of December has no entries.

The close of the first year of war found the following results. The Confederates had captured the large arsenals at Harper's Ferry and near Norfolk. They had been successful in two battles of the year, Bull Run and Wilson's Creek. They had also found success in minor engagements at Big Bethel, Carthage, Lexington, Belmont, and Ball's Bluff. The Federals had saved Fort Pickens and Fort Monroe and had captured the forts at Hatteras Inlet and Port Royal. They gained victories at Philippi, Rich Mountain, Boonville, Carrick's Ford, Cheat Mountain, Carnifex Ferry and Dranesville. They had also saved to the Union, the states of Missouri, Maryland and the area of Western Virginia which would become the state of West Virginia. Most important, they had thrown the whole South into a state of siege, the Federal armies on the north and the west by land and the navy in the east by sea maintaining a vigilant blockade of southern ports. The South's economy was starting to decline due to lack of imports and exports.

With the New Year 1862, the Federal army now numbered 500,000 while the Confederate had about 350,000. During the first year, there had been random fighting; the war now assumed a general plan. The year's campaign on the part of the North had three main objects: (1) the opening of the Mississippi to Federal forces (2) the blockade of the Southern ports and (3) the capture of the Confederate capitol Richmond.

The war in the West had the Confederates holding a strong line of defense to include fortified posts at Columbus, Fort Henry, Fort Donelson, Bowling Green, Mill Spring, and Cumberland Gap. To open up the Mississippi and other western rivers, the Federal government decided to pierce the line near the center, along the Tennessee and Cumberland rivers. This would compel the evacuation of rebel forces under General Albert Sidney Johnston at Bowling Green and General Leonidas Polk at Columbus, Kentucky. With the rebel forces gone, the river to Vicksburg and road to Nashville would be open.[41]

The January 1, 1862 entry has a passage copied from a Nashville newspaper, the *Union and American*. Maggie makes entries throughout the journals which indicate the importance of newspapers to the citizens of that time.

January 1st/62.

Copied from the Union American. 1861 has gone forever! Its exit sealed, a period which will always stand preeminently marked in the annals of Time. It will afford the historian as rich material as ever engaged his pen. It sank into past Eternity laden with as grand events as ever seen by man. It was a year of commotion, deep and universal, among the nations of earth. Within its cycle we have beheld a great Republic dismembered and from the ruins of the old estate a nation arise, distinct in its character, harmonious in its parts, and soon destined to lead a grand and glorious career among the Powers of the world. It has been a

---

[41] Barnes, *A Brief History of the United States*, Epoch V, pages 223-224.

year of gloom, and relieved only by the hope that the star of Southern Independence now emerging from the clouds of the present Revolution will provide a future in which we shall enjoy the blessings of peace and prosperity.

The New Year sets in minds as this Revolution which has brought upon the country never before realized by the American people. We feel deeply grateful to a kind Providence for the success which has thus far attended our armies wherever they have been thrown against our enemy; and we humbly beseech Him to continue His gracious care over us and our people during the year upon whose threshold we stand today. We trust that before the ensuing twelve months have rolled away, we may look up to a sky of peace while our afflicted country shall be rid of its enemies adorning again in its prosperous career....

Maggie begins her New Year in the following manner: "1862 A <u>miserable year!</u>" Often she will make entries in her journal explaining how 1862 was a very miserable year in her life. Some of these would be added to the journal text at a later date, most likely at the end of the year.

Maggie goes on to add the following statement to open the year:

The year 1861 with all its perplexities and sorrows has mingled its self with things which have been. I began it with earnest resolves to prefer God's love to all other things, to resist temptations, and break snares when they were turning most alluringly around me. The thoughts and prayers were not without <u>some</u> effect. Never the less my sins need washing in my Lord's blood. How can I grieve him who gave his life for me? I have many friends whose smile is clear to me as the light of morning, and whose voice is melody to my soul. <u>Them I do not forget</u>. Yet I am unmindful of Him whose eye is ever on me, whose ear marks every word on my tongue, who loves me far better than any human being can love and who will call me to account for all my days of negligence and coldness. Great God take me and make me holy; take me now in the flower of life and let me live to thee alone!

Saturday, January 11th 1862.

This morning I arose early and studied my tasks for Monday; after school I dressed and went to town to bring out Uncle James Armstrong. I then returned home and studied my history. It is so warm that we can almost comfortably do without a fire. I have just commenced the New

Year. It may produce many changes but I will leave the future all in God's hands. Mean time may it be spent to his glory. There are some points I would aim at: 1. More <u>openness and confidence</u> with my dearest mother 2. Self denial 3. Improvement of every hour; Lowliness, esteeming others better than myself; not wishing to be admired for my looks, conversation or playing.

Sunday, Jan 12th/62.

Did not go to church to day on account of it's looking so much like rain. About 3 o'clock it turned cool and commenced raining and by night the ground was covered with sleet.

Monday 13th.

It was so cold and disagreeable that I was compelled to remain at home but I have spent the day profitable in studying and practicing.

Wednesday 15th 1862.

I am again at home on account of the weather. Have employed my self in various ways. Practiced 2 hours.

Sunday, January 19th/62.

I am again prevented from attending church on account of the inclemency of the weather. A sad death has occurred within the last few days. Cousin Ben McCulluch Nichol departed this life on the 17th after a long and painful illness of typhoid and pneumonia. Cousin Ben was the second son of our old and esteemed fellow citizen James Nichol Esq. Only a few weeks since, he was seen upon the streets of Nashville in robust health, giving of a long and useful life. Today a large circle of adoring friends and a devoted family mourn him. Stricken down in the morning of his career which - though unostentatious and confined to the private walks of life - daily evinced the possession of the genuine and sterling virtues which go to make up the true man. Cousin Ben was gentile and kindly in his deportment, steady and correct in his habits, faithful and industrious in the discharge of his duties, a model son and brother, and a sincere friend. His death leaves a large void not to be filled. His memory will long linger with those who have enjoyed his friendship, while in the bosom of his bereaved family, it will live a tender cherished, and hallowed recollections.

Monday, January 27th, 1862. "The last time I ever saw him!"[42]

Uncle James went today to Bowling Green to join his Brigade. Tomorrow I start school after an absence of two weeks with the full determination of improving myself in all my studies so that I may be in after years an ornament to society and the delight of my dear parents. At the same time that I want to gain worldly knowledge, I don't want to remain in ignorance of that learning which is of far greater importance than all worldly gain.

Sunday, Feb. 2nd 1862.

It is so cold and disagreeable that I have concluded not to go to church. Spent the day in reading my Bible and performing other religious duties.

---

[42] James Trooper Armstrong II, Captain 13th Arkansas Infantry CSA, was killed in action during the Battle of Stones River. The underlined entry is believed to have been added over a year later to emphasize her loss. Refer to her February 22, 1863 entry.

Chapter Four
The Panic

*"This night our city will be surrendered to the Yankees
and how many peaceful and happy homes will be made desolate!"*

On the Western front, the clouds of war were rapidly gathering. The war department deemed Columbus impregnable; General Ulysses Grant with his army and Commodore A. H. Foote with his naval gun boats moved from Cairo, Illinois upon Fort Henry located on a poorly located area of the Tennessee River. On February 6, a naval bombardment from the gunboats reduced the place in about one hour. The army's land troops were to cut off a retreat but upon arriving too late, the rebel garrison was able to retreat to Fort Donelson. With Fort Henry captured, the fleet went back to Cairo and by way of the Ohio River ascended the Cumberland to hook up with Grant in an all out attack upon Fort Donelson. Due to stiff resistance and a well constructed fort, the battle would last three days before the fort would be surrendered due to worn out troops and dwindling supplies. A fresh last minute reinforcement of Federal troops aided Grant in its capture. When Confederate General Simon Buckner, the post commander wrote to Grant offering capitulation, Grant replied that no terms other than "unconditional surrender" would be accepted and that he "proposed to move immediately upon their works." On February 16, 1862 a total force of about 15,000 rebels were captured with the fort. A small number of troops to include Generals Floyd, Price, Pillow and Cavalry Colonel Nathan Bedford Forrest were able to break out and reach the temporary safety of Nashville. With both Fort Henry and Donelson now in Federal hands, as expected, Columbus and Bowling Green were evacuated. Within a few days, Union General Don Carlos Buell occupied Nashville. General Johnston retreated with his Confederate forces to Murfreesboro by way of Nashville. He finally met with Polk's forces in Corinth, Mississippi. Grant's Union army ascended the Tennessee River to Pittsburg Landing where the Battle of Shiloh would be fought during the early part of April, 1862.[43]

---

[43] Barnes, *A Brief History of the United States*, Epoch V, pages 224-225.

At this time, events far beyond Maggie's control begin affecting her life. With the fall of Fort Donelson, the Cumberland River is wide open to Nashville, the capital city of Tennessee. The February 16, 1862 entry announces the surrender of Nashville. In parentheses next to the entry Maggie writes, *"The most miserable year of my life."* This is the beginning of Maggie's heightened acknowledgement of the war within the pages of her journal, whereas her writing had previously been dominated by her religious exercises. She is forced to deal with the reality of the war only when it hits close to home and affects her own very priviledged life. In later years in the journal, she mentions not the anniversary of the beginning of the war, but the anniversary of the "Great Panic" when Nashville was surrendered.

With the Fort Donelson surrender, she writes of families forced to desert their homes. For safety, family members residing in Nashville leave for the safe confines of Williamson County. They take Maggie and her two younger sisters along to West View, the home of cousins living in Triune. The parents stay behind at Mt. Alban to protect the family possessions. On February 23, 1862 she comments on a cousin going back to his home in Nashville and asks him to check on her parents. The February 25, 1862 entry finds 10,000 Federal troops in Nashville and prominent men being arrested. Note the February 15, 1862 journal entry regarding her plans for Monday.

The Attack on Fort Donelson

Saturday, February 15th 1862.

Rose this morning very late and studied my lessons for Monday. I hope that I may know them perfectly. Nothing has occurred worthy of recording. Had a visit from a friend (Sallie House) which was a very agreeable surprise.

Sunday, Feb. 16th 1862. (The most miserable year of my life)[44]

Oh! what a miserable wrenched unhappy day I have spent! This night our city will be surrendered to the Yankees and how many peaceful and happy homes will be made desolate! We will have to leave ours and fly to some place of safety but wherever we go may God shield and protect us. May our country soon be rid of its enemies and may we look up to a sky of unclouded peace and prosperity.

The Flight to Safety

---

[44] Entry in parathesis is believed to have been added at a later date to emphasize how horrible the year was.

West View, Feb 18th 1862.

We arrived here[45] after many adventures about ten o'clock last night broken down in body and spirits. I left Mother and Father[46] at home to pack up and it is probable that they will also come up to Triune, but I hope and pray that if they do stay God will bless and protect them. I try very hard to keep my usual spirits but it is with great effort that I do it. Oh! what a horrid thing is war. Everyone is deserting their homes in order to seek a place of safety. Where we are now is about 22 miles from Nashville and on the Nolensville pike. It has been raining all day.

West View, Feb. 19th/62.

I rose very late this morning as it seemed nearly impossible for me to get to sleep last night on account of thinking about home and wondering where they were and what they were doing. Our baggage came last night and we were greatly relieved as we were in fear of our waggons being pressed. I feel perfectly miserable at times, but when I do feel so I always retire to my room and find my greatest consolations in meditation and prayer. No words can tell how happy I feel after hours thus spent. I intend going on with my French so as not to fall back for God only knows when I can finish my education.

Almost-daily journal entries begin to show how much the war is starting to affect Maggie's life. The family home, Mount Alban,[47] is on Franklin Pike. Entries over the next several years show the home to be very much in the midst of military activity. Immediately following the flight to safety, she is writing from West View, [the Triune, TN home of cousins Sam and Ella Brown Perkins] her parents having stayed behind at Mount Alban to try to protect their property. They stay in touch with their daughters and send along parcels and treats, but Maggie is very anxious to return. At West View, she goes horseback riding, walking, and even tries fishing. She wants to stay to herself and has to be made to leave her room and socialize in the library with others.

West View, Thursday Feb 20th 1862.

Nothing has happened worthy of being recorded only there have been confused rumors that Nashville has been taken by the Federals. Ma sent us some cakes and clean clothes which proved very acceptable.

---

[45] West View was the Triune, Williamson County estate of Samuel Fearn Perkins.
[46] Parents Joseph Vaulx (1799-1878) and Eleanor Ryburn Armstrong (1816-1895).
[47] Refer to April 26, 1861 and October 30, 1862 entries.

West View, Feb 21ˢᵗ 1862.

I rose this morning very late and was for the first time ready for breakfast. Took a long ride on horse-back and returned home feeling much better as I had a severe headache before I started. The house is now crowded with soldiers, some from the late fight at Ft. Donelson who gave us many interesting particulars of the battle. I am still anxious by hope each day may bring mother and father to us but it closes with my hopes scattered to the four winds of Heaven. I however earnestly commend them every night and morning to God's keeping and hope that He will watch over and protect them and soon bring them to us safe.

West View, Feb 22ⁿᵈ 1862.

Got up early this morning and poured forth my prayers to God thanking Him for my peaceful sleep during the past night. I fully intended taking a ride on horse-back this evening but it rained so hard that my intentions were naught. I still lean on the strong arms of Jesus for support and guidance under this great affliction and my happiest hours are spent in returning to my room and pouring forth my heartfelt prayers to my Maker.

Sunday, Feb 23ʳᵈ 1862.

I rose up early this morning and spent a delightful hour in prayer. This has been the most pleasant day this winter; just as mild as spring. Quite a contrast with yesterday for it was pouring torrents all day. I have been more homesick today than I have been since I have been up here, but try to console myself that father and mother will soon be here or we will return to our dear and happy home. Charlie Percy went home this morning and I gave him strict injunctions to go by to see how they all are at our house. I do miss going to church so much but I nevertheless spend my Sabbaths in devotional exercises.

~~Monday,~~[48] Feb 25ᵗʰ 1862. (Tuesday)

I rose up early this morning although I sat up very late last night writing a letter to Brother Joe and Uncle James Armstrong. We heard today that 10,000 Federal troops had arrived in Nashville and had arrested Gen. Barrow[49] one of our most prominent men. Oh! how I long

---

[48] In the original manuscript, a strike through has been made on Monday. No entry was recorded for Monday the 24ᵗʰ.

[49] George W. Barrow was appointed by Governor Harris as commissioner to negotiate Tennessee's entry into a civil and military league with the Confederacy. Barrow was arrested

for mother and father were up here, but it is impossible to wish it for I received a letter from them saying that they would remain at home to protect their property, leaving the future in God's hands. I have been more gloomy and home-sick today than any time since I came up. I do wish Ma would come up or send for us to come to her for I am sick and tired of this way of being with no <u>mother</u> or father to consult about anything. I <u>earnestly</u> <u>hope</u> and <u>pray</u> that the time may soon come when we will all be restored to our happy homes and our sunny South freed of its enemies, and may we be a people whose God is the Lord! Ma wrote me a long, kind and affectionate letter giving me some excellent advice, and telling me as I was the oldest of her little flock she very naturally looked to me to advise and direct the other two.[50] I felt that I was very incapable of filling so important post, and I rushed to my room and gave vent to many bitter tears. I at length controlled myself enough to fall on my knees and pour <u>forth</u> my prayers beseeching Him to give me aid to cheer, encourage and direct them to the path of duty.

The Occupation of Nashville, Tennessee[51]

---

and charged with treason. He was later incarcerated at Fort Mackinac, a federal prison in Detroit, Michigan. After being released, he would live in St. Louis. See Durham's, *Nashville, the Occupied City 1862-1865*, pages 71-72, 167 (Knoxville, The University of Tennessee Press).

[50] Maggie's younger sisters Catherine (Kate, 1847-1931) and Martha Vaulx (Mattie, 1852-1919).

[51] The 51st Ohio Infantry Regiment as assembled on Nashville's Court Square February 25, 1862. The photograph is courtesy of the Ohio Historical Society.

West View, (Wednesday) Feb 26th 1862.

I rose very late this morning with an awful headache in consequence I suppose of spending such a miserable night. What would I not give to be at home with dear father and mother! All my relations complain of me talking so little. It is not because I am cold or distant but who can be talkative under such gloomy circumstances? Not I, surely! Took a long walk, hoping that my head would be better but it is nearly bursting now as I write.

West View, (Thursday) Feb 27th/62.

This morning I got up before sunrise and spent such a delightful hour in prayer before anyone else had risen. We walked about 2 miles to-day fishing; when we arrived at the place specified we waited a long time for our beaux's to come but our patience at length became exhausted and we went home, and found that we had misunderstand the boys and went to the wrong place. I would give my weight in gold to be at home just now. I never thought of remaining up here so long, if so would not have come and left mother and father by themselves. We heard today the Yankees had extended their pickets some 8 or 10 miles; if that is the case they are some distance beyond our house. There is no more hope of my dear parents coming up. Will I ever see them again? I feel so wretched that I just go to my room and remain there until someone comes and reproves me for staying by myself so much. I go to the library and there sit as if I was family. Words fail to tell what a relief it is for me to get off by myself to muse undisturbed with my own thoughts. Why will they not let me enjoy those peaceful hours alone?

Friday, Feb 28th 1862.

I rose early this morning, not withstanding I was just in time for breakfast. Afterwards I heard Mattie all her lessons thoroughly although I was compelled to deny myself the pleasure of a walk with the boys and Cousin Sam [Perkins]; I feel much happier as my conscience told me that I had performed my duties instead of indulging in pleasure. Ellen Percy and I took a ride on horse-back this evening and went about 12 miles so I necessarily feel very much fatigued.

Maggie will continue to relay rumors on the national and international scenes and of battles happening close by. Maggie's first journal entry in March contains a rumor that England, France, and Belgium have recognized the Southern Confederacy and ordered the Federals to leave Southern soil.[52]

---

[52] This entry relates to the ongoing effects of the Trent Affair. It was a diplomatic incident which could have caused problems between the United States and the European nations of England

Saturday, March 1st 62.

I have been unwell today with a sick headache. Wrote a note to Ma today begging her to let me come home or for them to come up here, but I expect that it will be useless. We heard that the pickets were not on the Franklin road, if so it is probable that she will send or write to us. Today is the beginning of a new month and I earnestly pray that when it expires, it may find us peacefully settled in our homes. There is a rumor that England, France, Belgium have recognized the Southern Confederacy and ordered the Federals to leave our soil; and the Confederates to abandon Northern ground. Alas untrue!

Sunday, March 2nd/62.

I was very tardy in rising this morning and was late at breakfast, much to my shame. I then returned to my room and performed my religious duties, afterwards I heard Mattie her Sunday lessons, and then took a long walk. I fully intended going to church to-day but it looked so much like rain I was compelled to deny my-self that privilege.

On March 7, 1862, Maggie is allowed to return to the Nashville area with her grandmother, but due to safety concerns stays with Aunt Jane.[53] Mount Alban has been turned into a Federal encampment. It is reported to her that all the fences have been burned around their property and soldiers are encamped in their woods. She will be in Nashville for quite a while. This temporary home gives her a chance to record some interesting observations about what is going on around her; such as the funeral of a Federal soldier, the daily marches, and other military actions.

West View, March 7th/62.

So many things have happened in the past week that I have been prevented writing in my journal. On the night of the 5th as we were eating our supper, Uncle Alex [Nichol] sent a carriage and a pass from Genl. Buell for Aunt Jane to come immediately home. After

---

and France. On November 8, 1861 Captain Charles Wilkes of the United States Navy halted the British ship Trent and removed Confederate commissioners J. M. Mason and John Slidell. The two envoys were detained amid sharp British protest. The matter was defused when the U. S. Secretary of State William H. Seward sent a notice disavowing the action and releasing the men. The incident is included in Maggie's list of important dates of the War for Southern Independence. See appendix.

[53] Jane Ramsey Nichol Brown (1818-1899). Residence at 33 N. Cherry Street. Today it would be 4th and Union, but then it was known as the Josiah Nichol block.

considering the question for some time, I concluded to remain with Grandma and the children, as I had a great many things in wash. Yesterday, Aunt Jane sent a carriage for all of us to come home. Fortunately, I had all my things packed and therefore we did not lose much time. We started about 10 o'clock and reached Nashville just about dark. We had great difficulty getting through the pickets as they had just received an order not to let anyone come or go. Grandma pleaded very hard and at last succeeded as one the officers promised to take all the responsibility. I never felt so grateful to any one in my life, for if he had refused us, we would have been compelled to remain all night in the carriage as there was no <u>respectable</u> house within 4 miles. Two or three mornings before we left, a portion of our cavalry ventured down as far as 5 miles of Nashville and captured 4 prisoners about day light. One of the pickets remarked to us that some of their men had been captured and that that was the source of the strict order.

The Return

Chapter Five
Ensconced at Aunt Jane's

"Ma is very anxious for us to come home but as yet Pa thinks it is unsafe."

Nashville, Monday, March 10th/62.

I was dilatory in rising this morning as it seems to be impossible for me to get over my ride on Saturday. Pa came in to see us today and is very low spirited. The federals have destroyed and burned all our fences and a large cavalry is now encamped in the woods just immediately back of our house. Father is much undecided whether to stay or come into town. All our things are up at Triune and it seems little hope of getting them. There is a report today that our army at Manassas[54] entirely defeated the Federals and taken a large number of prisoners; also that Gen. Price had gained a glorious victory for us and was in full pursuit of the enemy.[55] Oh! that all this war would soon cease and our invaders be driven from our once happy land. Jesus is my only support in these dark days of adversity; for no matter how grieved and troubled I am about earthly things, my mind is calm as I know that Jesus is my friend.

Tuesday, March ~~10~~ 11th 1862.

Rose early this morning notwithstanding I spent such a sleepless night. We had a visit from our minister (Dr. Hendrick) who is now filling in Mr. Bardwell place, who has gone to Mississippi. He is such an agreeable man. He was forced to leave Paducah when the Federals took possession of that city. Pa comes in every day to see us and is very gloomy. Charlie Percy managed to get out to our house and reports that the entire side of our hill is a perfect encampment. Ma is getting on very well and regrets that we did not remain in Triune.

---

[54] Reference to The First Battle of Bull Run fought on July 21, 1861 near Manassas, Va.
[55] The Battle of Pea Ridge was fought in March 1862 in northwest Arkansas. The outcome of the battle gave the Union control of the border state of Missouri. Barnes, *A Brief History of the United States*, Epoch V, pages 230. The reader may note Maggie's false report and euphoria of victory at Pea Ridge.

Wednesday, March ~~11~~ 12th 1862.

I was rather lazy in rising this morning but I think that I am excusable as I was compelled to be up through the night with Mattie who was a little sick. Went up to see Cousin Lizzie Lea[56] and then took a long walk. I have just returned from church and feel so unhappy; but alas this is no proof of my nearness to God! Oh! That I could serve my Maker more than I do. Some times when I kneel in prayer, my mind wanders and I arise without knowing one single word I have offered. I <u>must</u> correct this evil. Ma has not yet come in. I wonder if she thinks I can do without seeing her forever. It's now nearly a month, but it seems as if it were four. Oh! How earnestly do I pray that our once happy land may soon be freed of its enemies and our home and firesides made cheerful by the safe return of my dear brother, relatives and friends. Such is ever the fervent prayer on my soul. I have received no letter or news from Brother since he left Winchester [Virginia], and therefore perfectly ignorant of his whereabouts but I hope and pray that God will protect and shield him from all danger wherever he is and if it should be his lot to fall bleeding for his country, may bright angels convey his noble soul to a purer and better world, to dwell forever with his Savior in whose sacred promises I hope he puts all his trust!

Thursday, March ~~12~~ 13th 62.

I have been busy all day sewing and reading the "Life of Napoleon Bonaparte" which is one of the most interesting works I have ever read. I want to break myself of the habit of reading novels (I am happy to say I am not as much addicted to it as I was once) and accustom myself to reading histories and the lives of great men, which I am now fully convinced of greater pleasure and at the same of more importance than all those frivolous works of fiction. I am determine hereafter every morning after breakfast to steal to my room and hold communion with my Heavenly Father, for whenever I kneel in prayer when anyone else is present my mind wanders and I utter "solemn sounds on a thoughtless tongue." We engaged a man to go to Triune to get our trunks and so I hope I will be prepared to attend church next Sabbath.

---

[56] Elizabeth Overton, daughter of Judge John Overton. She married John McCormick Lea in 1843. He served as Assistant U. S. District Attorney (1843-1845), Mayor of Nashville (1849), and Circuit Judge after the Civil War. He was part of the commission which surrendered Nashville to the Federals in February 1862.

Friday, March ~~13~~ 14th 62.[57]

I was up before any one this morning and spent those moments in prayer and praise to God thanking Him for my peaceful night's rest and imploring his protection through the day. I fully intended going to see a friend[58] to-day but it has been raining so constantly that I was denied the privilege. What is this compared to [being] deprived of attending church tonight? I am very much afraid our clothes will get wet if it continues raining as it is now. Ma has not yet come in. If it goes much longer I think I shall try to induce Pa to let me go out and stay a few days and then return. I am almost afraid to ask that favor! Just to think I am only three miles from home and still cannot go to that sacred spot, where I have spent so many happy hours.

Saturday, March 15th 1862.

Went to see my friend this morning and spent the time delightfully. Ma sent us a portion of our clothing and some delicious cakes. She is very anxious for us to come home but as yet Pa thinks it is unsafe. The man who went for our baggage returned saying they positively refused to let him pass the lines. So I will be compelled to absent myself again from worship to-morrow, but it will not however prevent me from passing the day in performing my religious duties.

Sunday, March 16th 1862.

I expect I rose this morning sooner than I have done for some time. I have spent the day very profitably. I passed two hours alone this morning. It is needless to say how they were employed. I love solitude so much; my heart delights in its own company and finds this a richer engagement than any which can befriend in social life. Really I am in no way indebted to external sources of amusement; in contemplating God in nature and in holding sweet communion with Him in the solitude of my chamber. I find more pleasure than in crowded halls of mirth. Indeed I am rather unsocial; I do not like company; I am quite miserly in selecting my sources of happiness. To hold sweet intercourse with my own heart in my dear closet with my Bible are the greatest delight I can enjoy.

---

[57] The original manuscript shows strike throughs and corrected dates for March 10th through 14th. I believe the excitement of going home and added stress of having to stay in Nashville with relatives to have caused Maggie to lose track of her days.

[58] I believe this friend to be fellow schoolmate Irene A. Watkins, identified on the journal's inside front cover page as a particular friend.

Monday, March 17th 62.

A month today since I have seen my dear mother and home. I have retired to-day to mediate and pray. Took a long walk with my friend this evening. Oh! that I could be the means of reconciling her to her Saviour. We would then be the helpers of each other's sorrow and joys in this world, and we could look forward if death should [point] to a happy reunion in the better world. Let us pray that I may be enabled to bring her to choose the better portion. I feel that I am very sinful and at times am almost determined to give up trying to become one of Christ lowly children. A funeral of a Federal soldier came by our house this morning. It was the saddest sight I ever witnessed and I think I can say with Washington Irving, "Who can look upon the grave even of an enemy and not [feel] a compunctious throb, that he should have warred with this handful of dust that now lies smoldering before him." Sometimes when I look at the large regiments of Federals that daily march through our city, I can scarcely view them with any kind of feeling but <u>hatred</u>. Is this Christian like? Is it in accordance with Him who said "Bless them that curse you and despitefully use you? Love your enemies?" Let me pray that God may put it into our enemies' hearts to stop this war and bloodshed and may we be a people whose God is the Lord!

Tuesday, March 18th 1862.

I was late in rising this morning in consequence of taking so much exercise the previous evening. Pa came in to see us to-day and thinks there is a chance of us getting the trunks from Triune. I have had a wretched headache all day but took a walk which partially relieved it. I have felt so home-sick and sad to-day. It is now over a month since I have seen mother and words fail to tell how many sad hours I spent longing to see her, from whom I have been separated a greater length of time than I ever knew.

Friday, March 21st 1862.

I was late in getting up this morning in consequence of not being well for the last few days. I took a long walk with some friends on the 20th and returned and had I think a chill; as the night was warm and I was shivering as if it was in the middle of December. Mother has not yet come in, but we hear from her regularly every day and Father comes in nearly every day. He says there are such a vast number of troops on our road that he was two or three hours getting in. I have been quite unhappy to-day not on account of anything I have said or done but about my little sisters whose tempers are not easily subdued, and it makes me as unhappy seeing them display it as if it were myself who committed the fault. I am thankful to say that I have by the aid of Providence almost conquered mine, and I must now assist and encourage my little charges to overcome their enemy. Wilt thou look down oh! my Heavenly Father and smile upon my undertaking, and may my efforts be crowned with success. I must expect to encounter [many] difficulties but I will then have occasion to exercise patience which is I think one of the holiest traits in a Christian's character. Let me commence with a stout heart putting all my trust in Him.

By late March 1862, Maggie is back to her studies and religion begins again to be a frequent topic. The girls' trunks containing their clothes have not arrived, thus church and other social activity is limited. She serves well in her role as big sister and substitute mother during those trying days. She continues to wonder about the fate and location of Brother Joe and Uncle James Armstrong, and the war hits home as she learns of the death of a young friend.

Saturday, March 22nd 1862.

I was quite indolent in rising this morning as I thought but upon going down stairs, I found myself "alone in my glory." Have felt very unwell all day but I took some medicine to-night and I hope I will soon be well to attend to my usual duties. Another Sunday has rolled around and I find myself compelled to remain at home from church. Pa came to see us and brought us some eatables, which were received with many thanks. Little Mattie came to my room last night just crying fit to kill herself. After much difficulty I fathomed the cause of her distress which was that she and Sissie had been playing a game of cards and Mattie being more lucky than Kattie, the latter accused her of cheating, at the thought of which Mattie's proud spirit revolted. She immediately came up to me to make known her grief. I talked very kindly to her and she promised me she would not give way to her temper anymore and as night has come, I can say that she has kept her promise as far as I can see. O! may I ever be thus successful.

Sunday, March 23rd /62.

Have spent a long pleasant day although I passed it alone which gave me a fine opportunity to indulge in my greatest delight - prayer. Still continue a little sick, but I hope by doting to soon get well again.

Monday, March 24th /62.

I have nothing to record today but once or twice I have given away to my temper; and I am necessarily unhappy.

Wednesday, March 26th 1862.

I was very brisk in rising this morning notwithstanding I spent such a wretched night. Our trunks came very unexpectedly late last night and oh! I can't tell how glad I was to get a new dress to put on. Pa didn't come in to-day as he promised. I have felt very miserable all day because I have failed to be as strict in my religious duties as heretofore. I must endeavor to steal away from the family and give a portion of time to my religious observances which are to me of far greater delight than all worldly amusements. Besides neglecting the above, I have not guarded as closely as I ought my enemy temper which is at times beyond control, but I hope by praying to soon entirely overcome it. Just as I am writing Ellen is playing that beautiful song "Home Sweet Home". O! how to my eyes will that song bring bitter tears. That sacred spot whose memory is so dear to his heart is perhaps left desolate and is now only occupied by an evading face. Such is the fate of war.

Thursday, March 27th 1862.

I have been kept very busy to-day attending to the making of some dresses and consequently feel somewhat fatigued. Pa came in to-day and brought us some nice eatables which were received with many thanks as anything particularly nice is always devoured with great [delight] during such times as these. I have failed again to perform my religious duties to-day and my conscience is therefore not at rest. Can I ever be faithful to my God?

Friday, March 28th /62.

I don't think I was as lazy rising in my life as I was this morning. I have always desired to form a habit of early rising, but I think it will be impossible to acquire it at this rate. Been very busy all day attending to my duties but is this a sufficient excuse for my neglecting my duties to my God, which are of so much more importance than all worldly affairs. I must and I shall commence to pay more attention to my religion than I have heretofore done. Assist me my God and heal my many backslidings!

Saturday, March 29th/1862.

I was again lazy this morning, but upon going downstairs I found I was up before the lady of the house which partially compensated for my indolence. I heard sad, sad news today on the death of a young friend who was killed in the failed engagement at Fort Donelson (or rather mortally wounded). He was the youngest son of Rev. P. S. Fall[59] and the idol of his father and mother. Seldom does this world of ours produce such a youth so pure, so noble! It seems as though this world was too gross, too wicked for so noble, so pure a spirit to inhabit and he was called away to a world better suited to his disposition. I am now conscience to the agony of parting with a friend never again to see him until the trump is sounded and the sea and earth is required to give up their dead! Yet it is a <u>great</u> <u>consolation</u> to think that I will there see him sitting there on the right hand of the Father, arrayed in the garments of angels as bright and pure as his noble spirit joining with his voice in the unanimous praise to the Almighty King, the Maker of all things! But this is what we must all come to. Death seizes with its iron grasp alike the humble, the proud, the rich and the poor from dust we were all made and at some future day each and every one of us will return to the dust. But this blow will fall with the greatest force on the relations of the deceased; on the venerable father and two loving sisters who now mourn the loss of <u>a</u> <u>younger</u> <u>son</u> and <u>brother</u>! Farewell Albert! Never more shall thy affectionate sisters await the sound *of* thy welcome footsteps. Never more shall "thy dear familiar voice" gladden the heart of a dear father, they shall watch in vain for thy coming, for thou art gone, gone, gone! "The home is broken that can never unite again." We know that it is hard to part with a dear friend but it is harder still to imprint the farewell kiss on the cold icy lips of a fond brother! Oh! may divine grace reconcile them to this severe stroke of an All wise Ruler, teach them to humbly say "not my will but thine be done." Farewell dear Albert!

Monday, March 31st, 1862.

Another month has fled and I find my-self no nearer to my God and my home than when it commenced. I had no heart to write in my journal yesterday for upon that sacred day I allowed myself to fall into a passion at my little sister, to whom I should endeavor to be a

---

[59] Dr. Philip S. Fall was a respected pacifist and leader of the local Christian Church. He would later be exempted from taking the oath of allegiance being imposed upon citizens by the Johnson government.

sister and mother. Oh! What a vile creature I am and how much more so must I appear in God's sight. O may I begin tomorrow to act more judiciously that I have been doing hitherto, and may I begin to serve my God more faithfully, kind and much [injured] Father. I own my guilt before thee, I have sinned against heaven and in thy sight. God be merciful to me a sinner. No tears of penitential grief can wash away my sins. Teach me to plead the Savior's death, and cleanse me in his atoning blood. "Create in me a new heart and renew a right spirit within me. Let no more of the precious days of my youth be spent careless as many have already been. Grant these request, O most merciful God for thy dear Son's sake to whom I could flee as my only refuge; and to whom be kingdom, power, and glory forever and forever. Amen!"

Tuesday, April 1st, 1862.

I was rather dilatory in rising this morning; but I think I made up for lost time by dressing very quickly and found that my room-mate didn't beat me much. We were very agreeably surprised this evening by the arrival of Cousin Sam and Cousin Ella who intends remaining a week with us. I have been very, very unhappy to-day on account of indulging in my temper and not acting to my intention of retiring and communing with Him whose ear is ever opened to the cry of the distressed. Can I ever expect to become one of Christ's lowly children without "praying unceasingly?" Oh! no words could tell how much I desire to be one of the humble followers of Christ, and ought I not make a greater effort to become one. I want to possess all those noble qualities which should adorn a Christian's character viz: patience, forbearance, holiness, justice, goodness and truth, and a host of others which are of so much more importance than the most precious jewels. The latter quality I must regard with the most rigid strictness, for at times when I become so engrossed in <u>conversation</u>, I let things fall from my lips where upon a moment's reflection, I find are not according to the strict principles of truth. This is a serious fault and if not corrected at once will lead I fear to serious consequences. I should take warning and correct this evil.

Wednesday, April 2nd.

Another wretched day has gone, over which I will pass without recording as my heart is bursting with grief; <u>at the many faults I have committed.</u>

Friday, April 4th 1862.

I spent last evening at a particular friend of mine, Irene Watkins and was rather early rising not withstanding I took a long walk with her and then returned and then sat up until 10 or 11 o'clock. This morning I was most agreeably surprised to see that long wished for – Ma. Oh! How glad I was to see [her]. It seems as if the time was two years since I last saw her.

Saturday, April 5th 1862.

I have been a little unwell to-day but Ellen Percy and I took quite a long walk and visited some friends whose lively conversation served as a cure. Ma did not come in this morning but promised to do so the first opportunity. To-morrow is the Sabbath, may I be enabled to keep holy that precious day and act in a different manner from last Sunday. It is also the beginning of a new week and may I commence it with a full determination of living nearer to God. Immediately after breakfast I retired to a small room (where I intend holding communion with my God each day) and I enjoyed a delightful hour of meditation and prayer. I expect to resume my studies in a few days. I must confess I would much rather remain at home under such sad circumstances, but at the same I consider it a great privilege to attend school and I therefore am determined to store [my] mind with useful knowledge during the remaining months of the session.

Tuesday, April 8th 1862.

I have failed to perform my duties and am therefore not at all happy. Cousin Sam came for Cousin Ella who will return [home] to-morrow morning. We will miss her a great deal. Ma came in to-day and has not yet decided about my going to school. I would much rather not attend as long as I remain in town for there is so much confusion. It would be impossible for me to fix my mind on my books. However, if mother thinks it best for me to go, I will do so without a murmur and perform my duties to the best of my abilities.

The Battle of Shiloh or Pittsburg Landing was a major battle in the Western Theater of the war. The two day southwestern Tennessee engagement was fought on April 6 and 7 1862. The Union army under Maj. Gen. Ulysses S. Grant had moved via the Tennessee River deep into Tennessee and was encamped principally at Pittsburg Landing on the west bank of the river. Confederate forces under Generals Albert Sidney Johnston and P.G.T. Beauregard launched a surprise attack on Grant there. The Confederates achieved considerable success on the first day, but were ultimately defeated on the second day.

The Confederates determined to rout Grant's army before the arrival of General Buell.[60] On Sunday morning, at daylight, moving out of the woods in line of battle, they suddenly fell on the Union camps. On the one side were the Southern dash, daring, and vigor; on the other, the Northern firmness and determination. The Federals slowly yielded, but for twelve hours stubbornly disputed every inch of the way. At last, pushed to the very brink of the river, Grant massed his artillery, and gathered about it the fragments of regiments for the final stand. The Confederates, to meet them, had to cross a deep ravine, where, struggling through the mud and water, they melted away under the fire of cannon and musketry from above, and the shells from the gunboats below. Few reached the slippery bank beyond. At the same time, Buell's advance lines came shouting on the field. The tide of battle was stayed. The Confederates fell back. They possessed, however, all the substantial fruits of victory. They had taken the Union camps, three thousand prisoners, thirty flags, and immense stores; but they had lost their commander, General Albert Sidney Johnston, who fell in the heat of the action. The next morning the tide turned. Buell's army had come, and fresh troops were poured on the wearied Confederates. Beauregard, obstinately resisting, was driven from the field. He retreated, however, in good order, and, unmolested, returned to Corinth. General Halleck now assumed command, and by slow stages followed the Confederates. Beauregard, finding himself outnumbered, evacuated Corinth, and Halleck took possession of it on May 30, 1862.

The Confederates, on retreating from Columbus, fell back to Island No. 10. There they were bombarded by Commodore Foote with little effect for three weeks. General Pope, crossing the Mississippi in the midst of a fearful rain-storm, took the batteries on the opposite bank, and prepared to attack the fortifications in the rear. The Confederate garrison, seven thousand strong, surrendered on April 7, the very day of the conflict at Shiloh.

The results of the Battle at Shiloh were now fully apparent. The Union gunboats moved down the river and on May 10 defeated the Confederate iron-clad fleet. On the evacuation of Corinth, Fort Pillow[61] was abandoned. The gunboats, proceeding, destroyed the Confederate flotilla in front of Memphis, took possession of that city, and secured the Memphis and Charleston railroad. The great State of Kentucky and all Western Kentucky and Tennessee had been taken from the Confederacy.[62]

The news of the Battle of Shiloh reaches Nashville, first with fear and then high thoughts of success. Later news will show the former.

---

[60] General Don Carlos Buell, commanding the Army of the Ohio, was enroute from Nashville to provide reinforcements for Grant's army.
[61] A rebel stronghold located north of Memphis on the banks of the Mississippi River.
[62] Barnes, *A Brief History of the United States*, Epoch V, pages 224-228.

Thursday, April 10th 1862.

I was late in retiring last night on account of hearing some very distressing news and I therefore sat up in the hopes of hearing some better tidings; but all failed! This morning however the tide has turned in our favor and it seems that we are the conquerors; but at what a cost! As I now sit by [a] comfortable fire, I cannot help but think of the many friends and relatives that are now perhaps tossing over beds of sickness and suffering with no loved one to minister to their wants; or are left to die on the bloody field of battle. Brother Joe is expected to be at Chattanooga and was therefore (I hope) not in the fight; but while my mind is at rest about him I am uneasy for fear Uncle James is in the battle. Oh! how earnestly do I hope and pray that God will shield them from all danger and bring them safely to us! To Him alone I flee in every hour of peril and I feel confident that he will guide me safely through the stormy scenes of life and land me on the peaceful shores of heaven.

Saturday, April 12th 1862.

I have just finished my Saturday nights task namely washing myself and the children and I consequently feel very tired. Each day confirms our victory at Corinth, but with all our joy, there is sorrow mingled with it. Our brave and gallant A.S. Johnston fell while leading his men on; struck by a cannonball on the leg and severing one of the leading membranes which produced his death. I am very uneasy about Uncle James for from the papers I see that his Gen (Hardee) made the attack and Gen Hindman (whose brigade Uncle is in) was wounded very badly. O! If I could only know that he was safe or if he was dead would be a relief for to be held in this kind of suspense is dreadful. Still I trust he is safe; and hope that God will shield him for He has the lives of all creatures in his hand.

Tuesday, April 15th 1862.

I have been so busily engaged during the past two days that I have failed to perform this duty. There seems as yet no chance of hearing from Brother Joe and Uncle James. We are pretty certain the former was not in the fight at Corinth, but some think that there has been more fighting and if that is the case he will be in it and will sacrifice, perhaps his life for country. But I commit him to God and hope that he will shield them and soon bring them to us.

Wednesday, April 16th 1862.

I have been very [busy] all day sewing and having my teeth plugged. Nothing worthy of note; but I think I am again straying from the path of God.

Friday, April 18th 62.

I have been quite unwell to-day with a severe headache, but Ma came in which served a measure to cure it. I am not all satisfied in regard to my progress to Heaven. I think I am neglecting Him to whom I should flee in every hour of distress and make God the hearer of my supplications. O may I be more diligent in prayer hereafter.

> The one year anniversary of Maggie's commencing her journals allows her to reflect upon her now changed life and the long-lost, carefree days of her youth at her beloved Mount Alban.

Nashville, April 26, 1862.

I have been prevented from my duty for a long time since I have many things to attend to. It is just one year since I began to write in my journal and how many events have happened in that time! Then I was settled in my home surrounded with all those I love best on earth; now I am absent from that sacred spot; and my only brother's spot is vacant around our fireplace. Pa came in today and gave us some distressing news of Ma being sick. O! how I wish that I were home to wait upon her. Every day I become more and more disgusted with my way of living and often wish for those hours I used to spend at "Mount Alban." But we never appreciate a blessing until it is withdrawn.

Nashville, April 28th 1862.

I was very late in rising this morning but I was [reassured], covered my laziness by their having a very late breakfast. Sissie has been very unwell all day and most of my time has been devoted to her. Pa didn't come in to-day on account of Ma's not being well; but Charlie says she is much better and intends coming in very soon.

Nashville, (Wednesday) 30th 1862.

I have been very busy to day waiting on sister who remains quite sick; and assisting Ellen Percy in her duties of the house on whose shoulders all that drudgery devolves. I readily avail myself of this opportunity of learning to attend to the household affairs and at the same time

I prove myself grateful to Aunt Jane for her unwavering kindness and consideration to Sister. Pa came in today and said Ma's eye is inflamed and that prevented her from coming today.

Friday, May 2nd/62.

Sister still remains quite sick with a very severe headache. I have been very busy waiting upon her and assisting Aunt Jane in her duties. I have been a little unwell but I hope that by doting I may evade a spell of sickness. Pa says Ma's eye is better but was afraid to venture out on account of so much wind.

Sunday, May 4th 1862.

I rose very late this morning having to get up in the night with poor little sister who suffered a great deal with her head, but I think she is much better and I hope may soon regain her health.

Sunday, May 11th 1862.

I was up last night until twelve o'clock waiting upon little sister who is now slowly recovering from her illness. She is so weak that she needs our constant attention. Mattie is now at home quite sick and it is on that account Ma has not been in. I am so sleepy and tired it is impossible for me write more.

Tuesday, May 13th/62.

I rose very early this morning; notwithstanding I sat up until 12 o'clock waiting on Sister who remains very sick and weak. Little Mattie is much better and I look forward to see them tomorrow. Nothing more.

Wednesday, May 14th 1862.

Ma and Mattie came in to-day and brought us some beautiful flowers which were very acceptable. It is very probable the troops will leave our place soon and I look forward with great pleasure to that happy day when we will again be settled at Mount Alban.

Tuesday, May 20th 1862.

Was up this morning at 5 o'clock and am sorry to say that I did not employ those solitary hours in prayer. Sister is getting on very well but is quite weak. The cook of Brother's regiment arrived and says he is quite ill and is now at Columbus with friends who will [supply] his comfort. Oh! how earnestly I pray he may be brought in safely to us.

Thursday, May 22nd 1862.

I have been very busily engaged to-day assisting Aunt Jane in various ways and attending to my own affairs.

Sunday, May 25th 1862.

I was very early in rising this morning and had ample time for my devotional exercises; but I am sorry to confess I neglected. I was compelled to be absent from church on account of having none of my summer things, they being up at Triune.

Monday, May 26th 1862.

Tis midnight! and midnight reigns triumphant o'er the still world. This is the hour when man must feel his nothingness- this is the hour when solemnity gains possession of the untutored Soul- this is the hour when the guilty conscience shudders beneath the pressure of a preponderous load- and this is the hour <u>when the hardened Sinner</u> sees himself unpenitent and his soul shrinks back from the prospect of eternity! But this ah yes! This is the hour when the Christian holds communion with his God or sleeps in undisturbed repose while guardian angels watch around his couch in the Spirit of their Lord they seem to say- "Sleep child of Heaven; thy Father's eye is on thee! No ill awaits thee here, but peace eternal waits [thee in] Heaven."

Friday, May 30th 1862.

I was more dilatory in rising in consequence of not being well. Oh! How I long to go home. I am so tired of staying in this hot and dusty town. The troops are still on our place and it is on that account Father is so much opposed to our returning. Ma is however very anxious for us to come home, and I do hope her opinion will sweep away all oppositions. I can truly say "there is no place like home." It is so lonesome without Aunt Jane who has gone to Triune. The house seems so desolate without her. I trust that better and happier day are in store for us; but I leave it all in the hands of God who disposes of all things for the best.

Sunday, June 1st 1862.

I was up this morning at the late hour of six and was very much hurried in my dressing. I again failed to perform my duties. Will it always continue thus. Today a new month begins and may I commence it with the determination of preferring God's law above all other things;

but I must not expect to overcome my weakness without some difficulty; and therefore beseech the aid of my Heavenly Father.

Monday, June 2nd 1862.

I have been very busy all day sewing my dresses and performing other duties. When I rose this morning I retired after dressing to the little room and there spent a delightful hour in communion with Him who heareth in secret. Each day I look forward to returning home; but I am almost afraid to anticipate much joy; as Pa is undecided about our returning owning to the insolent conduct of the troops now encamped on our place. If he thinks it is best for us to remain in town, I will obey without a murmur; although it is a great sacrifice.

Tuesday, June 3rd 1862.

I was dressed this morning just as the six o'clock bell struck and performed as yesterday my religious duties and then assisted Kattie in dressing as she has not yet regained her strength. Ma could not come in owing to its raining but I confidently expect her to-morrow. Nothing more.

Wednesday, June 4th 1862.

It was just before six when I finished my toilet. I am unhappy to-day but strange to say I can give no reason for it. Oh! how I long for some pious friend to instruct me in the way I should go. I often regret that I have not confided to mother my religious view for who would enter in to my feelings, and encourage me to cling strongly to the cross more readily than my very dear mother? Let me hereafter when we are again settled at home make her more my confident.

Friday, June 6th 1862.

As yesterday I have failed to perform my duties and can I be otherwise than happy? I must rise earlier or I never will form a habit of devotion. Went to see dear Mrs. Holcombe and I don't remember of ever spending such a delightful evening.

Monday, June 9th 1862.

I was rather lazy in rising this morning, so late that I could not perform my religious duties and therefore have not been as happy to-day as I might have been. Ma came in to see us to-day after staying from us for a week, oh! How long it seemed! I practiced a good hour to-day and employed myself in many other ways.

Wednesday, June 11th/62.

I was awakened last night about 2 o'clock by the alarm of fire and it seemed impossible for me to get to sleep for some time and when I did accomplish it I found it very difficult for me to awake as breakfast was on the table and they were eating before I could make up my mind to get up. I hope I never [again] will be guilty of such laziness. When I rise early and take a walk in the garden or practice I feel so much brighter and more in the humor of eating Aunt Amelia's delicious rolls than I would do in wasting those delightful hours in sleep. I have again to acknowledge my fault, viz: of failing to pour forth my prayers to Him in the morning. When I neglect doing it I lose the savor of divine things and trifles often cause me to forget my Heavenly Father. The course to take is to determine that; whatever are the employments of the day; I will make this the first object and seek to get my thoughts disengaged from earth and fixed on divine things. It too often happens my thoughts surrender, and I do not know what I need and to ask for. It is true there are many hindrances and I often am compelled to hurry through my devotions for fear of causing some inconvenience to the family; but may God pour upon me the spirit of prayer and supplication and may I ever consider it my dear delight. Now let me seek solemnity in coming before Jesus, remembering to whom I speak and a more knowledge of my sins, and more confessions and casting away of each; and to feel the Spirits teachings: and then my times of prayer will be very, very precious.

Thursday, June 12th 1862.

I was up this morning just as the bell struck six but was so slow in dressing I was compelled to perform my duties after breakfast; but I hope I performed them in accordance with my previous resolutions. I spent the day with Mrs. Holcombe and my old school mates and time never flew so fast and of course pleasantly. I am not satisfied with some parts of my conduct: for example when conversing with my school-mates I often in relating little anecdotes exaggerate the story, consequently I am not happy for though the beginning be ever so small it may cause me many bitter hours of remorse hereafter, so let me pluck this evil in the bud. Another source of error to me is that I continually find my-self indulging envy and jealousy, the meanest traits of a fuscous [dark] character. If I see a person with anything better than mine I immediately begin to wish for them when at the same time mine are as good as theirs. Oh! <u>may</u> <u>God</u> <u>root</u> <u>these</u> <u>evils</u> <u>from</u> <u>my</u> <u>heart</u>.

Friday, June 13th 1862.

I was up quite soon this morning but not liking to keep breakfast waiting I retired after eating to pour forth my prayers to the Most High. None of the family were in to-day, I trust nothing's wrong. I have felt a little unwell to-day owning I suppose to my being so low spirited. There is as yet no prospects of my going home but I hope the time is soon to come when I will once again enjoy undisturbed those hours of solitude at Mount Alban. When I retire to pray I am always in constant dread of being disturbed and therefore I have to shorten my prayers. I will however ask not to be disturbed.

An interesting event takes place in June 1862. Aunt Jane's son, John Preston Watts "Bul" Brown Jr., and his friend, John Kirkman, both about fifteen years of age, are arrested for trying to leave Nashville to join the Confederate army. They devise a plan to collect needed supplies and sneak out of the city and joining the army in Murfreesboro. Their plan is thwarted when the Federal police learn of the plan and arrest both. Maggie shows concern over this due to Aunt Jane's opposition to her only son, John, joining the army. It seems his scheme was to be accomplished while his mother was visiting his sister, Ella Perkins, in Triune. John will later join up and distinguish himself at the Battle of Resaca.[63]

Saturday, June 14th/62.

I was just in time for breakfast this morning; but I afterwards retired to Aunt Jane's room which is unoccupied and there engaged myself in communing with the Great Father of Spirits. Father came in to see us and on my expressing my regret at mother's not coming in he gave me a sad piece of intelligence that mother's again on the sick bed. Tomorrow is the Sabbath and may I be enabled by divine aid to keep that day holy. I will I hope attend church tomorrow and I trust my mind will be in such a state as nothing will distract it from the service. Quite a scene occurred this morning. About breakfast time we were seated at the table when the bell rang and someone inquired for John on <u>particular business</u>, but the latter being unwell had not risen and consequently his visitor failed to see him, but he returned after a little, [again] meeting with no better success. Just as we had finished eating, the bell again rang and a strange gentleman inquired for Bul. The servant informed him that the former had not risen but upon the man's insisting that he must see him she took him up to John's

---

[63] Walter T. Durham, *Nashville, The Occupied City 1862-1863*, pages 197-198 (Knoxville, The University of Tennessee Press).

room. They soon returned with Bul seeming very much agitated, Grandma hastened not to inquire the cause of it, when Bul informed her that he was under arrest. We immediately commence questioning him but the man laughed and told us nothing was the matter. We afterwards learned that something was the matter for it seems that Bul and some other of his associates had formed the plan of going off and joining a cavalry company and in preparing for the occasion had been detected by the Federal police of this city. He is now in the penitentiary and will I expect remain there for a week. Aunt Jane is in Triune and will remain there for some time. Bul went with her but becoming dissatisfied he returned and has I expect been forming this escape ever since. I am thankful he was detected before he succeeded in getting off; for he being Aunt Jane's only son she was always opposed to his joining the army and Bul thought I suppose this would be a fine opportunity of carrying into effect his wishes during her absence.

Sunday, June 15th 1862.

I rose this morning at six but having so many things to attend to I was compelled to defer my duties until after breakfast. Went to church this morning for the first time in six weeks and heard a most excellent sermon from our pastor Mr. Hendrick the text being IV chapter of Revelations 9th verse: "And they sang a new song, saying, Thou art worthy to take the book and to open the seals thereof: for thou wast slain, and hast redeemed us to God by thy blood out of every, and tongue and people and nation..." Oh! how fervently he exhorted us to come and partake of the body of Jesus broken for our many iniquities. I remained at the ceremony of the Lord's Supper and don't remember of ever witnessing such an imposing rite. How fervently do I pray that I may be brought to show forth his loving kindness at some future day by partaking of his supper. He sees all of my sins and the coldness of my heart – my readiness to forget the Rock whence I was hewned. Oh! that he may help me to live near to him, to watch my wayward heart and to be so humbled by my sins as to receive gladly my Saviour offers of guidance, and to feel that "without Him I cannot go" "Create in me a new heart and renew or right-spirit within me. O Lord. Farewell earth! Farewell all the allurements of a dying world! my God demands my heart; my God shall have it."

Monday, June 16th 1862.

I rose this morning late but had ample time for my prayers which I enjoyed exceedingly. After breakfast I attempted to make some tatting but it being so warm I found it impossible to do it. I then commenced to practice but was interrupted very pleasantly by the coming of Ma. This evening Bul was released from the Penitentiary and I hope and trust he will be prevailed upon to go up to Triune with his mother, for I know she is miserable if she has heard of the conduct of Bul. We had a hard rain and a severe thunderstorm this evening which was at times grand and awful. I bring home the question "Am I ready to die?" Would that I were sure for the hour of each day draws nearer. I think I would go to heaven through my most blessed Saviour; but O, the coldness of my heart.

Tuesday, June 17th 1862.

Just as I had finished pouring forth my prayers to God the bell rang for breakfast. Pa come in to-day and brought us the welcome intelligence that our linens and summer clothing had come and it was on that account mother was prevented from coming in. I have been very miserable to-day on account of being so low-spirited when I do get so I speak as cross to dear Grandma who is so kind and good to me. Can I be other wise than unhappy? O God root the evil from my heart.

Wednesday, June 18th.

At half past six this morning Sissie awoke me and after hurrying through my prayers and dressing, I found breakfast nothing like ready. Pa came in to-day but having so much business to attend to he neglected coming to see us. Ma wrote me a note and says all our clothes were dripping wet. I don't think I have said or done anything that is wrong but I must beseech Him to give me aid to resist temptation for without God's help, I can do nothing.

Thursday, June 19th 1862.

I was up and dressed by half past five and I then retired to Aunt Jane's room and performed my accustomed duties. I was just about <u>doing a very</u> sinful act but the still small voice of conscience warned me and therefore I was [able] to resist temptation. But I want the time to soon come when no sinful thoughts will enter my mind and to this end I will constantly pray. Pa was in this morning and brought us some fruit; and I am sorry to confess I was so much *disappointed at Ma's not coming, I gave away to a <u>little temper</u>. Why should it be so when I know full well the many duties Ma has to attend to? Let me be more reasonable hereafter.*

Friday, June 20th 1862.

I was up much earlier this morning and enjoyed a delightful hour of prayer. I don't think I have said or done anything that is wrong to-day and I trust God will give me grace to resist temptation when it is staring me most boldly in the face. Ma was in and spent the day with us so I didn't attend to my duties, but I practiced an hour before breakfast.

Saturday, June 21st 1862.

Not up as early this morning as yesterday; but had ample time for my duties. Pa was in and brought us some vegetables and our summer clothing which we were delighted to see. Nothing more.

Sunday, June 22nd 1862.

I arose this morning very early and after dressing I performed my religious duties in my own room owing to the others being occupied. Went to church this morning and heard a very impressive sermon from Dr. Hendrick; but owning to the noise, I failed to hear the text. I have been very much interested in reading a little work "Counsels to the Awakened." It gives me excellent advice and encouragement to further my prayers to Zion and I hope I will profit by them. Late this evening, Ma sent for Charlie and also some delicious cake. She wrote me a note and says she hopes we will soon be at home and when we do get there she thinks she will never let us go away from her. She will <u>not</u> have much trouble in accomplishing that!

Monday, June 23rd 1862.

It was very early this morning when I rose notwithstanding I spent a sleepless night. Sunday night we were in the sitting room having a very nice chat with Grandma when someone gave the alarm of "fire" under our window; we hastened out and found a stable immediately back of us in flames. We were very uneasy for a time but the engine and the house foreman did their work nobly and soon the angry flames were quenched without doing further injury. None of the family were in to-day and I must confess I am surprised at Ma not keeping her promise. I have spent a very miserable day on account of being home-sick, and giving away to my temper.

Tuesday, June 24th 1862.

Very late this morning but had sufficient time to my religious duties. Practiced a good hour this morning and employed myself in many other ways. Pa came in and gave me $10 which I intend laying out very usefully. Mother wrote me a very kind and interesting note giving me some excellent instructions and says she hopes we do-not think she advises us too much. No indeed <u>dear</u> <u>mother</u> could you have seen how many times I read your sacred epistle you would never have had any fears on that score. Your excellent advice will ever be treasured up in my mind and remembered and practiced through life.

Wednesday, June 25th/62.

I rose late this morning on account of not being well and after hurrying a great deal I was compelled to perform my duties after breakfast. It rained so hard none of the family could come in but after the rain had ceased Harry [family servant] was sent in with some delicious fruit which is a great treat. In the evening I assisted Ellen in cleaning and arranging the china closet which proved a tedious task. I don't know of anything that I have said or done that is wrong but I will lay open my heart to the Great Searcher of Hearts and trust he will wash away all guilt from it in the blood of his crucified Son.

Thursday, June 26th.

It was I expect 5 o'clock when I got up and I therefore had plenty of time for my beloved devotions. The rain again prevented the family from coming in, but I trust there will be no obstacle in their way tomorrow. I have felt very unwell to-day on account of having such a wretched cold; but I hope it will soon be well, at least before Ma comes in. Heard from Brother to-day. He is in Cousin Frank McNairy's[64] cavalry and is at Chattanooga. I scarcely know what to believe concerning his whereabouts as we heard some days since [he's] on Gen. Maney's[65] staff. Watch over and protect him O God, wherever he may be!

---

[64] CSA cavalry Colonel Frank McNairy was killed on February 3, 1863 during the Second Battle of Fort Donelson.

[65] George Earl Maney, a family friend and native of Franklin, TN, who became a Major General with the Confederate army. After the war, he died in Washington, DC, and is buried in Mt. Olivet Cemetery, Nashville.

Friday, June 27th.

I was up before five this morning and went through my usual devotions. Ma sent us some delicious fruit and I must confess I was very much disappointed at her not coming in but when I read her note I could readily account for her non-appearance as Pa is confined to his bed with his old complaint the - gout.[66] I hope he will soon be well not only on our account but his own for when laboring under one of these attacks he suffers the most excruciating pain.

Saturday, June 28th.

I was up again this morning very early and had a full hour for communing with my gracious Father. I made a yard of crochet work before breakfast. Pa came in and brought little Mattie with him; but the former's foot is not quite well. I have not spent a very happy day having given way to my temper. Oh how I hope soon to conquer this enemy; but I must expect to accomplish naht [nothing] without employing His aid. Tomorrow is the Sabbath; is my mind in Sabbath frame? I trust it is.

Monday, June 30th.

Very late in rising this morning but had plenty of time to perform my regular duties. In consequence of not feeling well, I did not write in my diary yesterday but it is sufficient to state I spent that holy day profitably. Ma came in and spent the day with us; but it seemed so short. Once or twice I have been a little impatient. There are I find many sins concealed in my heart which are ready to burst forth when the flame of temptation is applied. Let me pray to my Father to wash away my sins and purify my sinful heart.

Tuesday, July 1st 1862.

I was awakened this morning by the report of a gun [fire] and as on a former occasion I could not get to sleep until very late, and the consequence was I over slept myself. It rained very hard. Ma was prevented from coming in. I have again indulged in my temper and therefore I am far [from] feeling happy. For sometime past one thing has troubled me, and that is I have never tried as I ought to bring my little sister to her Saviour. Conscience has often told me this but I have waited for "a convenient season." I know that my conduct is such at times as did not become a disciple of Christ. Oh, may I be enabled to act more wisely toward her and both by

---

[66] **Gout** refers to a form of arthritis caused by deposits of barbed crystals of uric acid.

precept and example win her to that blessed Saviour who said: "Suffer the little children to come unto me, forbid them not for of such are the kingdom of Heaven."[67]

Wednesday, July 2nd.

I was again dilatory in rising this morning but nothing ever prevents me from performing my duties. None of the family were in to-day except Pa who had so much business to attend to he was prevented from coming to see us. Once I gave way to my evil temper and as is always the case I spend many bitter moments.

Thursday, July 3rd/1862.

Very late in rising this morning but performed my accustomed duties. Spent the morning in making crochet work and then read a very interesting and instructive work to Mattie and Kattie. Visited some friends this evening and being so little accustomed to walking I feel a little fatigued. I don't feel exactly as I ought though I have not given away to my temper. I have fostered sinful thoughts which I would much rather never enter my mind. I was very agreeably surprised to see a friend who has been some months in the South. I promised to go and see her tomorrow but if it continues as warm as now, I don't think I will keep my promise.

The Federals celebrate the nation's 1862 Independence Day with booming cannons and strains of martial music. The holiday still finds Maggie and Sister Kate confined at Aunt Jane's. The day is far from being joyous for Maggie. Later in the month, she will long to escape the noise and dust of the city.

Friday, July 4th/1862.

I was awakened this morning by the booming of the cannon and the strains of martial music. I must confess it is the saddest 4th I ever spent in my life. I pray that we may soon be able to celebrate our day of independence when the sunny south can declared herself a free and independent nation. Pa came in today but it being so warm, Ma and Mattie decided to seek the cool shades of "Mount Alban" in preference to this hot and dusty Yankee town. Spent the morning in sleep as I lost a great-deal last night, owing to the confusion. In the evening I again laid down but spent the time more profitably searching for those beautiful and sublime passages of Scriptures. There is nothing that I said or done that is wrong but still there are

---

[67] Matt. 19:14

many sinful thoughts which I must try to dispel. I have been very home-sick today and when I am in those fits I appear as if I were angry with those around me and as dear Grandma told me it made her feel unhappy at seeing me look so miserable. Hereafter I must try to conceal my feelings better for I have no notion of making my relatives unhappy on my account.

Saturday, July 5th.

I was not late in rising this morning but it being so warm I was very sluggish in dressing and was compelled therefore to attend my duties after breakfast. I have not spent a happy day at all on account of giving away to my unruly temper. Will this always be my day's record, I trust not. I fear that I rely too much upon my feeble endeavors instead of beseeching Him to make my sins, though they be as scarlet, as white as wool "Search me oh God and know my thoughts; try me and know my heart: and if there be any wicked way in me lead me in the way everlasting."[68]

Sunday, July 6th.

I rose quite late this morning but had sufficient time for my devotions. Did not attend church this morning as our pastor is absent and the other ministers are confined in the Penitentiary. Spent the day profitably in reading religious works.

Monday, July 7th.

I rose this morning just as the six o'clock bell rang. Had a visit from a friend who promised to use her influence in persuading Pa to let us return home. I hope her efforts will be crowned with success. The family was in and spent the day. This has not been a happy day and I have given way to my temper and fostered sinful thoughts.

Tuesday, July 8th/62.

I was awakened this morning from a profound sleep by the tolling of the six o'clock bell. Had abundance of time to perform my tasks, and spent an hour in communing with my most gracious Father. Have not given away to my temper although temptation stared me boldly in the face. Have been quite sad on account of hearing such discouraging news from our army.[69]

---

[68] Ps. 139:23-24.
[69] The Seven Days Battle was fought near Richmond, Virginia from June 25 to July 1, 1862. Barnes, *A Brief History of the United States*, Epoch V, page 239. Maggie, along with others, feared that the Confederate Capital of Richmond could fall to the enemy.

I trust that the dark cloud that is now impending over our ill-faded South will soon be dispelled and the sun of peace and prosperity will pour his brightest rays upon us.

Wednesday, July 9th 1862.

Very late rising this [morning] and as is always the case I was obliged to attend to my duties after breakfast. Pa came but mother was prevented from fulfilling her promise of yesterday on account of the dining room servant being quite sick. This has been a very warm day and don't remember of ever feeling so inert. My temper has not troubled me but I think if I were irritated it [would] burst forth with great violence notwithstanding my many resolutions. Consequently I will have to guard it very close and extinguish the flame when it is about to ignite. Assist me oh my God and cleanse me from all guilt.

Thursday, July 10th 1862.

I rose this morning quite late but had an hour for my duties. None of the family were in to-day on account of its being so warm. Had a hard rain which in a measure cooled the atmosphere. I have once again given away to my temper and consequently I am not satisfied with my-self. Spent the day in various ways and in the evening I undressed in the hopes of getting cool, but I soon dropped off to sleep reading an instructive work, and when I woke I found my clothes drench in perspiration.

Saturday, July 12th 1862.

Not very late this morning and had time for my devotions before breakfast. Pa came in; all the family with [him] but Mama was prevented from coming in on account of having no bonnet. Don't think I have said or done anything wrong but my heart still needs cleansing and purifying in the blood of [the] ransomed Saviour. Was prevented from writing in my diary on account of being out very late but I am thankful to say my account of yesterday is as good as to-day. May it ever be so is my constant prayer. I have a plan which I hope will be attended with success. It is this: every Friday and Sunday evening I intend to learn an epistle, committing to memory three verses regularly. I have an old school-mate though differing in politics we have always regarded each other as sworn friends. Judging from the tone of many of her letters, I was brought to conclude that she had "chosen the bitter position." I trust that I am not mistaken! I mention Friday and Sunday because I have an especial love for those evenings when Christians though far distant unite in spirit to entreat the outpouring of the Spirit on themselves, the church, and the world at large.

Sunday, July 13th, 1862.

Very late this morning dressing and after Ellen and Hettie went to Sunday school, I retired to my room to pour forth my prayers to the most High! Again compelled to be away from church owing to our pastor being still absent; but I now feel the truth of that beautiful text; "For we know that if this earthly tabernacle be dissolved we have a building of God, a house not made with hands eternal in the heavens."[70] After breakfast I employed myself in writing to Mrs. Smith and mentioning to her my plans and entreating her to join me. I trust she will approve of them and will write me soon. In the evening I undressed and acted according to my resolutions, and committed to memory a beautiful hymn and reviewed a portion of my catechism. I fervently hope that I will spend every Sabbath like to-day. I have formed another resolution which is that I have determined to guard for one week against saying <u>a single</u> word against any living creature. I much wish to have that deep sense of my unworthiness which will make me charitable to all. Not that I wish to lose the power of judging between a good and a bad character, but I think it is well to seal my lips for fear of speaking in an unendorsed way.

Tuesday, July 15th, 1862.

Very late again in rising this morning not because I had any inclination to do so but on account of Ellen once expressing her liking to dress alone. I thought I would take the hint and lie in bed until she had finished her toilet. Failed to write in my diary yesterday but it matters little as there was nothing worthy to record. Ma came in and spent the day with us, and I made her promise to let us go and pass some time with relatives in the country. I hope that time will soon come for I am perfectly disgusted with city-life. In regard to keeping my resolutions of Sunday, I have to record many failures, but I will set forth with a stout heart and a full determination to conquer this evil passion which has often caused me much grief.

---

[70] 2 Cor. 5:1

Wednesday, July 16th, 1862.

It was seven o'clock this morning when Grandmamma woke me from a profound sleep but I found I had sufficient time for my duties although I was sluggish. I expect Father was in but his business consumes so much of his time he can't spend much with us. Nothing more worthy of record but upon reflecting I find I have indulged in my old enemy temper toward my litter sister whom I should set a better example. I must have patience and persevere in spite of failures.

Thursday, July 17th 1862.

Very late rising this morning on account of being so rainy and dark. I was compelled to shorten my devotions on that above reasons. I feel very comfortable to-day but I am again getting home-sick.

Chapter Six
Ensconced at Hedge Lawn

"When will our distracted country become quiet and we exiles return to our homes?"

After the defeat at Stones River, Jefferson Davis, in late June 1862 replaces General Beauregard with Braxton Bragg. By July of 1862, the Union army held a line running from Memphis, through Corinth, nearly to the city of Chattanooga, toward which point General Buell was steadily pushing his troops. We shall next consider the efforts made by the Confederates to break through this line of investment. At this time they were concentrated under Bragg at Chattanooga, Price at Iuka and Van Dorn at Holley Springs, Mississippi. The first movement was made by General Bragg, who with rapid marches, hastened toward Louisville. General Buell fell back to Nashville, where he found out his enemy's plan. Now commenced a race between them of three hundred miles. Buell came out one day ahead. He was heavily reinforced to the number of one hundred thousand men. Bragg fell back with Buell slowly following. By the middle of September, 1862, events in Mississippi were starting to heat up. Every one of Grant's veterans who could possibly be spared had been sent north to help Buell. Price and Van Dorn, taking advantage of the opportunity, were maneuvering to get possession of Corinth. Grant, thinking that he could capture Price and then get back to Corinth before Van Dorn could reach it from Holly Springs, ordered Rosecrans to move upon Iuka. Through some mistake on September 19, Rosecrans failed to occupy Price's line of retreat, and after a severe conflict, the latter escaped. Thereupon the two Confederate generals joined their forces, and attacked Rosecrans in his entrenchments at Corinth. The Confederates exhibited brilliant courage, but were defeated, and pursued forty miles with heavy loss.[71]

Friday, July 18th 1862.
Not quite as late as yesterday in rising. Ma and Pa were in and the latter procured us a pass to go to Cousin Jane Morgan's[72] next week. According to my resolves of last Saturday I

---

[71] Barnes, *A Brief History of the United States*, Epoch V, pages 227-229.
[72] Jane L. Williams Morgan, 1817-1882. Jane was the niece of Joseph Vaulx.

retired to my room after ma left and committed [to memory] three verses of the Bible. I must confess I had almost forgotten it but the voice of duty soon urged me to my performance. Had quite a severe thunder-storm accompanied by rain which cooled the heated atmosphere. Nothing else.

Saturday, July 19th, 1862.
It was not quite six when I rose this morning and had an hour of solitude to give to my God. Pa came in but could stay but a short time with us as he had so much business to look after. Have spent a very wretched day as my temper was at one time beyond control.

Sunday 20th/62 - Monday July 21st 1862.
Not late in rising today and spent a very short time in prayer. After getting my accustomed Sabbath duties, I dropped off to sleep and when I woke it was too late to write in my diary. Went to church this morning, the last time I fear for some time to come as our present pastor has been recalled to his formal congregation in Paducah.

21st- Ma was prevented from coming in owing to Pa's not being well. Cousin Jane Morgan and Frank came to see and staid sometime. They insisted on our going out [with] them today but I declined not wishing to go before seeing Mother as she intends going with us herself. On looking over the first day I find my enemy temper gaining ground and if not instantly repelled will stand victorious in the contest.

Tuesday, July 22nd 1862.
I was quite late this morning and had just finished my duties when the bell rang for breakfast. After breakfast, I employed myself in variety of ways in the hopes of passing off the time as it always seems so long before Mama comes! I was <u>destined</u> to be disappointed as wished, for [Ma] failed to make her appearance. In looking over the past day I can think of nothing that is objectionable in my conduct. I don't think I am as ardent in my devotions as I [was] last week and my frame of mind is of course not calm. Let prayer oh, God ever be my dear delight!

Wednesday, July 23rd, 1862.
I rose late this morning for just as I had finished dressing the bell rang and my duties were therefore neglected. After eating I became so much engrossed in making crochet work my

devotions were forgotten and on reflecting I can readily (or account) for the many sins I have this day committed owing to the omission of religious duties. Pa came in and brought us some delicious fruit and vegetables. He told us he thought it very improbable whether we could go out to Cousin Jane's but I intend keeping up a stout heart and hope for the best.

Thursday, July 24th/1862.

I rose early this morning and had time to atone for my negligence of yesterday. I am happy to record a perfect account of myself and I clearly see how it was I prayed to my Heavenly Father "to lead me not into temptation" and he has heard my supplication. Ma was prevented again from coming down due to the strict orders of Gen Campbell[73] not to let anyone go or come in. I was again longing for home or for some quiet spot where I will be out of the noise and confusion of this dusty town. I never knew I loved my dear, dear parents and my own sweet Mount Alban until after our absence of six months and I know I can truly say "the dearest spot on earth to me is home sweet home."

Friday, July 25th, 1862.

I arose quite late this morning and had sufficient time though for my accustomed duties. Pa came in this morning and gave us some encouragement as to our going over to Cousin Jane's. He had a letter of introduction from the Secretary of State to Gen Campbell and he was in hopes of procuring a pass by that means. We are certain of mother's coming in and I eagerly look forward to that event as it's has been a week since we have seen her. I have said or done nothing that is wrong although my mind is filled with many sinful thoughts. "Heavenly Father, let the words of my mouth, the meditation of my heart be acceptable in thy sight." In the evening I retired to chamber and committed to memory my usual number of verses from the Bible. I trust those sacred words may sink deep in my heart and take firm hold there.

Pa's letter of introduction went forward and General William Bowen Campbell ordered a civilian pass to be issued to Joseph Vaulx. Ma is permitted to take the Vaulx sisters and travel to Hedge Lawn, the ancestral home of the Vaulx family. The 1860 federal census lists the household members as Widow Jane Morgan with sons Berry, Calvin, and Frank and daughter Kate. Hedge

---

[73] William Boren Campbell, a native Tennessean. During the war, he served as Brigadier General in the Union Army, resigning in 1863. He had previously served as Whig Governor of Tennessee from 1851 to 1853. He died in August, 1867 and is buried in Cedar Grove Cemetery, Lebanon, TN.

Lawn was located on the Murfreesboro Pike, about six miles from Nashville. The girls stay with Cousin Jane and cousins Frank and Kate Perkins. Berry, Calvin, and Kate's husband Daniel are serving with the CSA. For a moment in time, Maggie's life is much happier.

Hedge Lawn, Wednesday, July 29th, 1862.[74]

Have been enjoying my self within the last few days that I have failed to perform this duty. Ma brought us over on the 26th, Gen. Campbell having given Pa a pass. Went to town yesterday and spent the day with Grandmamma and the rest of the family and I was glad enough to escape the noise and dust of the city. In regard to my keeping up my devotional I have to acknowledged many failures and when I do perform them, it is with so many faults that I fear that my prayers are not acceptable in God's sight. Take me under thy care, oh Lord and let me be a wanderer no more!

Thursday, July 30th 1862.

I rose quite early this morning and had sufficient time for my religious duties before breakfast. It has been raining all day and from appearances it seems as if it had set in for some time to come. Look for mother and father over to spend the day with us very soon. Employed the day in a great many ways reading, practicing, &c. Kate and I fully intended taking a ride with some friends but owing to its raining so hard we were prevented from doing so.

Hedge Lawn, July 31st 1862.

I rose very late this morning and had therefore a very short time to engage in my devotional exercises. Kate, Fannie Wilson and I took a long ride this evening and enjoyed myself exceedingly. O! how beautiful the country looked and it seemed so hard to think that this sunny land should be desolated with so much blood!

Hedge Lawn, August 1st 1862. (Friday)

I was awakened this morning by darling little Mary Perkins[75] who came into my room laughing and trying to talk her baby language. Cousin Jane and Kate went in town this morning and I

---

[74] The original manuscript shows wrong-day entries for July 29 through 31. July 29, 1862 fell on a Tuesday, not Wednesday. I believe the excitement of changing places of abode caused Maggie to once again lose track of her days.

[75] Mary Perkins, one-year-old daughter of Cousin Kate Morgan and husband Daniel Price Perkins. Cousin Dan is serving with the Rebel army.

decided to remain at home with Sister. Cousin Jane saw Ma in town and thinks she will be over some-time next week. I am continually straying from the path of God. Oh how many things from time to time are striving to wean my heart from God, who in love commands me to give it to him? Often it is so cold, perplexed, polluted, fearful and unbelieving, that at every hour needs renewed pardon. And will it ever continue thus? Oh then who alone canst offset this mighty change, do thou speak the work, and thy servant will be healed!

Saturday, Aug 2nd 1862.

I rose very early this morning, had scarcely time to engage in my devotions before the bell rang. Employed myself in various ways during the day. In the evening Kate and I took a long walk over to Mr. Weaver's[76] to see the family and spent a delightful evening.

Hedge Lawn, Aug 3rd/62. (Sunday)

I was more dilatory in rising this morning. How different how I spent this in comparison with my former Sabbaths. There are so many things constantly occurring that tend to lead me on the broad path of evil. Tis true I have many obstacles to overcome, but there will be more glory in knowing that I have "fought the good fight of faith and have vanquished them all!" I am sorry to confess that I am again speaking in an unadvised way – Set a guard oh Lord, before my mouth; keep thou the door of my lips[77] – Preserve me, from a vain conversation; give me grace never to be ashamed to speak of Thee and Thy law![78]

Hedge Lawn, Aug 4th 1862 (Monday)

I rose quite early this morning but I found when the breakfast bell rang I was still undressed as little Mary came up in gale of good humor and I of course could not refrain from joining in her merriment. After Cousin Jane and Kate went to town, I retired to my room and engaged in my devotions with more warmth than I have done for many days. I then dressed very neatly but I soon found that I could go in for looks no longer and gave myself up to

---

[76] Dempsey Weaver, family friend and business associate of Joseph Vaulx, Sr.
[77] Ps. 141:3
[78] *The Sacra privata*: the private meditations and prayers of the right Reverend Thomas Wilson, the Anglican Bishop of Sodor and Man between 1697 and 1755.

comfort. I have said or done nothing that I can regret and I now find that with the help of God, I can accomplish everything but if I neglect my Heavenly Father he will [allow] me to pursue my course until I see the folly of my conduct.

Hedge Lawn, Aug 7th (Thursday)

I rose very soon this morning but had scarcely finished my devotions when Kate came in and announced her intention of taking a horseback ride and insisted on my doing the same. I readily assented and after eating a hearty breakfast we donned our habits and were soon mounted on our gallant steeds. I enjoyed myself exceedingly notwithstanding the warm morning. Nothing else.

Hedge Lawn, Aug 8th/62. (Friday)

I rose very soon this morning and had therefore sufficient time for my devotions. After breakfast Kate proposed to walk over and see the pressing machine work, but it was so warm and I being a very corpulent person, I declined her invitation promising to comply with it at a future day. Cousin Jane gave me some <u>welcome</u> intelligence, viz: that she intended going in and getting us a pass to go over and spend the day at "Mount Alban." What a happy day it will [be] for us all once again to be gathered under that hallowed roof where I have spent so many blissful hours.

Hedge Lawn, Aug 9th/62. (Saturday)

It was so warm this morning I found it impossible to sleep so I rose very early and had an hour of quiet to devote to my duties. I was most agreeably surprised to see Ma, Mattie and Pa who spent the day with us and brought me some letters from my dear absent friends. Mrs. Weaver sent us word that there would be preaching in the neighborhood tomorrow. If the weather will permit I will attend and I trust that those sacred words I now hear will take firm hold in my heart and be a means of bringing the stranger to the fold of Christ. I will tomorrow renew my Sabbath duties and I hope God will enable me to continue them not with the allurements that are constantly appearing.

Hedge Lawn, Sunday Aug 10th.

Rose very soon this morning and after attending faithfully to my duties I found I had an hour of leisure so I employed it in copying "The Self Examination" which I think will greatly further my progress to Heaven. At 10, we went over to the school house and heard an excellent sermon by Dr. Provine from the expressive text 22 Chap of Matthew 42nd verse, "What think ye of Christ." After eating my dinner I retired to my room and there performed my long neglected tasks and of course I feel happier knowing that I have not left undone those things which I ought to have done.

Hedge Lawn, Aug 12th/62.

It was very early this morning when I rose and had therefore sometime before Kattie got up to give to my devotions. It is I think the warmest day we have had and as yet there is an appearance of the long wished for rain. In the morning I tried to fix my underskirt, but owing to its being so hot I found it impossible to work so I lay down to read and soon found myself in the "land of dreams." Kate Perkins and I visited some friends in the evening and had a delightful ride home.

Hedge Lawn, Wednesday Aug 13th.

The sun had not peeped from behind the hills when I found myself dressed and all my devotions performed. I employed the remainder of the morning before breakfast in reading a very interesting magazine. I intend hereafter when I rise so early to practice an hour or two for I find I am neglecting my music as the weather is so warm it is impossible for me to perform this, my dear delight. Kate and I took a delightful ride this evening on horseback and after starting we thought we would go over and see some friends as Frank warned us not to go far on account of the insolent conduct of the pickets.

Hedge Lawn, Thursday, Aug 14th.

It was quite late when I rose this morning on account of not sleeping much as I took a long nap on the day before. I have repeatedly tried to settle myself at some work but I find it so warm my endeavors were fruitless. After dinner I read a very interesting article to Cousin Jane from the magazine entitled the "battle of Saratoga and Stillwater" which proved one of the most interesting pieces. If our fore fathers endured so many privations before they gained that precious Liberty why cannot we battle on putting our trust in Him and [at] length stand victorious with "freedom" granted on our banners!

Hedge Lawn, Friday, Aug 15th.

I rose quite early this morning notwithstanding it being an excellent morning for sleeping. Cousin Jane and Kate went to town with Mrs. Buchanan and I concluded to remain at home as I had no particular desire to go to the town where I was compelled to five months. Spent the day very pleasantly reading and talking to Frank and playing with sweet Mary Perkins.

Andrew Johnson

Had a visit from Ellen and Mrs. Fall in the evening and was therefore prevented from committing my Bible verse but I fully intend performing this delightful duty tomorrow morning as I am sorry that I have so long neglected. Yesterday, Cousin Jane, Kate and I had a delightful drive over to Mrs. Weaver to hear the news which gave us every encouragement as to our "noble boys" coming back and redeeming old Tennessee. I trust that it is so for our citizens are sick of the tyranny of old Johnson's government.[79]

Hedge Lawn, Saturday, Aug 16th, 1862.

I rose late this morning on account of it being so cool but had sufficient time for my devotions. In the evening, Kate and I took a walk through the woods and after reading a short time we concluded to go over to Mrs. Weaver's and see how the baby was coming on. Had a pleasant, though dusty walk home.

Sunday, Aug 17th 62.

I rose very early this morning and after performing my duties faithfully I read a long letter from Ma which Mr. Weaver was so kind to bring out. The Yankees had called upon Pa to

---

[79] In March 1862, Senator Andrew Johnson from Unionist East Tennessee was appointed by President Lincoln as the military governor of occupied Tennessee with the rank of brigadier general. During the three years in this office, Johnson "moved resolutely to eradicate all pro-Confederate influences in the state." Likewise Johnson's "unwavering commitment to the Union" was a significant factor in his being chosen by Lincoln as his vice presidential candidate in 1864. Johnson vigorously suppressed the Confederates, telling his subordinates, "Whenever you hear a man prating about the Constitution, spot him as a traitor."

furnished six negroes to work on the fortifications at St. Cloud hill[80] but not having that number to spare he gave three of the _best_ working hands on the place. O' I trust their work will _serve_ our boys.[81] After eating dinner I retired and performed my accustomed duties and then took a refreshing nap.

Monday, Aug 18th 1862.

I rose very early this morning and dressed for town as Cousin Jane wished to go in before the heat of the day. Saw Aunt Jane [Brown] who has just returned from Triune and I regret exceedingly that Cousin Ella left before I went in. None of the family were in on account of Pa's having the gout. There are many rumors to-day about the advancing of the "CSA". I trust when they do come they will have abundance of force to hold the city.

Tuesday, Aug 19th 1862.

I rose quite early this morning and after dressing I read some very interesting and improving pieces from the periodicals. Cousin Jane and Kate went to town this evening and brought us welcome news that Gen. McCook and his staff who left Nashville a few days since had been taken by Forrest and his men.

Wednesday, Aug 20th 1862.

I rose early this morning and think I engaged with more ardor in devotions than I have done for a long, _long_ time. The day has been excessively hot and as always the case my lazy pores were developed to a great degree.

Thursday, Aug 21st 1862.

I rose this morning very soon but was unusually lazy in dressing and was compelled therefore to shorten my devotions. After eating breakfast I made a great deal of crochet work and then read and played with Mary Perkins. Have been quite low spirited notwithstanding the good news I heard yesterday of "_our boys_" making a forward movement from Chattanooga. What a

---

[80] The fort was a star-shaped limestone structure atop a hill south of the city. The construction was overseen by Captain James St. Clair Morton. It was constructed using the labor of slaves, both local and contraband, that had flocked to Nashville once it was taken by Federals. The fort was named for Union Army General James Negley.

[81] From the sarcasm of Maggie's text, perhaps Pa supplied some hands that may have been more on the lazy side. Note the underlined words "best" and "serve".

glorious day it will be when our troops plant the southern flag on the capitol from whence it has been so ruthlessly torn. Nearly two years has passed since I have seen Brother Joe and yet how thankful I ought to be that his life has been spared during all the toils and dangers he has encountered. I heard some days since through a friend that Uncle James was at Mobile with Uncle Harris, whether in the army or not I could not ascertain. I often wonder if I will ever see my dear friends and relatives who are now so far from me, but my mind is at ease when I pray to my God to shelter them and if He should see fit to break the tie that binds us here on earth, prepare each and every one of us to look forward to a happy reunion beyond the skies.

Friday, Aug 22nd 1862.

I arose very soon and had a short time to pray as Cousin Jane has such early breakfast. After breakfast Mrs. Sharp and Miss Buchanan called on Kate and me. After they left Cousin Jane, Kate, and myself went over to see some very entertaining friends which consumed our time until dinner. After eating a hearty meal we set ourselves to peeling apples for drying which occupied the whole evening.

Sunday, Aug 24th 1862.

I rose very early this morning notwithstanding my being a little unwell. I decided on that account not to go to church and it was well I did as Cousin Jane soon returned as Dr. Provine was prevented from fulfilling his engagement. After dinner I performed my usual duties but not, I am sorry to say with the attention that I have hitherto [given] them. I think I am again growing negligent about my devotional exercises and <u>many, many</u> are the solemn sounds I utter on a thoughtless tongue.

Monday, Aug 25th 1862.

I rose very late this morning owing I suppose to my spending such a sleepless night. After breakfast I made a great deal of crochet work and practiced a good hour. I have felt a longing to see mother and my home and at times I feel as if I am destined never to see that hallowed spot. Every day brings news of the advance of our boys. O! if we were certain of their coming how many anxious hearts would be gladdened by the thought.

Friday, August 29th/62.

I rose very early this morning and prepared myself to accompany Cousin Jane to town but I found to my great disappointment that mother was not in. Saw Uncle Alex who told us that "our boys" (1st Tenn. Regiment) were well and were better clothed and in finer spirit then they had been for a long time. He heard the above from Mr. Fogg who has just returned from the South having gone there to see his son Melbourne whom he heard was quite low but was most happy to find him in fine health. He could give us a great deal of comfort concerning our army but dare not for the fear of being thrown in prison by the tyrants. Cousin Jane gave me a very nice scrapbook to fill with interesting articles from the daily papers. Wrote a note to ma by Mr. Weaver asking her to collect me every interesting piece she would think suitable for such a book. After returning from town I tried to go to sleep but found it impossible owing to its being so warm and knowing that I had more important duties to perform. I wrote a long letter to Queeny Humphreys and sent them by Mr. Weaver to Pa to put in his office but [am] doubtful about her getting them owing to the irregularity of the mails.

Saturday, Aug 30th/62.

I rose very early this morning and after hurriedly performing my devotions, I cleaned and arranged my drawers which proved very tedious. Late last evening Mary Weaver came over and brought me an "extra" containing glorious news from our army in Virginia. Our gallant troops had beaten the "so called invincible Pope and McClellan" and taken Manassas Junction[82] after a hard fought battle. The sun of prosperity is again smiling upon us and I trust it may never be darken by defeats and disasters. Cousin Jane and Kattie went to town this morning and I am anxiously waiting their return to hear more good news. I received a long letter from Ma yesterday and in it she says she is afraid we will become weaned from her and our home. O dear ma could you know how I long for home you never would have fears on that score.

Sunday, Aug 31st/62.

I rose quite early this morning notwithstanding I spent a sleepless and uncomfortable [night]. As is my custom, I retired to my room and there performed my accustomed duties. Nothing else.

---

[82] The Second Battle of Bull Run (Manassas) was fought in August 1862. (Barnes, *A Brief History of the United States*, Epoch V, page 241) The battle was on the same ground as the First Battle of Bull Run, but of much larger extent.

Tuesday, Sep 2nd/62.

I rose very early this morning and after <u>neglecting</u> my duties I went to town with Mr. Weaver. None of the family came in much to my regret as I wished particularly to see Ma on business. Heard more encouraging news from our army. Genl. Kirby Smith had defeated and succeeded in routing Gen. Nelson. The latter was severely wounded and has been sent to Cincinnati.

Wednesday, Sep 3rd 1862.

I rose very early this morning and after performing my accustomed duties I found breakfast inviting. I spent the morning practicing, reading, sewing, viz. After dinner Kate and I went over to see Fannie and Lucy Wilson. The evening passed very pleasantly. From there we walked to Mrs. Weaver's. Franklin is now in "Dixie" as is also Frankfort and Lexington, Ky. It is reported that Kirby Smith intends marching in and taking Covington and then shelling Cincinnati. When will we gain our independence and this unnatural war end![83]

Thursday, Sep 4th. 1862.

I rose very early this morning and it is strange to say as I spent a sleepless and unhappy night. The day has been excessively hot and consequently I have been very lazy. I thought for a while of going to town but I am thankful I decided not to as the road has been completely crowded with army waggons and belonging to Mitchell's and Rousseau's divisions[84] who are retreating from the South.

Friday, Sep 5th 1862.

I rose very late this morning. Spent the morning in various ways. In the afternoon Kate, Frank and myself walked over to Mrs. Weaver's and there learned an amount of good news. Received a note from Pa as follows: "Several companies of Kentucky cavalry are in Dr. Berry's hill opposite us. Genl Negley's command is just below on Capt. Foster ground; a large

---

[83] This reference was to the Kentucky Campaign, a series of maneuvers and battles fought in East Tennessee and Kentucky. The summer of 1862 found Confederate forces under the command of Generals Braxton Bragg and Edmund Kirby Smith going against the Union forces of General Don Carlos Buell. The aim was to gain a rebel victory which was hoped to be the catalyst for drawing the border state of Kentucky into the Confederate States of America. After some early rebel success, the cause was stopped at the Battle of Perryville. Kentucky would remain in Union hands for the remainder of the war. [Barnes, *A Brief History of the United States*, Epoch V, page 228]

[84] Union forces belonging to the army of Maj. General Don Carlos Buell.

drove of cattle with their attendants are in Mr. Armistead's meadow. Several large pickets are stationed near, one at the end of our lane and one last night in the lane at the hedge. I am constantly annoyed by the soldiers getting in the orchard taking cabbage, potatoes, &c. Many come to the house and ask for something to eat and if not given them they will steal anything they wish. I am nearly worried out. I have a safe guard[85] 'but that frequently does no good'. Life under such circumstances is a torment. Fortifications are being erected on Mr. Campbell's hill which is not over 1¼ miles from our house. In the event of a fight we shall be in danger, indeed those much further off. We shall have to quit using coffee, sugar at present prices. I paid 40 [cents] a pound for sugar yesterday."

Hedge Lawn, Sep 6th/62 (Saturday)

I rose very early this morning and fixed myself for going to town with Mr. Weaver but owing to the great number of troops constantly passing I was disappointed in going. Sometime when I think of my once happy home (in all probability to be destroyed) never more perhaps to be visited by me, I can scarcely choke back the bitter tears. Oh, may peace soon be restored to our Sunny South!

Hedge Lawn, Sep 8th 1862. (Monday)

I rose this morning quite early and after faithfully performing my tasks I employed myself in finishing the "Self Examination" but at length failed to finished. This has been quite an eventful day. About 3 o'clock this evening we were quietly conversing when Frank noticed some cavalry men riding through the lane by the barn. He immediately went back and on inquiry he found out they were Confederates belonging to Col. Forrest's command. We will hear more of them tomorrow and the meaning of their strange movement. O may they soon return to their homes!

Hedge Lawn, Sep 9th 1862. Tuesday

I rose very soon this morning notwithstanding I spent [a] sleepless night thinking of the confederate cavalry. They went down the road but finding the Yankees in too great a force they returned intending to try again [another] day. They say that Cheatham is now at Lebanon, Bragg and Price are advancing but at what pace they were not at liberty to tell. The Federals are still working on the fortifications but some think it is only a front as they

---

[85] A military order used to protect private citizens from the unlawful intrusion or removal of personal property. See also the journal entry from December 17, 1862.

are evacuating Nashville as rapidly and secretly as they possibly can. What a happy day it will [be] when we can [ride] to town without having to show our passes to the Yankee pickets. It will be more joyous to sister and I as we look forward with "joy" "unspeakable" to that time to return to dear Mount Alban.

Hedge Lawn, Sep 10th, Wednesday

I rose rather late this morning and after performing my religious duties I employed the hours before breakfast in selecting [articles] for my "scrap book." Had a refreshing rain this evening which was very acceptable as the dust had become almost intolerable. It is thought that the lime-stone of which the road is composed will cause the death of many of the horses and all probability the men. Received a note from Ma. All the family is well. Sent her keys to my trunk to get my under skirts fixed as I am tired of making crochet work. It is believed that two divisions will remain to defend Nashville. I trust they will quietly give up Nashville. Oh! How terrible it will be if they do make a stand. We will now know horrors of war!

Hedge Lawn, Thursday, Sep 11th 1862.

I rose very early this morning and had a long, long time for devotions. Cousin Jane and Kate went [to] town. Had another hard rain to-day. Mrs. Weaver came over this [morning] and says she heard our troops are at La Vergne, a small town 10 miles from here and 15 from Nashville.

Hedge Lawn, Friday, Sep 12th 62.

I rose very soon this morning but was so slow in dressing I found I had barely time for my devotions. Cousin Jane went to town this morning and returned very late bringing Cousin Lou Ewing. Nothing more.

Hedge Lawn, Saturday, Sep 13th/1862.

I rose this morning very early and had an hour or more for my beloved devotions. Have passed the day very pleasantly with Cousin Lou and Kate. Heard nothing from home to-day and am rather uneasy for fear something has happened. I hope tomorrow I will perform my religious duties better than last Sunday. This will be far different from the last as the place was swarming with Federal soldiers. Heard from Brother through Dr. Harris who has just returned from the South. All our friends and relatives are well and are under Bragg who has gone over to Kentucky. Brother Joe[86] is not in the regular service but intends joining very soon. Oh! that they were all at home and this horrible war at an end!

Hedge Lawn, Sunday, Sep 14th 1862.

I rose very early this morning and after performing my duties I read a very interesting little work titled "A Token of Friendship". After dinner I retired to my room intending to attend to my Sabbath task but I soon found myself in the land of dreams. Mrs. Harris came out from town this evening and says it is believed that Stonewall Jackson is within 4 miles of Washington and gives them four hours to surrender having already thrown some shells in the city.

General Thomas "Stonewall" Jackson

Hedge Lawn, Monday, Sep 15th 1862.

I rose quite soon this morning. Dr. and Mrs. Harris left this morning for La Vergne. Have felt rather home sick and unwell all day. Oh! how I long for home and dear father and mother. Will I ever be peacefully settled at Mount Alban again? I am very sorry to say I am again growing negligent about my religious duties. I don't take the same interest in my devotions as formerly, as my mind is too much taken up with worldly affairs.

Hedge Lawn, Sep 17th 1862.

After rising very early I retired to Cal's room and there spent a most delightful hour in meditation and prayer. Have spent a very pleasant day, mostly by myself as I find solitude the best remedy for home sickness and I sure was indulging in this to a great extent. Have at last finished copying "Self-Examination and Rules for Domestic Happiness."[87] Had such a dreadful headache I was compelled to neglect writing in my diary but it is sufficient to state Cousin Jane went to town and brought us home most welcome intelligence from the "Southern Confederacy." It is reported and most generally believed that Secession flag now floats over the

---

[86] Brother Joe's enlistment had ended while in Virginia. He returned to East Tennessee and would re-enlist there in time for the Kentucky Campaign.
[87] Maggie copied "Self-Examination and Rules for Domestic Happiness" onto the opening pages of Volume Two of her journal. Refer to the appendix for more details about this work.

federal capitol and that "Stonewall Jackson has his headquarters in Baltimore. Someone was telling us that Breckenridge was at Murfreesboro having his pickets at Le Vergne. Received a long letter from mother this morning and I think that increased my home sickness. There are now 16,000 troops all around our house, the rear of Buell's army from Corinth. (Rousseau's division) they have been making forced marches of 40 miles a day. Ascending to their account they were fired on by our cavalry near Columbia and the consequence was the shelling of that beautiful town. I trust however that it's not so. The greater part of them says they are tired of the war, and as the South is right they want her to gain her independence. On count of the insolent conduct of the troops, Father is compelled to have 6 guards who sleep and eat at the house. When will our distracted country become quiet and we exiles return to our homes! In the evening I retired to my room and there spent some time in solace.

Hedge Lawn, Sep 18th 1862.

I rose very late this morning on account of feeling very unwell. According to the wishes of our President we have spent the day in fasting and prayer; but on reading the daily papers we find that it was a day appointed for thanksgiving,[88] prayer and praise. Received a long letter from my dear friend Mollie Berry. Speaking of the many happy hours we have spent together at dear Mount Alban and Elm Wood, I could scarcely suppress the rising tears, but I succeeded after much difficulty not liking to indulge in weeping again for fear of making my relatives unhappy. Heard nothing from home to-day but most certainly look for a letter from mother to-morrow.

Friday, Sep 19th 1862.

I rose quite late this morning in consequence of feeling still unwell but had sufficient time for my devotions before breakfast. Nothing has happened worthy of recording. Went over to see Mr. Weaver in the hopes of hearing something from home but I found nothing awaiting me. The weather is very cool. Heard a sad piece of intelligence this evening namely the death of

---

[88] This refers to the 1862 Thanksgiving Day Proclamation for victory by Jefferson Davis. To the People of the Confederate States: "....Now, therefore, I, Jefferson Davis, President of the Confederate States, do issue this, my proclamation, setting apart Thursday, the 18th day of September as a day of prayer and thanksgiving to Almighty God for the great victories vouchsafed to our people, and especially for the triumph of our armies at Richmond and Manassas." This should not to be confused with the national holiday which we observe on the 4th Thursday of November.

Tom Wilson the brother of a friend of mine. He was killed in the fight in West Tennessee. Many seem to think it is a mistake, so the bereaved family has some hope to cling to.

Saturday, Sep 20th.

I rose this morning quite soon. The weather continues cool and pleasant. Heard nothing from home again. Tomorrow is the Sabbath and I trust that it will be spent far differently from the last. I am not taking the same interest in my religious duties as I have hitherto. I am also neglecting my verses from the Bible which I am in the habit of committing. In the evening Cousin Jane and I took a long ride and on our return we drove [past] the Asylum[89] but it being so late we were prevented from alighting.

Sunday, Sep 21st/62.

I rose very late this morning and had scarcely time for my devotions. I lay down the greater part of the morning owing to my being a little unwell. Spent a very quiet evening attending to my tasks and reading my Bible. Oh! how I long for my home and dear mother and father. Seven long months have passed since I have been to my home and at times a fear comes over me that I am never destined to visit it. May my fears never be realized!

Monday, Sep 22nd/62.

I rose as early as usual this morning. Cousin Lou and Kate went to see Cap. Hopper (paymaster of the 1st Regiment) who reports our army well which when he left they were at Sparta Tenn.

Tuesday, Sep 23rd 1862.

I rose very early this morning and as Cousin Jane intended going in I concluded to accompany her and well I did as I was most agreeably surprised to see Ma and Mattie. I expect them over on Friday. No news from our army to-day.

Wednesday, Sep 24th.

I rose very early this morning and after breakfast I practice a good hour and then employed myself in various ways. Went over to Mr. Weaver's and there met a portion of Forrest's men who had a little skirmish with the Yankee pickets. The news to-day is that 17,000 men had

---

[89] The asylum is the present-day Central State Hospital, Donelson, TN.

surrendered with all their arms, ammunition and without any blood being shed at Harper's Ferry;[90] also Genl. Stonewall Jackson had whipped McClelland at Fredericksburg.[91]

Thursday, Sep 25th 1862.

I rose quite late this morning on account of setting up past my accustomed bed-time. Some of Forrest's men took breakfast with us. Started over to see Fannie and Lucy Wilson but it being so warm we thought best to defer our visit until a more pleasant evening. I hope Ma will be over to-morrow according to her promise.

Friday, 26th 1862.

I rose very soon this morning and after faithfully performing my devotional exercises I employed myself in arranging pieces for my "scrap book." I had just given Ma out when the old cab made its appearance bringing the precious burden. She had just seen Aunt Julia Nichol who saw all of our boys. Brother had so much business to attend to he was prevented from writing. He was well and that in a great measure compensates for his not writing. More of Forrest's men passed the night here after giving the Yankee pickets a good scare. Every day confirms our recent victories in Virginia.

Saturday, Sep 27th 1862.

I rose quite early this morning and after devoting a half an hour to my prayers I employed myself in writing to Mollie Berry. Cousin Jane and Sister went to town this morning and brought me a note from Ma. She had great difficulty in getting home as the pickets above us were fired on and three or four killed.

Sunday, Sep 28th 1862.

I rose at my accustomed time this morning. Spent the morning in fixing my Scrap book, reading my hymns and Bible. Nothing more of interest. We heard to-day that a flag of truce had been sent in demanding the surrender of Nashville, but Gen. Negley intends holding the city at all hazards.

---

[90] Harpers Ferry was a strategic West Virginia town located on the railroad at the northern end of the Shenandoah Valley. Barnes, *A Brief History of the United States*, Epoch V, page 241

[91] This reference is to skirmishes leading up to military actions at Fredericksburg, VA. The main battle was fought in December 1862. Barnes, *A Brief History of the United States*, Epoch V, page 242.

Tuesday, Sep 30th 1862.

I rose as early as usual this morning. Cousin Lou Ewing came from Franklin last evening and returned this morning. Cousin Jane tried to pass the pickets but they refused to let her do so. Mr. Weaver and Father were the only persons that got passes to leave the city. Kate, Mr. Taylor[92] (a confederate soldier) and my-self took a long ride on horse-back and on our return rode through the Asylum grounds.

Wednesday, Oct 1st 1862.

I rose quite late this morning on account of taking such a long ride. Cousin Jane and Kattie went over to Mrs. Harris this evening and there heard that a courier had been sent to the pickets stating that Breckenridge[93] and his command had arrived in Murfreesboro and his advance guard was at La Vergne. It is reported that Genl Negley intends leaving Nashville but Gov. Johnson determines to apply a torch to every house. I hope it is not so! The vile wretch is capable of doing any mean act.[94]

Thursday, Oct 2nd 1862.

I rose at my accustomed hour this morning and I am sorry to confess I performed my duties very unprofitably. Kate, Sister and myself went over to see Mrs. Gurley and other friends. No news whatever to-day.

Friday, Oct 3rd 1862.

I rose quite early this morning and employed myself after practicing and sewing on my underskirt. In the afternoon [cousin] Kate, Sister, Mrs. Taylor and myself went up to the Asylum and there spent a delightful afternoon among the flowers, and looking at the many other curiosities which that institution affords.

---

[92] Mr. Taylor, a Morgan family friend.
[93] Prior to the war, Confederate General John C. Breckinridge served as both U. S. Representative and Kentucky Senator. He also served during the James Buchanan administration as the 14th vice president of the United States.
[94] This journal entry clearly shows the disdain the people of Nashville held toward this man, whom they viewed as a traitor and tyrant.

Saturday, Oct 4th 1862.

I rose quite early this morning and employed the morning in variety of ways. Mrs. Luter and Miss Fannie Holcombe[95] came out this evening with two gentlemen who had escaped from the penitentiary and they were taking them to La Vergne to get them to their homes in East Tennessee. Went over to Mr. Weaver's this evening with Mollie King and there received a note from Ma. The place is still over run with the Yankees and it is with the greatest difficulty that father gets in town.

Sunday, Oct 5th 1862.

I rose quite early this morning and attended to my accustomed duties. The day has been so exciting that I have not been able to attend to my other duties. Just before dinner, Mr. Edmunson came having been absent from his home since the fall of Donelson. Mrs. Luter and Miss Fannie Holcombe returned from LaVergne this evening being successful in getting off the gentlemen to Knoxville. Heard this evening through Mrs. Goff that a large foraging party was expected out tomorrow. Frank, Mr. Taylor and Mr. Edmunson made preparation for going to LaVergne as they were afraid of being arrested. We had just got to bed and were fixed for a good night's rest when Kate came up to our room in haste telling us that Mrs. Holcombe had walked all the way from Nashville to warn us of danger. She heard from Dr. Ford that the Federals intended sending troops out on this pike by the [railroad] cars to cut off Genl. Anderson. She obtained the above from a Federal officer. Frank immediately mounted his horse and left for LaVergne to warn Genl. Forrest of the danger. Oh! I trust they will be prepared for the worst. Mrs. Holcombe left to-night as she had to return to attend to her school duties.

Monday, Oct 6th 1862.

I rose quite late this morning, after spending a very sleepless night. Have been perfectly miserable all day as we know not what day the Yankees may come to plunder our houses. Aunt Jane wrote me a note and sent me a very nice shirt which I intend giving to Mr. Taylor if I ever see the poor fellow again.

---

[95] The 1860 United States Federal Census lists Miss Fannie Holcombe, age 18, as a daughter of Mrs. Emma Holcombe.

Tuesday, Oct 7th 1862.

I rose very late this morning again on account of being awake the greater part of the night by the noise of troops going to LaVergne. Kate and I went to Mrs. Weaver's and there witnessed the return of the troops that went to LaVergne. According to their statement they are the conquerors. The whole of Negley's command went out and that in a great measure accounts for our being whipped. We are all very uneasy about Frank for he is always ready for killing the Yankees.

Wednesday, Oct 8th 1862.

I rose very early this morning. Cousin Jane, Kate and Mrs. Mooney went up to LaVergne this morning to hear the particulars of the fight. Mr. Smith and Edmunson came over and stayed the greater part of the day. After dinner Alice and Sallie Brunston paid me a long visit which passed the evening. Cousin Jane came home about 5 o'clock. We were not so badly beaten as the Yankees represent having only two killed and six or eight wounded. The Federals burnt several houses and stole everything from the private residences as the families were compelled to leave on account of the shelling.

Thursday, Oct 9th 1862.

I rose this morning very early and employed myself before breakfast in pasting my <u>Scrap book</u>. Cousin Jane and Sister went to town this morning but Kate and I spent a very pleasant day with Mrs. Taylor. In the afternoon the latter went to Lavergne to get us a pass to go up and see some of our relatives; but I think our visit will be interfered with as Cousin Jane says she heard that a large foraging party was coming out on this pike, and they were to proceed to Murfreesboro and destroy that place. I hope it may not be so.

Friday, Oct 10th.

I rose very early this morning. Mrs. Weaver came over and spent the greater part of the day and it was well she did as we were very lonesome on account of Cousin Jane's going to Mrs. Smith's to see about Frank's coming home. Mr. Taylor returned from Lavergne this morning and brought us a pass from Col. Morgan. It has been raining all evening and it is now cool and disagreeable.

Saturday, Oct 11th/62.

I rose at my accustomed time this morning. Cousin Jane went to see about Frank's coming home. We were most agreeably surprised to see him slip in this evening. Mr. Taylor staid all night with him. We heard to-day that Genl. Forrest intends retaking Nashville as soon as he reorganizes his army.

Sunday, Oct 12th 1862.

I rose quite early this morning and spent that time in reading my Bible and hymns. Mr. Edmunson and Taylor staid all night.

The Johnson's Family Flag of Truce

An interesting incident occurred with Maggie meeting the family of Military Governor Andrew Johnson. While on a scaly bark hunt, she and some friends met the Johnson family enroute to Nashville. Mrs. Eliza Johnson, along with other members of the family, had traveled by rail from East Tennessee to

Murfreesboro. From Murfreesboro, General Forrest sent them safely under a flag of truce through rebel lines to their destination.[96]

Monday, Oct 13th 1862.

I rose very early this morning and dressed to go scaly bark hunting with Fannie and Lucy Wilson. Spent a most delightful day and coming home our conveyance broke down and we [found ourselves] under the necessity of returning in Mrs. Wilson's cart. When we returned we met the flags of truce and Gov. Johnson's family who were on their way to Nashville. Expected some Confederate soldiers to take supper with us but were in some way disappointed.

Tuesday, Oct 14th.

I was rather lazy in rising this morning on account of feeling very much fatigued after my yesterday's exertions. Taylor spent the day with us and as Frank was afraid for him to stay all night he went on a scouting expedition. Wrote a note to Ma for our winter clothes and begging her to come over and spend the day.

Wednesday, Oct 15th.

I rose quite early this morning and employed my time before breakfast in reading. Mrs. Luter came out from town this evening and says the Yankees are building Pontoon bridges at Hyde's Ferry, whether to evacuate our poor old Nashville or for Buell's army to reinforce is a question not to be answered at present.

Thursday, Oct 16th.

I rose at my usual hour this morning. Nothing of interest to record.

The journal entry for October 17, 1862 brings news that Federals will leave the city. Maggie writes, "*I fear it is too good to be true.*" News also arrived through the rumor mill that the Confederates had won more victories in the Western theater. All would later prove to be untrue.

Friday, Oct 17th.

I rose a little after day [light] this morning and spent the time before breakfast in reading my Bible. Mr. Taylor returned from Murfreesboro this morning and brought us very cheering

---

[96] Walter T. Durham, *Nashville, the Occupied City, 1862-1863*, pages 194-197 (Knoxville, the University of Tennessee Press)

news from our army. Bragg had whipped Buell's army in Kentucky and Price has cut Grant's army all to pieces. Heard that Andy Johnson had left and the Federals are leaving the city. I fear it is too good to be true. Three more Confederates took dinner with us to-day. Mr. Weaver is prevented from going to town and thus I can hear nothing from home. I am again indulging in home-sickness on account of not seeing mother and father in so long. When I do go home I never intend leaving it, under any circumstances. Another thing that causes me much sorrow is that I am neglecting my Heavenly Father, and am consequently falling into my old sins. O! how I wish religion, could always be kept alive in my heart.

The Battle of Perryville, Kentucky was fought on October 8, 1862. Confederate General Braxton Bragg's Army of Mississippi won a tactical victory against a single corps of Maj. General Don Carlos Buell's Union Army of the Ohio. The battle is considered a strategic Union victory and is sometimes called the Battle for Kentucky because Bragg withdrew to Tennessee soon thereafter. The Union retained control of the critical border state the remainder of the war. Considering the casualties related to the engaged strengths of the armies, the Battle of Perryville was one of the bloodiest battles of the Civil War. It was also the largest battle fought in the state of Kentucky.

Saturday, Oct 18th 1862.

I rose quite early this morning. Employed myself in hemming my skirt and attending to many other duties. Received a long letter from mother this morning and our winter clothes. Mr. Taylor came this morning. He had been over by our house and had a little skirmish with the Yankee pickets who are stationed at the end of our lane. We are all quite low-spirited tonight on account of hearing such discouraging news from Price's army. I hope that it is not as bad as it is represented.

Sunday, Oct 19th 1862.

I rose at my accustomed hour this morning. Mr. Taylor and Frank went to Lavergne, the former to get me a pass for mother to pass our pickets[97] and the latter to hear some more cheering news from our army. Major Morgan (a cousin of Kate's) took dinner with us and he in a great measure cheered [us] up. He says we were not so badly whipped at Corinth, the

---

[97] The Rebel pass would allow movement from Mount Alban to Hedge Lawn without having to travel through occupied Nashville. This indicates the Rebel pickets were within seven miles of Nashville.

Federals having evacuated the latter place. Bragg has cut Buell's demoralized army to pieces, but with all our joy there is sorrow mixed with it as I see from the papers that 200 of the 1st Tennessee regiment were killed and wounded, and Genl. George Maney was killed. This is the Federal account which I hope is exaggerated. Oh! I wish we could hear from them and know they are safe. Major Morgan says he firmly believes the Federals are preparing to leave Nashville. Sometimes I am firm in my belief as to the Yankees leaving our poor sacred "City of Rocks,"[98] and then I hear something to discourage me in my belief.

Monday, Oct 20th.

I rose very soon this morning and spent my time in mending clothes. Mr. Taylor returned from LaVergne this morning but did not get a pass for mother and father as Col. Morgan was quite sick. Two Confederates [took] supper with us. All of them are of the opinion that Nashville will be given up as they are moving the sick.

Tuesday, Oct 21st.

I rose very early this morning. Passed the morning very pleasantly reading, sewing, and &c. Mr. Trabue came over in the evening and tells us that none of our relatives were killed in the late battles but so many of our friends were. I have no idea where dear Brother is. I hope God has preserved and watched over him.

Wednesday 22nd 1862.

I rose this morning at my usual time and spent my time before breakfast in reading my Bible to Cousin Jane. Frank returned from Murfreesboro this morning with cheering news from Bragg's army but with all our joy there is sorrow mixed with it; for how many dear friends are forever gone from us. Some are saying that there has been more fighting. O! I do wish this horrible war would cease before all our friends are killed. Heard nothing from home today. Why doesn't Ma write?

Saturday, Oct. 25th 1862.

Up this morning very early. Have been so much excited during the last two days that it seemed impossible for me to compose my mind to write, sew, or read. On Thursday we were

---

[98] Early nickname for Nashville derived from its being built upon the limestone bluffs of the Cumberland River.

again visited by our vile persecutors. They came out in full force thinking they would encounter some of our cavalry but the latter retreated to LaVergne to give the alarm to our forces in Murfreesboro. The Yankees went only two miles of the former place and then returned to pay the people for [aiding] the Confederates. They stole some of Cousin Jane's turkeys and some of them who were drunk attempted to search the house but upon Frank's coming down and reading the "safe-guard" they apologized for their rude behavior and left. Their force of about 8,000 went up but finding that our men had gone to Murfreesboro they "skedaddled". Our men stood picket at the Institute and the little Episcopal Church both of which the Yankees burnt. Mr. Taylor made a very narrow escape as he had just got off our lane when the Federals fired on him but the balls took no effect. Have employed the day in knitting and Ma is so anxious for me to learn. It has been cloudy and cool all day and it is now snowing fast. Dr. Harris staid all night with Frank. He is of the opinion that Bragg is now at Cumberland Gap and will soon be at Murfreesboro to attack Nashville.

Sunday, Oct 26th (Hedge Lawn).

I was rather late in getting up this morning on account of the fire being hard to make. The ground is covered with snow and is bitter cold. How I pity the poor soldier who has now no blanket or fire to keep him comfortable. Mr. Weaver brought us a bundle containing our thick flannels and a long letter from mother. She is anxious for us to come in but as Mr. Weaver has received orders not to come in any more I am cut off from all communications with my home and parents. Spent a quiet and pleasant day reading my Bible and &c. Mr. Taylor staid with us all evening.

Monday, Oct 27th.

I rose very early this morning. A heavy frost and very cold. Mr. Taylor went with us to gather scaly bark but we [met] with no success after walking about four miles.

Tuesday, Oct 28th 1862.

I was just in time for breakfast this morning as I could not get over my long walk yesterday. Nothing else has happened.

The end of October 1862 finds the weather cold with the remnants of an early snow on the ground. Maggie and Sister Kate, being homesick and yearning to see Mount Alban, decide to take the matter into their own hands. They "put their heads to thinking" and come up with the excuse of needing winter clothes. The sisters decide to run the federal blockade and visit home.

Thursday, Oct. 30th /62.

I rose very early this morning and after eating breakfast we put our heads to thinking and we at last concluded to run the <u>blockade</u> and visit <u>dear</u> Mount Alban as we were needing our winter clothes. We rode over on horseback and met with no difficulty whatever arriving at home about 9 o'clock. Mother was not home having gone into town to carry Aunt Jane. They were perfectly astonished to see us and I was surprised at our good luck as I had no idea I could get over.

Running the Blockade

Friday, Oct 31st (Mount Alban)

I rose quite early this morning considering how tired I was with my yesterday's ride. Ma went into town this morning to get us some things and returned just as breakfast was ready. I left very reluctantly but I hope to be at home soon and I know that no power can tear me from my parents again. We arrived at "Hedge Lawn" in safety and found that there had been a little skirmish the evening before on the place and it was well that we had staid all night at home.

Maggie records on November 1, 1862 that General Bragg has his Army of Tennessee headquartered at Knoxville. The general will bring the army back to Murfreesboro, Tennessee by the middle of December. Brother Joe is back in military service, having reenlisted with the Army of Tennessee in time to participate at Perryville.

Saturday, November 1st 1862.

I rose as early as usual this morning and employed the day in fixing my winter clothes. Mr. Taylor came from Lavergne this evening and brought us a great deal of good news. Just at dark we were seated around the fire playing with Mary Perkins who should come in but Berry with a hearty, "here's your Confederate soldier!" Oh! How glad we were to see him as he has been gone nearly two years. All of Bragg's army is now at Knoxville and will soon be advancing on Nashville. He was in the fight at Perryville, also Cousin Dan, Cal and Brother Joe. The latter is aid to Genl. Cheatham. None of our relatives were killed and how thankful I am to my gracious Heavenly Father for his many, many mercies.

Sunday, November 2nd.

I rose very late this morning on account of sleeping so miserable last night. Spent the day before dinner in reading my Bible and &c. After dinner Kate and I walked over to Mrs. Weaver's and passed the evening very pleasantly.

Monday, Nov. 3rd 1862.

I rose late again this morning. Spent the day in knitting, sewing and &c. I have been quite home-sick this evening but hope I may soon go to my beloved Mount Alban.

Tuesday, Nov 4th 1862.

I rose quite early this morning. Cousin Jane and sister attempted to go to town but failed to get through the pickets. Heard this morning that our army had been ordered to cook three days rations and make a forward move on Nashville.

The sound of cannon fire was heard early on the morning of November 5th. It was the general consensus that the rebel army was making an advance upon the city. The noise actually came from the south, where Forrest's guns were making a demonstration. The intent was to divert the Federals' attention away from Morgan[99], who was advancing from Gallatin with the intention of making a rapid dash into Edgefield to destroy the railroad station and as many freight cars as possible. Forrest was able to drive the pickets back into the city and fire upon Federal fortifications, including St. Cloud hill. The Federal guns opened up in response, which caused even more excitement with the city's inhabitants. At the end of the day, Morgan had less progress than expected and retreated back to Gallatin.[100]

Wednesday 5th/62.

I was up very late this morning as I lay awake the whole night. Our forces came down this morning and had quite sharp fighting on the other pikes. Some say three miles out on the Franklin road. We could distinctly hear the booming of cannon from the different forts surrounding Nashville. It is believed that this attack was made to give John H. Morgan time to burn the [rail] cars in Edgefield.

Thursday, Nov 6th 1862 - Sunday Nov 9th 1862.

I rose very late this morning as I have been quite unwell for the last three days with my usual sore throat and sick headaches. I think I must have taken cold getting up and very imprudently exposing myself on the night of the 5th. We have heard very discouraging news from Price's army as Mr. Caldwell has just returned from their division and according to his statement it is a perfect mess. Everyone is of the opinion that our army will be compelled to fall back as the Federals have been largely reinforced. We know nothing of the movements of armies and I therefore flatter myself with the belief that there are perhaps brighter days in store for us. For fear that the above rumor may be true Cousin Jane hastily prepared Cousin Dan and Cal some clothing (as the latter wrote he marched from Camp Robinson to Knoxville barefooted and started to Murfreesboro last evening with the intention of forwarding them to whatever point, she hurried home from there. I fully intended writing to dear Brother as I have nothing to send but was prevented from doing so by my head aching so bad.

---

[99] John Hunt Morgan, Confederate general and cavalry officer, June 1, 1825 – September 4, 1864.
[100] Walter T. Durham, *Nashville, the Occupied City 1862-1863*, pages 126-127 (Knoxville, The University of Tennessee Press).

Monday, Nov. 10th. Hedge Lawn.

I rose this morning quite late as I passed a very sleepless night. Mrs. Luter, Miss Brown came out this morning on their way to LaVergne to carry Fenton Hadley some clothes. Miss Cassie Harris spent the morning with us. Cousin Jane has not yet returned. Some think our army is falling back from Murfreesboro but there will be a <u>bloody</u> battle fought in old <u>Tennessee</u>. Oh! <u>how we all dread it</u>! Will this horrible war ever end! Kate has an intention of going to Murfreesboro to meet Cousin Dan if Cousin Jane should telegraph to her and I think I will accompany her as I may in all probability meet dear Brother.

Tuesday, Nov 11th.

I rose very early this morning and spent the whole of the morning in knitting. Cousin Jane returned from Murfreesboro this evening and heard that Brother Joe was there but Cousin Jane could not get to see him. Cousin Dan is there also and Kate intends going up to see him to-morrow, but I cannot leave. In all probability I will go up the first of next week to see Brother. Wrote him a long letter however which I hope he will get. Heard from home today. In the little fight the other day several shells fell in the meadow and exploded portions which flew in the rooms above mother's and shattered the windows to pieces.

Wednesday, November 12th.

I rose early this morning and finished writing to Brother and assisting Cousin Jane and Kate to get ready for Murfreesboro. After breakfast we heard the Yankees were coming up so Cousin Jane concluded not to go as she was almost afraid to leave us. Kate and the baby went up. Mr. Edmunson's family came down this evening and as nothing was fixed Cousin Jane invited Sallie and Lena to come over and stay several days with us. Taylor <u>came to see us for the last time</u> tonight.[101]

Thursday, Nov 13th 1862.

I was very lazy in rising this morning. Sallie and Lena spent the morning with us and then returned home to assist their mother in arranging their house. Little skirmishing this evening between the Yankee and Confederate cavalry but the former were driven in. Wrote a note to Ma

---

[101] Mr. Taylor, the family friend, was killed at Stones River. I think the last line of the journal entry was probably entered at a later date.

and Pa for some clothes for Brother but as Mr. Weaver is prevented from going in I can't send the <u>poor</u> <u>fellow</u> nothing. I wrote a letter to him as Cousin Jane intends going up tomorrow explaining the wherefore. Sallie and Lena intends staying with us during her absence.

Friday, Nov 14th.

I rose very early this morning notwithstanding I sat up until 11 o' clock last night helping Cousin Jane make Cal a needle book. She left for Murfreesboro this morning with Lucy Wilson. Sallie and Lena spent the day with us and their company is a small measure compensated for her absence. She intends returning in a few days and I anxiously look for that day as everyone apprehends an attack on Murfreesboro.

Saturday, Nov 15th 1862.

I rose quite late this morning as we again sat up very late listening to Frank's consuming stories. We still hear that the Federals intend making a forward move from Nashville but I trust it will not take place until Cousin Jane returns.

Sunday, Nov 16th 1862.

I rose very late this morning. A large Yankee force came out from Nashville and encamped on the <u>Asylum</u> grounds. They will move to Murfreesboro to-morrow I expect. We are all anxious for Cousin Jane and Kate to come [home].

Monday, Nov 17th.

I rose very late this morning as Lena and I sat up very late teasing Frank. Cousin Jane and Kate have not yet returned from Murfreesboro. The Yankee troops are still encamped on the Asylum grounds but are disturbing no one.

Wednesday 19th 1862. (Hedge Lawn)

I rose very soon this [morning] but I am sorry to record I am neglecting my religious duties. Can I ever become a consistent Christian? I fear not; if I do not pay more attention to my God and the salvation of my soul. Sallie and Lena spent the morning with us. We are so uneasy about Cousin Jane and Kate. I do wish they would come home as I am getting very tired of housekeeping. Finished knitting my sock. As Mrs. Weaver was going in, I wrote a long letter to dear Ma and sent a note and a pair of stockings to little Mattie. Nothing else.

Thursday, Nov 20th.

Nothing worthy to record to-day.

Friday, Nov. 21st.

I rose very late this morning as Lena and I had a good [chat] before going to bed. I again failed to perform my religious duties and of course have not been happy. Cousin Jane has been gone one week to-day.

Saturday, Nov 22nd.

I was up very late this morning. Cousin Jane and Kate and the baby returned from Murfreesboro late to-day.

Hedge Lawn, Nov 24th 1862.

I rose very early this morning. Mrs. Edmunson and Cousin Jane went up to Genl Sill[102] to get a pass but he had no authority to give. They intend going in to-morrow. Heard from home. All are well. Cousin Ella Perkins was down. Brother was up at Triune and sent letters to us all but I expect mother was afraid to send them.

Hedge Lawn, Tuesday Nov 25th.

I rose quite late this morning. Cousin Jane and Mrs. Edmunson went to town and they saw Pa. He sent Brother Joe several bundles of clothes by Mrs. Overton to Brentwood. Cousin Jane intends going in on Saturday and if Mrs. Edmunson don't accompany her I think I will go in to meet Ma. Three Federal officers took dinner with us. Kate and I had a little dispute with them but it was all in a quiet good humored way.

Hedge Lawn, Sunday, Nov 30th.

I rose at six o'clock this morning. I have neglected writing in my diary for several days as we are all surrounded by Yankees and have to put up with their many insults and I not being accustomed to it; has completely unstrung me. Five of them quartered themselves on Cousin

---

[102] Union Army Brigadier General Joshua Sill, a 13th Brigade, XVI Corp commander later killed at the Battle of Stones River. Fort Sill, Oklahoma was named in his honor.

Jane with all the army cattle attendants &c. Joseph E. Johnston[103] has won command of our forces. A <u>bloody</u>, <u>bloody</u> battle will be fought in old Tennessee and how many aching hearts will throb for the loved ones that will fall. Will our distracted country ever become settled!

Hedge Lawn, Dec. 2nd 1862.

I rose very early this morning. As it cleared off Kate and I went over to Mrs. Smiley's to see Anna Hays.

General Joseph E. Johnston

John "Bul" Brown once again causes stress for Aunt Jane. Earlier in June, John and his friend John Kirkman were released on parole from the penitentiary. In hopes of being part of a prisoner exchange and being sent south, the two men now make a false claim of being paroled prisoners and are again arrested. Their plan is exposed when it is discovered that they were citizens and not soldiers. They are returned to the penitentiary until they agree to take the oath of allegiance. In the spirit of Nathan Hale, the two young men in their fervent patriotism could not take the oath. They join in a plot to escape and on a wet December night, led by a convicted rebel spy, they along with eighteen others slip over the wall. They make their way to the home of Dr. John Hudson, a staunch rebel sympathizer. They soon reach the safety of rebel lines. Both Bul and John Kirkman were welcomed into Confederate service just after the Battle of Stones River.[104]

Hedge Lawn, Dec 4th 1862.

I rose quite early this morning and spent the morning very pleasantly knitting, &c. Received a note from Aunt Jane. She is in great distress about Bul. He reported himself as one of the paroled prisoners and was instantly sent to the Penitentiary. Heard from home. There are no

---

[103] In early March 1862, Joseph Eggleston Johnston assumed command of the Army of Northern Virginia. After being wounded in battle, he lost his command to Lee. He was later reassigned and would assume a command in the Western theater.

[104] Walter T. Durham, *Nashville, The Occupied City 1862-1863*, pages 197-198 (Knoxville, The University of Tennessee Press).

troops on our poor old Mount Alban; fortunately the creek was dry. Genl. Jeff Davis[105] is encamped on Mrs. John Thompson's[106] front yard.

Hedge Lawn, Dec. 5th 1862. (Friday)

I rose very early this morning and prepared myself for going to town but owning to its snowing so fast my visit was postponed. Nearly three long months have passed since Mother has paid us one of her cherished visits. When will I ever return to my home!

Hedge Lawn, Dec. 11th 1862. (Thursday)

I rose quite early this morning. Spent the day as usual in knitting socks, &c.

Maggie endures a miserable birthday on December 17, 1862. She turns eighteen years old.[107] The Vaulx home continues to have trouble with Federal soldiers. She records them stealing bacon and lard and raiding the carriage house. These lawless acts of forage compel Pa to ask for a guard. Pa had earlier sought after and received a safeguard order dated July 28, 1862 and signed by Colonel John F. Miller of the 29th Indiana Volunteers. The back of the order was signed by Brigadier General Lovell H. Rousseau and noted as approved by Major General Rosecrans. Even with the document in hand, and heavily agreed upon by officers of high command, the pillage of Mount Alban would continue.

Thursday, December 17th 1862.[108]

I rose quite early this morning. Eighteen years old today! Would that they all had been spent in my Makers service! Have been home sick and low spirited on count of having such bad news from home. On Tuesday morning, Pa went over to Capt Morton's headquarters and appealed for a guard. He was insolently refused, the Capt. telling him that the President of the U.S. did not protect private property. About 3 o'clock, a regiment or more greeted themselves on Pa, The rain was pouring in torrents when they came. They immediately broke down the carriage house door; pulled the Cab carriage and buggy out and then occupied the stables and sheep houses. They threw the servants out in the rain and ordered them to go to

---

[105] General Jeff Davis had risen from a lieutenant at Sumter to rank of general after the Battle of Wilson Creek. He, after having his face slapped and being offended, shot and killed his superior officer General William Nelson. He was arrested and imprisoned but soon released because of the need of experienced field commanders for the Union Army.

[106] The John Thompson Franklin Pike residence, Glen Leven. It sat on a tract of land below Mount Alban.

[107] Mt. Olivet obelisk grave marker shows birth year as 1845. Maggie should know how old she is. Her birthdate should read Dec. 17, 1844.

[108] The December 17th through 22nd journal entries for the days of the week are off. On Christmas day, Maggie catches up on her days.

the house and make a fire. Six <u>officers</u> were quartered on Pa. Safe guards had we sought, whatever! They stole about 600 lbs of bacon and almost all the lard. The officer of the day promised Pa to report them to Genl Rosecrans. He seemed very much worried about it. Says such conduct is "death to my soldiers." He obtained the names of all the officers, what company and regiment they belonged to. I trust they will be severely punished.

Friday, Dec 18th.

Nothing of interest to-day to record.

Saturday, Dec. 19th 1862

I rose very early this morning and assisted Cousin Jane in getting ready for town. Heard nothing from home today but she saw Pa and all are well but worried to death with the Yankees who are encamped on our ruined Mount Alban. Bul Brown and John Kirkman escaped from the Penitentiary a few nights ago. How they affected it, I have not yet heard. Passed the day in knitting for the boys.

Tuesday, Dec 22nd 1862.

I was very late rising this morning on account of sleeping so miserably. Cousin Jane and Kate went over to Mrs. Brown's, the latter wishing to go to Triune with Mary Hadley but they were betrayed by their driver. <u>Heard from home yesterday</u>. The troops are all over the place.

Thursday, Dec 25th 1862.

I rose early this morning. Colonel Howard[109] who is encamped in the woods invited us to witness a flag presentation. We all went but I felt sorry that I did as I thought those men were going to fight our dear ones. The Colonel, I think is becoming thoroughly disgusted with the war and thinks the old Union can <u>never</u> be restored. Major Dresser and the Colonel took dinner with us. This is the first Christmas I have ever spent from home and my dear parents and oh! how fervently do I pray that it may be the last.

Because Middle Tennessee holds strategic rail and river transportation facilities, there is much fighting around the area. Maggie records the Confederate prisoners coming through and makes multiple references to a looming battle which would later be known as Stones River.

---

[109] Lt. Colonel William Howard, commander of the 59th Ohio Infantry regiment.

Chapter Seven
Stones River

"Every relative and friend that I have is in this battle!"

The Battle of Stones River or also known as Murfreesboro was fought from December 31, 1862 to January 2, 1863. The engagement took place near the sleepy Middle Tennessee town of Murfreesboro. Although the battle itself was inconclusive, the Union Army's repulse of two Confederate attacks and the subsequent Confederate withdrawal were a much needed boost to Union morale after Eastern Theater defeats including the Battle of Fredericksburg. It further dashed Confederate aspirations for control of Middle Tennessee. Stones River had the highest percentage of casualties on both sides. It was one of the bloodiest contests of the war, the loss being one-fourth of the total number engaged. The Battle of Stones River closed out the year in the Western Theater of war. The effect of the battle was the attempt of the Confederates to recover Middle Tennessee and Kentucky was now abandoned. The way was open for another Union advance on Chattanooga. Bragg's force was reduced from an offensive to a defensive attitude.[110]

The close of 1862 finds Maggie and Sister Kate residing with Cousin Jane Morgan at Hedge Lawn, located six miles outside Nashville on the Murfreesboro Pike. Pa, Ma, and little sister Mattie are at Mount Alban which is under the heavy burden of a Union military encampment. Pa still feels that Hedge Lawn is a much safer place for his teenaged daughters.

Friday, December 26, 1862.
I rose quite early this morning and after dressing I am almost finished knitting my socks for Cousin Dan. All of the troops moved up the road this morning. As Colonel Howard's regiment passed the band struck up "Dixie" according to the promise of the Colonel. We may expect to hear of a <u>bloody</u>, <u>bloody</u> battle.

---

[110] Barnes, *A Brief History of the United States,* Epoch V, pages 229-230.

Saturday, Dec 27th.

I was very early rising this morning, notwithstanding I lay awake a greater part of the night expecting every moment to hear the booming of the cannon and how many sad, sad thoughts passed through my mind as in all probability some near and dear friends or relatives [would] passed from this world of strife to a land of peace and eternal happiness. This morning my expectations were realized as we could distinctly hear the booming of the cannon but at what front we could not ascertain. Cheatham's Division is at Lavergne, but I hope and put my trust in God for the preservation of dear Brother.

Sunday, Dec 28th/62.

I rose very early this morning. Have spent a very lonesome day as Cousin Jane and Kate went over and spent the day with Mrs. Weaver. I did not spend my Sabbath as I would wish but I hope I will soon return to my God from whom I have so often wandered.

Monday, Dec 29th 1862.

I rose very early this morning and as is my custom, I spent the entire day in knitting socks. Cousin Jane went in town with Mrs. Weaver. Heard from home to-day. There is general concern on account of the Yankees moving up the road. Heard that Cheatham's Division was at Nolensville. I think it is hard to tell their whereabouts.

Tuesday, Dec 30th 1862 – Wednesday, Dec 31st 1862.

I rose very early this morning expecting to go to town to call on some friends, but we found that we had no driver so our visits are postponed until tomorrow. Frank went over to Mr. Edmunson's tonight and has returned telling us that there has been fighting ever since Sunday up about Murfreesboro. Two Yankees who were taken prisoners but made their escape told him that their forces after shelling Murfreesboro were driven within two miles of Lavergne. Five regiments were taken at the onset and it was reported that Genls. Sill, Rousseau and Crittenden were killed.[111] They have evidently received a great thrashing. Oh! how I hope that all of our dear friends and relatives are safe.

---

[111] The report was partially wrong; General's Lovell Rousseau and Thomas Crittenden survived the war. General Rousseau died in 1868 and Crittenden in 1893.

The close of the second year of war found the following results. The Confederates had gained the victories of Jackson in the Shenandoah Valley; of Lee in the peninsular campaign and those against Pope; Bragg's great raid in Kentucky and the battles of Cedar Mountain, Chickasaw Bluff and Fredericksburg.

The Federals had taken Forts Henry, Donelson, Pulaski, Macon, Jackson, St. Philip, and Island No. 10; had opened the Mississippi to Vicksburg, occupied New Orleans, Roanoke Island, Newbern, Yorktown, Norfolk, and Memphis; had gained the battles of Pea Ridge, Williamsburg, Fair Oaks, South Mountain, Antietam, Iuka, Corinth, and Murfreesboro, and had checked the career of the Merrimac.[112] The marked successes were mainly at the West and along the coast; while in Virginia, as yet, defeats had followed victories so soon as to hide their memory.

The plan for the third year of the war was the same as in the preceding year, but included also the occupation of Tennessee. The Federal army was about seven hundred thousand strong; the Confederate, not more than half that number. The Emancipation Proclamation[113] was issued at the opening of the year.[114]

Thursday, January 1st 1863.

Another sad new year! I thought the last first was the saddest but it seems as if each gets more melancholy. There has been fighting at or near Murfreesboro all day. We could distinctly hear the booming of the cannon. It seems as if all their army waggons came down and some think they will be compelled to retreat or starve as all their provisions are cut off by our cavalry. Every relative and friend that I have is in this battle![115]

The reader can observe the anxiety within Maggie's journal entries. Her lack of knowledge about the fate of loved ones is consuming her daily thoughts.

---

112 Refer to the appendix for Maggie's list of dates for War of Southern Independence.
113 The Emancipation Proclamation was President Lincoln's executive order proclaiming the freedom of slaves living in states not under federal control. The state of Tennessee was considered under control; thus it was exempt.
114 Barnes, *A Brief History of the United States*, Epoch V, pages 243-244.
115 Maggie's great-grandmother, Mrs. Josiah Nichol, had thirteen grandsons in the Battle of Stones River. Walter T. Durham, *Nashville, the Occupied City*, page 208 (Knoxville, The University of Tennessee Press). Refer to Maggie's journal entry, dated Sep. 1, 1861.

Friday, January 2nd 1863.

I rose very early this morning notwithstanding I lay awake the whole night thinking of dear brother who was perhaps lying wounded or dead on the battle field with no loving hands to supply his needs. This is the fourth day the fighting has been raging and it seems as if neither side will give up.

Saturday, Jan 3rd 1863.

I rose again early. We have again heard the booming of cannon. This morning a large provision train went out and about one hour after wards we heard firing and it is thought the whole train was captured.

Sunday, Jan 4th 1863.

Nothing to-day. There has been no fighting at all. Oh! I wish we could hear from our dear friends and relatives.

Monday, Jan 5th 1863.

I was up very early this morning. From all accounts our forces have evacuated Murfreesboro and fallen back to Tullahoma which is from all accounts strongly fortified. The Federals received a good whipping losing three to one. We captured 40 odd pieces of artillery.

Wednesday, January 7th

I rose very early this morning and assisted Cousin Jane in getting ready to go to Murfreesboro where I hope she may hear of our boys being <u>safe</u> and <u>well</u>. Employed the day in knitting Mary Perkins stockings. Mr. Weaver is prevented from going to town and it is on that account I am cut off from communication from home. When will I ever return to my <u>dear parents</u>.

Thursday, January 8th 1863.

I rose early this morning. Frank and Mr. Trabue went over to see Mrs. Jones who has just returned from Murfreesboro. Cousins Dan, Cal and Berry were in the fight but came out safe. He inquired of Brother but she could not give me news of that dear relative. O! I trust he is safe. Heard through her of the sad death of Mr. Taylor. Poor fellow he fell in a noble cause. His leg was shot entirely off and lock jaw was the consequence. We all loved him as dearly as a brother and are greatly grieved to hear of his sad death.

Friday, January 9th 1863.

I rose very early this morning. After breakfast, Kate and I went over to see Mrs. Harris to look at the Confederate prisoners who encamped in the Asylum field but we found much to our disappointment. They had gone by two hours before. She told us that there was a young soldier up the road very badly wounded. He is a very intelligent young man from Mississippi. Several of the neighbors have sent him many delicacies and comforts. I intend knitting him a pair of socks and Kate thinks of making him a warm under shirt. Cousin Jane has not yet returned from Murfreesboro.

Saturday, January 10th 1863.

I rose very early this morning and employed the day in a variety of ways; knitting, reading and practicing. Cousin Jane returned from Murfreesboro this morning. She heard nothing from the boys; but they are all safe or else we would have heard of any mishaps. Heard nothing from home. Oh! I hope nothing is the matter!

Sunday, January 11th 1863.

I rose late this morning on account of being awake the greater part of the night thinking of home and all the happy hours I have spent there. Several friends call on us.

Monday, January 12th 1863.

I rose quite late this morning employed my time before breakfast in playing with Mary Perkins. Kate said Cousin Jane started to town but the pickets refused to let her pass. Sallie Sharpe came to see us this morning. She told us that our forces were at Fosterville and that there had been a battle fought at that place. Whither there is any truth in it I cannot tell.

Tuesday, January 13th 1863.

I rose very early this morning and employed my time in knitting Mary Perkins stockings. Received a long letter last night. All were well. They had received a letter from Brother Joe. He has received all my letters and intended answering them. All communications are now cut off from our dear boys.

Wednesday, January 14th

I rose quite late this morning on account of not being all well. Spent the day in knitting, &c. Have spent a very home-sick and miserable day. Heard nothing from home to-day.

Saturday, January 17th 1863.

I rose very late this morning as I spent a very miserable and sleepless night. Spent the day in knitting Cousin Jane's stockings. Wednesday it rained all day and at night it turned intensely cold and commenced sleeting and snowing, continuing two days. This is the cause of my not hearing from home as Mr. Weaver cannot go in such bad weather.

On January 19, 1863, the Vaulx family is faced with some very bad news. A prisoner who had been taken at Murfreesboro tells the family that Uncle James Armstrong had been killed. A month later, a letter from Brother Joe will confirm the sad news to be true.

Monday, Jan. 19th 1863.

I rose very early this morning. I received a long letter from Ma and Pa, the one containing $15 and the other all the news among which there is sad. The Confederate prisoners who were taken at Murfreesboro told Mrs. Tom Smith that her son was wounded and that poor dear Uncle James was killed. Mother tried to get to see them, but they were so strictly confined, she failed. Aunt Jane and Mrs. Smith have gone to Triune and I hope and trust that they may find that [the] dear and only brother of poor mama's is alive and well.

Tuesday, Jan 20th 1863.

I rose unusually early this morning although I spent a very sleepless night thinking of dear mother sorrowing for her only brother who now lies moldering in the earth, where, none can tell. Little did we think when he parted from us this day a year ago, promising to come again in June that this would see him taken from this world of strife and discord to a realm of peace and eternal harmony. Let us earnestly endeavor to prepare ourselves to meet our dear relatives and friends in the land of peace.

Friday, Jan 23rd 1863.

I rose this morning at day break and spent the time before breakfast in knitting Mattie's stocking. I have been very homesick and it is on that account I have not written in my journal for several days. Yesterday Kate and I spent the day with Fannie and Lucy Wilson and their holily conversation and engaging manner soon dispelled my low spirits. Mr. Weaver met with so much difficulty in getting out of town on Monday he has not been back until to-day and I am <u>again</u> disappointed about [not] hearing from <u>poor dear mama</u>. Another great battle has been fought on the glorious soil of Virginia.[116] Whether victorious or not, I cannot tell. Oh! How fervently do I pray we have given them another Fredericksburg's defeat.

Saturday, Jan 24th 1863.

I rose very late this morning. It has been a very gloomy rainy day and thus as always the case, I have been low spirited. Mr. Weaver went to town this morning but brought us nothing from home and consequently the gloom settled more deeply on my spirits. This week I have been unusually sad about our political affairs, but far, far more so concerning the welfare of my immortal Soul, which ought to be the great object of my life. My prayers sure are short and hasty and many are the solemn errands I utter on a thoughtless tongue. Oh! My Heavenly Father make the miserable sinner to a true sense of his guilt, support his tottering footsteps and enable him to walk through the stormy scenes of life with a firm and steady tread, his soul pure and spotless as his Divine Maker after whose image he is made.

January 27th 1863. (Tuesday)

I rose this morning at day-break and spent the time before breakfast knitting Mattie's stocking. I have felt very unwell for the past two days and on that account I have not been as punctual in writing as I should be. Yesterday, I received a large bundle from home and on opening it what should meet my eyes but a long letter from Brother Joe. It was the first I had received from him since he was sick at Winchester, Va. The place from whence it is dated is a mystery to see, but it is now a measure solved when I reflect how restricted one's thoughts must be during such times as these. Mrs. Buchanan sent word to us that she had procured a pass for 20 days and kindly offered to lend it to us any time we may wish to assail our selves of it. Mrs. Sharp sent word to Cousin Jane that she was going tomorrow and as I am anxious to see Mama, Kate and I have concluded to go in on Thursday so that she may meet us.

---

[116] This is a reference to the skirmishes following the Battle of Fredericksburg. Union General Ambrose Burnside tried to advance his army against rebel fortifications but was prevented due to bad weather. A few days later, General Joe Hooker replaced Burnside as commander of the Army of the Potomac.

Wednesday, Jan 28th 1863.

I rose this morning quite early. Have spent a very miserable day owning to my again giving away to my violent temper. I was so cold and disagreeable. Cousin Jane and Sallie concluded not to go in. I feel so sad and out done with myself that I have no heart to write here in my book. Heard nothing from home today.

Thursday, January 29th 1863.

I rose this morning very late and with a severe headache as I spent a sleepless and unhappy night thinking how sinful and depressed I had made myself in the sight of my kind and inspired Heavenly Father. Cousin Jane and Mrs. Sharp went in to-day and brought me out a most beautiful writing desk, a present from dear Mama which I intend keeping carefully. As the roads are so bad, Kate and I will not go in. It is very well as Pa says Ma is so busy that she cannot leave home.

Friday, Jan 30th 1863.

I rose this morning with a very bad headache on account of sleeping so badly. Spent the morning in knitting Cousin Dan Perkins a pair of socks. In the evening I wrote a good long letter to Brother as Frank told me Mrs. Sharp was going South in a few days. Received a note from Ma promising to come over next week.

Saturday, Jan 31st 1863.

I rose this morning early as Kate and myself slept up stairs in order to wean Mary Perkins. In the morning we went over and staid some time with Sallie Edmunson, who is quite sick with typhoid fever. Heard nothing from home!

Sunday, February 1st 1863.

I rose this morning quite late as Cousin Jane and I took Mary Perkins into [town] to-day in order to wean her. Two Yankees came to get something to eat and as they seemed to have an intention of staying sometime, I slipped out of the room and employed myself in writing a letter. Cousin Jane went over to Mrs. Edmunson to give our letters to Dr. Charlton to send to the army.

Hedge Lawn, Tuesday 3rd 1863.

I rose very late this morning as Kate and I had quite an adventuresome time yesterday. We started in with the expectations of being turned back but when we reached the toll-gate a very gentlemanly officer kindly sent us in with a guard, telling we could procure passes at the Capitol, from the Provost Marshal. After an hour's ride over the roughest of roads we reached our place of destination, which is without doubt the filthiest place imaginable. According to the directions given us by the officer at the picket, we went to the Provost Marshal, who is a true type of a ["devon Easter."] A thin raw bone Abolitionist with black hair, eyes and whiskers and upon his nose was perched one eye glass. The room was filled with dirty lazy soldiers, and if I am not mistaken some "intelligent" contrabands were conversing with their benefactors. We asked the Provost Marshal for a pass, and was directed into an adjoining room. Three officers were seated around a blazing coal fire, and on a table close by a decanter of wine were placed and from the odor that filled the room I came to the conclusion the gentleman had been regaling themselves. We were treated with great rudeness and upon my requesting the officer at the desk to give us a pass, he gruffly replied they were issuing none except to those of loyalty. As we were not of that strip Kate and I concluded to go, after being directed to the headquarters of Genl Mitchell as he alone could give us passes. Thither we went, and were treated with great rudeness. We then attended to our business; determine to rely on the kindness of our good officer at the gate, as our guard had strayed from us. I then went to Grandma's and was relating our adventures to Ellen Percy, who laughed and said as going out, "I bet I get you one." I thought she was joking. As it was nearly 3 o'clock and fearing our friend at the picket would be relieved, we determined to start on home. We went down College St. and there met Ellen, who had gone with a <u>Union</u> friend to Col Wm. Trunsdale, Chief of Army Police in the Zollicoffer house, to have our barouche searched, but he declined doing so as our ingenuous faces told him plainly we had nothing "contraband". He sent a guard with us to the toll-gate, and there found our friend still on duty. After reading the papers he gave us the military salute and told us to pass on. I gave him my thousand thanks and drove rapidly home over the rigid road. I am determined never to go to town without the most imperative business calls me thither. Pa was in, but it being so late I had no time to call to see him. Heard from Ma through Mr. Weaver. <u>All's well</u>.

Getting the Pass

Saturday, Feby. 7th 1863.

I rose quite late this morning as I was kept awake a great deal by Kattie who is suffering with her old complaint, the ear-ache. This is the reason I have neglected writing in my journal. The weather for the last few days has been intensively cold. <u>Rain</u>, <u>snow</u>, and <u>sleet</u>! It is now much warmer and will be raining before morning. Heard nothing from home. Spent the day knitting, sewing, &c. Received a long letter from my dear friend and school-mate Mollie Berry. She is expressing the deep interest she now takes in attending church and Sunday school, those blessed privileges which I am now denied. Oh! how fervently do I pray that she has become convinced of the error of her ways, and is now determined to choose the better portion promised to the humble followers of our Saviour, Jesus Christ. I wrote to her immediately encouraging her to leave off her sins and prepare for time and eternity. How often have I prayed for that dear friend, and now I thank thee, oh God for hearing my cry. Heal her many backslidings, enable her to resist temptations and overcome the many difficulties that will beset her in this turbulent world!

Sunday, Feb 8th 1863.

I rose this [morning] very soon but from some cause I was late at breakfast. Spent the day very quietly reading "Lights and shadows of Scottish life".

Monday, Feb 9th 1863.

I rose this morning quite late as it seemed impossible for me to awake. Spent the morning sewing on my skirt. Mr. Trabue spent the morning with us. Heard from home to day. Our poor ruined neighborhood is again infested with Yankees. Six large regiments, artillery, and their waggons were encamped on our place. A fleet of boats came up with provisions for the citizens.

Friday, Feby. 13th 1863.

I rose quite late this morning as the baby kept me awake the greater part of the night. The day has been clear and beautiful. O! that our distracted country was quiet and free from all this bloodshed. Heard nothing from home. Wrote a note to Ma, begging her to come over. I expect it will be like my other attempts -useless-. Nearly two months since I have seen her and four since I have seen dear Pa. I hope I will soon be at home with them all, never again to be separated. Spent the day in knitting Mattie's stockings, which I hope will soon be finished, as I am growing tired of the tedious job. I received a little note from her. I am glad to see the progress she is making both in writing, diction and spelling. Oh! I wish I was at home! What an interest and a pleasure I would take in learning her, now that I have no studies of my own to attend to.

A miserable Maggie records February 16, 1863 as the sad first anniversary of the "Great Panic". The thought of her long absence from home causes deep homesickness to once again fill the pages of her journal.

Monday, Feb. 16th 1863

This is the sad anniversary of "the great panic". A year has gone by; and the war "still" drags its slow length along. And I am still in exile from my home and there seems as yet no prospect of my ever returning to that dear spot, where I have spent so many happy hours. Yesterday I spent the day in reading my Bible and performing my other duties that I have so long neglected, but I hope religion is again beginning to revive in my heart never to be effaced by misgivings and back sliding. To-day I wrote a long private letter to mother and father opening my whole heart to them in regard to my religious opinions. It is a thing that I ought to have done long ago, for who would more earnestly cheer me onwards to Heaven, and assist me in removing the vanities of this world and pray for my eternal welfare than my dear parents. We never appreciate a blessing until it is withdrawn. In the evening Kate and I went over to Mrs. Weaver's to [see] Fannie. The time passed agreeably and as I expected a letter from home but in this I was doomed to disappointment. No letter came and I found myself indulging in home sickness. Who would help feeling so, after staying from my home a year, a whole long wretched year! "Let us hope for brighter days."

Tuesday, Feby 17th 1863.

I rose this morning very early. Spent the day knitting, sewing and practicing. A year ago to-day, I left my home and little did I think when I went that twelve month's would see me still absent. Oh! I can't stand it any longer. Heard nothing from home. How anxiously I wait the reply to my letter to Mama! Nearly finished Mattie's stockings but was compelled to strip some out on account of dropping some stitches. A great fault of mine I am sorry to say! I am again neglecting my prayers in the morning and it would be far better if I would leave off praying at night, for they are short, hasty, attired with a "thoughtless tongue" and of course are not heard by my Heavenly Father. Hence forward, I will rise earlier and have a secluded room for my devotions, where no one will disturb me. How many times have I wandered from my God and of course are the sins that I have committed by such folly. Will I ever become in every sense of the word a Christian, never faltering, but journey onward with steady steps, until I reach that heavenly land where I will dwell forever with my God whom I hope to serve faithfully on earth. How I wish religion would always stay fresh in my heart. Sometimes I fear that I too much long for that perfection which is never acquired by earthly mortals.

Wednesday, Feby 18th 1863.

I rose this morning very early being awakened by the servants coming in and informing us that three of the negroes had left in the night. We had expected this for some time. They will soon repent of this folly and wish they were back at this comfortable house! Finished knitting Mattie's stockings and intend sending them to her to-morrow. Heard nothing from home! Why don't Ma write to her exiled children! Have again failed to retire and perform religious duties. I must tear myself from conversation of Cousin Jane and Kate and spend the time before breakfast in prayer.

Friday, Feby 20th 1863.

I rose this morning very early. Cousin Jane and I went over to see Mrs. Weaver complying with an engagement of that lady but she was not at home; from there we went to see old Mrs. Harris who is quite ill. Heard yesterday from Pa. The place is covered with troops, more than ever before. I wonder if we will ever be rid of our enemies. Received a long letter from Mollie Berry. Dear girl! how I love you, you the companion of my happy childhood, and now my sister in Christ. I have always prayed for such a friend, and now my Heavenly Father has answered my prayer. Assist me oh God in becoming each day more and more like unto thee.

Saturday, Feby 21st 1863.

The day was cold out and gloomy. Raining all day and it still continues to pour. Heard nothing from home. Spent the day reading Miss Edgeworth's Helen, which is an excellent novel, expressing on one's mind the necessity of being so strictly truthful.

Sunday, Feb 22nd 1863.

I rose very early this morning and retired to a room upstairs and there engaged in prayer with some of the ardours of other days. On coming down stairs, I was most agreeably surprised at finding a long letter from Brother. In it he confirms the sad death of dear Uncle James. He fell in an open field leading his men in a charge under one of the most terrific fires of artillery, musketry witnessed in this war. His remains were taken charge by his Regimental Quartermaster and buried in the cemetery at Murfreesboro. Although qualified for a much higher position, he was not ambitious of military fame but desired only to contribute in vindication of the principles and country he loved so well. Dear Uncle James, how I hope you were a firm believer on the crucified Saviour, that your noble soul has been taken to a world where no sin will ever corrupt it. Let us strive to live in the fear of God and thus prepare ourselves for a happy reunion beyond the skies.

Monday, Feby 23rd 1863.

I rose this morning very early and spent the greater part of the day in writing a long long letter to Brother Joe. Kate Perkins intends going to Franklin very soon, and I hope she may have a chance of sending them. Heard nothing from home. I wonder if Ma ever intends writing to me. Sometimes I get so home-sick and low spirited that I feel like walking all the way home. I wonder how much longer I will be separated from my parents!

Tuesday, Feby 24th 1863.

I rose this morning quite late. Cousin Jane and Kate went to the funeral of Mrs. Harris. The latter saw Mrs. Goff who told her she was going to Franklin so Kate concluded to accompany her. She went to Mrs. Goff's to stay all night; they intend starting early in the morning. Sissie is now staying with Josey Mooney so there is no one at home but Cousin Jane and myself. Mandy and her family left this morning.

Saturday, Feby 28th/63.

I rose this morning very late on consequence of having to be up so much with the baby as Cousin Jane staid all night with Mrs. Mooney. Yesterday I received a long and interesting letter from Mrs. Snyder. Although differing from me in politics, I have always regarded her with the warmest affections, we have been friends in Christ and the heirs of eternal happiness. Received nothing from home today, but Cousin Jane saw Pa this morning and all [is] well at my dear home. It rained all morning but cleared off warm and beautiful in the evening.

Sunday, March 1st 1863.

I rose this morning quite late with a very severe headache but upon my eating my breakfast it was partially relieved. Spent the morning in reading my Bible, writing to Mrs. Snyder and helping Cousin Jane attend to Mary Perkins who is rather unwell, owning I fear to mismanagement on my part during Cousin Jane's absence. The day has been clear and beautiful and everything indicates an early Spring.

Monday, March 2nd 1863.

I rose this morning rather early. Spent the day knitting the servants stockings and trying to amuse Mary who still remains quite unwell, and I consider it my duty and pleasure to return Cousin Jane of any duty that I can perform, as she has in a small degree supplied the place of a parent. This evening I received a long and most satisfactory answer from Mama, in regard to becoming a Christian. It will ever serve to cheer me onward in the way I should go. I feel that I have been too long in unburdening my mind to her. I must always give her my entire confidence, and to her with all my youthful pleasures and troubles, for none that know and love me best can ever be as patient with me in my sins and transgressions as my own dear mother. Oh! that I was at home, what a different life I would live!

Tuesday, March 3rd 1863.

I rose this morning very early and after eating my breakfast I cleaned Cousin Jane's room thoroughly. I then finished knitting the servants stockings. Mary Edmunson spent the evening with us. The weather is cold and clear.

Wednesday, March 4th/63.

I rose this morning very late. Cleaned my room and then washed up the dishes and arranged the sitting room after Cousin Jane's going to town with Mary Edmunson. A slight snow in the morning but it cleared up and remained the rest of the day. Mary Perkins proved very troublesome to-day and I have therefore accomplished little or nothing. Cousin Jane went to the office but Pa was not in.

Thursday, March 5th/63.

I rose this morning very early and cleaned one room before breakfast. After eating, sister and I washed the dishes, cleaned the safe out, &c. I think under Cousin Jane's excellent control we will become pretty good housekeepers. Frank went in the morning with Mr. Weaver and staid all night. Heard from home – all well.

Friday, March 6th/63.

I rose this morning early and attended to my own regular tasks. The day has been cold out and gloomy. Frank returned this evening bringing me a large bundle of paper from Pa. The troops are still on the place. Spent the day writing and reading "Rinsells Diary North and South". Kate Perkins returned from Williamson [county].

Saturday, March 7th 1863.

I rose this morning quite late as the baby kept us awake owning to the little darlings being sick. Heard heavy firing this morning in town but have not yet [determined] the cause. Heard nothing from my dear home.

Sunday, March 8th/63.

I rose this morning very early and spent the morning writing to Ma and several friends. Heard to-day that our troops drove the "abolitionists" out of Franklin and they were soon fighting at or near Brentwood.

Monday, March 9th/63.

I rose this morning very early and finished cleaning our room before breakfast. Spent the morning in writing a long letter to my former friend and schoolmate Mrs. Fellows, as I think I will have an opportunity of sending it. I intend writing a short letter to Brother Joe [and sending it] by the same person. Heard nothing from home.

Tuesday, March 10th/63.

I rose this morning very early and attended to my household affairs. After breakfast I assisted Cousin Jane in peeling apples and quilting Lizzie's skirt. It has been raining all day but there is now a prospect of it clearing off as it has turned quite cool. Heard nothing from home.

Wednesday, March 11th/63.

I rose this morning very early and performed my regular duties. Spent the morning writing to Mollie Berry, knitting, practicing, &c. Frank went to town this morning and I anxiously await his coming for I expect something from home. Cold and clear and I hope we will have no more bad weather.

Thursday, March 12th/63.

I rose this morning very early. Spent the morning very usefully knitting the boys socks as we hope soon to have an opportunity of sending them. Kate and Mary Edmunson went in town this morning. Heard nothing from my home. Will I always be separated from the scenes of my happy child hood? I will put my trust in and hitherto gracious Providence with the fervent prayer that he will guide me through the trials and troubles of this world and at last take my soul pure and spotless to those realms of eternal happiness.

Friday, March 13th/63.

I rose very early this morning and after eating, finished cleaning the breakfast things. Spent the morning knitting, &c. In the evening Cousin Jane and myself went to the Asylum. After spending an hour or so viewing the flowers we called on Mrs. Jones. I knew her very well some years since when I went to school with Mrs. Fellows, but had almost forgotten her.

Saturday, March 14th/63.

I rose this morning early. The day has been clear and pleasant so Cousin Jane and I have spent the day out doors looking at Frank's garden. Nothing more.

Sunday, March 15th/63.

I rose this morning very early. Kate and I spent the morning over at Mrs. Weaver's. Cloudy all day and it now has the appearance of rain. Have not attended to my religious duties this day and on that account I am far from feeling happy and satisfied with myself.

Monday, March 16th 1863.

I rose this morning very early and assisted Kate in cleaning our room. Very much surprised at seeing such a lovely day. Clear and warm! After breakfast Kate and I cleaned the yard and made it look considerably improved. Heard nothing from home.

Tuesday, March 17th/63.

I rose this morning very early and cleaned our room. Cousin Jane went in town this morning with Mary Edmunson and intends staying all night as it takes a person a whole day to procure a pass. The day has been clear and warm. Walked down to the pond to see if we could catch any fish but like our many other efforts, our success were bad. Heard nothing from home.

Wednesday, March 18th/63.

I rose this morning very early and dressed the baby as Kate has been kept awake so much during the night. Cleaned our room after breakfast. Very warm, raining a little in the morning but it looks now (7 o'clock P.M.) as if it might clear off. Lena Edmunson spent the evening with us. Cousin Jane has not yet returned from town as she has so much business to attend to. I am again disappointed about not hearing from home.

Thursday, March 19th.

I rose this morning very early. Kate and the baby went in town this morning. Spent the day sewing and fixing Frank's hat for farming. Cousin Jane returned this evening, greatly distressed of hearing such sad news from Berry. A lady came to the office to see Pa. She told him that she had received a letter from Shelbyville, stating that a violent storm had occurred, destroying the railroad bridge and among the killed was poor Berry. An intimate acquaintance of Kate's has just returned from the same place, having left after the storm, she particularly mentions Cal as being well and in the finest of spirits. I hope that it is not so. Poor Cousin Jane, how much distress and anxiety she is in.

Friday, March 20th 1863.

I rose this morning quite late as I was kept awake a great deal by the baby. Our fears have been realized in regards to the sad death of dear Berry! Yes! he has been taken from his mother and sister to a world where parting or sorrow is known no more. He was in the telegraph office at Shelbyville and there met his sad fate. How deeply do I feel for Cousin Jane and Kate in their bereavement. May they look forward to a happy reunion beyond the skies, where parting is known no more!

Saturday, March 21st/63.

I rose this morning early. Cousin Jane went to town this morning to see a little girl who has just returned from Shelbyville bringing a handkerchief of poor Berry's. She has a letter from Cal but left it with Bishop Whelan at Murfreesboro. The storm occurred on the 8th about 4 o'clock P.M. Berry and several of his friends had gone in to the telegraph office some time before it took place. He was busily engaged in reading and had dropped off into a sound sleep, when the storm came up. His friends rushed out leaving poor Berry to perish in the ruins! Heard from home. All's well.

Sunday, March 22nd/63.

I rose this morning and have again commenced performing my religious duties. After breakfast I retired and finished getting my hymns, catechism and Bible verses. Cloudy and looks as though it might rain. Cousin Jane and Kate have determined to go to Shelbyville to see about Berry. I hope they will for they will be so much better satisfied.

Monday, March 23rd/63.

I rose this morning very early but failed to perform my religious duties. Went to town this morning with Kate. Saw Mr. Blunkhall who told me Pa was quite sick. Will I ever go home and again be the same happy child of former days. Grandma and Aunt Jane were both well.

Tuesday, March 24th/63.

I rose this morning very early and performed my devotions before dressing as I find I have no time to give to them after cleaning my room. The day has been cold, wet and gloomy. Nothing from home. Spent the day in making tatting for Mattie's dress and hemming some towels for Cousin Jane.

Wednesday, March 25th/63.

I rose this morning early and performed my devotions before sister rose. The day has been clear and cold. Heard from Ma this evening. All were well at my <u>dear home</u>. When will I ever return! Heard that Van Dorn had driven the Yankees to Nashville[117] and he was now at Brentwood. I trust it is so. I feel at times almost tempted to go back to town, that place where I have spent so many miserable hours, for I will there be able to see Ma every day. God only knows what is to become of us! It seems as if the times get more gloomy and sad each day. Well! let us not look for happiness in this sinful world but press more eagerly forward to those mansions of eternal bliss. Oh! that I could become an earnest Christian, never faltering, but with staff in hand pursue my course with a firm and steady step. Help me oh! my God, to become a child of thine and may the precious days of my youth be spent in thy service.

Thursday, March 26th/63.

I rose this morning early but from some cause I neglected my devotions and am consequently far from feeling happy. Employed myself in attending to Nannie Perkins and making my spool holder. Kate and Cousin Jane went to town this morning and I anxiously await them coming to hear from my dear home. The day has been clear and cold. Mrs. Caldwell came to see Cousin Jane and Kate and says the Abolition forces received a terrible whipping at Brentwood. When will this horrid war stop and brother quit warring against brother?

Friday, March 27th.

An unhapppy day for me, as I have committed a <u>great sin namely</u> prevarication. Oh! my Heavenly Father assist me in overcoming this great enemy and may I soon become a consistent

---

[117] A minor action associated with a reconnaissance mission which occurred from late March to April 10, 1863 by Confederate cavalry leader Major General Earl Van Dorn.

Christian and may my many failures only serve to convince me that without Thy divine aid I can do nothing. Heard nothing from home. The day has been <u>cold</u>, <u>wet</u> and <u>gloomy</u>.

Saturday, March 28th/63.

I rose this morning very early, but owing to my being so slow dressing, I found no time for my devotions. Cousin Jane went in this morning to see Bishop Whelan, who has returned, but brought no letter from Cal. I intended going in with her to see Ma, but Cousin Jane proposed to let us go through the country and stay all day and night at my dear home. I expect to carry her instructions into exertion tomorrow, if the weather will permit. Finished knitting Cal a pair of socks as Cousin Jane and Kate intends starting for Shelbyville in a few days.

Sunday, March 29th.

I rose this morning very early. Have neglected all my duties this day and oh! far am I from feeling happy! Can I ever expect to become a consistent Christian at this rate? How I wish I was at home, how much encouragement dear mother would give me. The weather has been so cold and disagreeable that I concluded not to go to our home. Cousin Jane received the letters from Cal stating the particulars of the death of Berry. He was returning from off picket duty when the storm came up and he and several of his friends stopped at the telegraph office. His left temple was struck causing concussion of the brain. He lingered four days perfectly unconscious of all around him. Edgar Nichol and Eugene Wilson (a grandson of Mrs. Kingsley) was slightly wounded. A few days before the accident Joe Carney clipped a <u>lock</u> of poor Berry's hair off remarking as he did so, "I will take this piece of him, for fear you may be killed Berry," where upon he replied "Don't speak so Joe, it might really happen." Poor fellow! how sad was thy fate.

Monday, March 30th/63.

I rose this morning very early. Spent the time before breakfast cleaning my room, but my duties to my God were neglected. The day has been clear and cold and I think Frank said there was a little ice. Sent Mrs. Haney some shoes by Cousin Jane. Heard from home this evening and was most agreeable surprised to receive a letter from Brother Joe. He complains of my not writing to him. I have written and rewritten several times, and none of them have ever been received. Ma is anxious for us to come in and stay a few days in town. I would much prefer going to our home.

Tuesday, March 31st/63.

I rose this morning very early and finished cleaning my room before breakfast. Neglected my duties this morning. After knitting some time I commenced a long letter to Brother Joe as I think an opportunity will soon present itself. The day has been cloudy, clear and at times a little snow fell. I wish it would clear off and be warm and pleasant. Heard nothing from home to-day.

Wednesday, April 1st 1863.

I rose this morning very early and cleaned my room before breakfast. Spent the morning knitting, practicing and making Aunt Jane a needle book as I intend going in tomorrow. Clear, but much warmer than yesterday. Heard nothing from home.

Thursday, April 2nd 1863.

I rose very early this morning and much to my sorrow I gave away to my unruly temper. I concluded not to go in as I had no pass, and none of the family are included on Cousin Jane's. I don't remember of ever feeling so lazy as to-day. The weather is very warm and clear. Again disappointed in not hearing from home. <u>Why don't Ma write?</u>

Friday, April 3rd Hedge Lawn.

I rose this morning very early. Cousin Jane and Kate went to town, but Pa not being in, I am disappointed in not hearing from home. Spent the day sewing and knitting. The weather's clear and in doors cold!

Saturday, April 4th/63.

I rose this morning very early and after breakfast Sissie and I gave our room a good cleaning. Spent the morning making the servants some underskirts. The day has been perfectly beautiful. The grass is green and many of the trees have just put forth their foliage. Have been perfectly miserable all day and was rendered still more so on Mr. Weaver's telling Cousin Jane that he could not bring out nothing more for us; on account of the strict orders of the military authorities. Oh! will I ever return to my dear parents!

Sunday, April 5th 1863.

I rose this morning very early and after cleaning my room I spent the time before breakfast in reading my Bible, hymns, &c. I wish I could spend all my mornings in this manner. Another day has passed. It seems as if each day grows sadder and sadder. If I am fully prepared to meet my Divine Judge I would willingly take leave off this world of sin and sorrow; and go to a land where all is peace and eternal happiness. I know not at what time I may be called and ought I not strive to bring myself nearer and nearer to my God. There is much sin and corruption on this vile heart of mine, but I have a Friend on High who knows my vileness and I trust he will forgive and help me to forsake whatever my besetting sin may be.

Monday, April 6th/63.

I rose this morning very early and finished my prayers before sister got up. Cousin Jane and Sissie went in town this morning and I anxiously await them as I expect to receive my last letter from home! Spent the day sewing for Cousin Jane, making Ma a needle book. The weather's clear and warm, but quite cool as I now write (6 o'clock P.M.).

Tuesday, April 7th/63.

I rose this morning very early. Kate and I went in town and were most fortunate in meeting Pa. I expect to start to school in a few days. I hope to improve every opportunity.

Wednesday, April 8th 1863.

I rose this morning very early. Pa came over to-day and carried sister over with him. I was very much disappointed at Ma's not coming over, but look for her in the course of a few days. The day has been clear and delightful outdoors and rather cool in doors.

Thursday, April 9th/63.

I rose this morning very early. Cleaned my room and employed the time before breakfast in reading my favorite book. Kate and Cousin Jane went to see Mrs. Hurley and take her some thing's Ma sent over. Employed the day making Mrs. Weaver a needle-book. Fannie and Lucy Wilson came over to see me. Nothing from home.

Friday, April 10th.

I rose very early this morning. Assisted Kate in making her dress as she expects to go to Williamson [county] in a few days. She and I went over to Mrs. Weaver's and spent some time. Heard from Pa this evening; perhaps Ma will be over to-morrow to take me to my beloved home.

Saturday, April 11th.

I rose this morning early and took a good bath after eating. Looked for Ma to-day but she disappointed me. Received a letter this evening from Mollie J. Berry. Precious girl; she has now acknowledged her Saviour before men, and I pray that she may ever be a consistent and humble Christian. I will soon see her and then what a long talk we will have.

Chapter Eight
Home at Last

"The whole country around my home is entirely changed, fences burnt, trees cut down and devastation is everywhere visible."

Union General Rosecrans, after the battle of Murfreesboro, made no formal movement until June. With sixty thousand men, he then marched against Bragg. By threatening his communications, he forced Bragg to evacuate Chattanooga on Sept. 8. One objection which Rosecrans opposed to a forward movement was his inferiority in cavalry. This was removed in July, when General John H. Morgan, with about four thousand Confederate cavalry, crossed the Ohio at Brandenburg, swept around Cincinnati, and struck the river again near Parkersburg. During his entire route, he was harassed by militia. At this point he was overtaken by his pursuers, while gunboats in the river prevented his crossing. Nearly the entire force was captured. Morgan escaped, but was finally taken and confined in the penitentiary at Columbus. Four months afterward, he broke jail and reached Richmond in safety. Rosecrans pushed on in pursuit of Bragg, whom he supposed to be in full retreat. Bragg, however, having received powerful reinforcements, turned upon his pursuers so suddenly that they narrowly escaped being cut up in detail, while scattered along a line forty miles in length. The Union forces rapidly concentrated, and the two armies met on the Chickamauga. The battle of Chickamauga was fought on September 19 and 20. The first-day's fight was indecisive. About noon of the second day, the Federal line became broken from the movement of troops to help the left wing, and then hard pressed. Longstreet seized the opportunity, pushed a brigade into the gap, and swept the Federal right and centre from the field. The rushing crowd of fugitives bore Rosecrans himself away. In this crisis of the battle all depended on the left, under Thomas. If that yielded, the army would be utterly routed. All through the long afternoon the entire Confederate army surged against it. But Thomas held fast. Thomas was thenceforth styled the "Rock of Chickamauga." He was in command of men as brave as himself. Col. George, of the Second Minnesota, being asked, "How long can you hold this pass?" replied, "Until the regiment is mustered out of service." At night he deliberately withdrew to Chattanooga, picking up five hundred prisoners on the way. The Union army, however, defeated in the field, was now shut up in its entrenchments. Bragg occupied the hills commanding the city, and cut off its communications. The garrison was threatened with starvation.[118]

Home at last. In the middle of April 1863, Maggie and Sister Kate are back together with Ma and Pa and little sister Mattie. After one year, one month, and twenty-six days, the exile is over. The family will enjoy the summer together at Mount Alban before the fall semester at South Side Institute commences in late October.

Sunday, April 12th/63.
Ma came over to-day and took me home!

Monday, April 13th. Mount Alban.
I rose this morning very early. Ma and I went in town to see about our boarding at Mrs. Holcombe's. Cloudy and cool. Saw Mollie Berry in town. She promised to come out and see me soon.

Tuesday, April 14th 1863.
I rose this morning very early. Miss May just returned from Triune. Several citizens were arrested. For what no one knows. A real April day.

Thursday, April 16th/63.
I rose early this morning, after eating, assisted Ma in making Mattie's dress and hearing her lessons. Clear and delightful out to-day. Spent the evening in writing to dear Brother Joe.

During Maggie's long absence from home, many changes had occurred. The journal entries reflect how the war is altering the land. She states "devastation is everywhere visible." The journal also shows how oppressive the Andrew Johnson government and Federal occupation is to the residents of Nashville.

Friday, April 17th/63.
I rose early this morning, after breakfast Ma and sister went in town. Employed the day sewing and hearing Mattie's lessons. The day has been bright and beautiful. Oh! how sad it makes me feel to think how happy I have once been, but it seems now as if I am destined to

---

[118] Barnes, *A Brief History of the United States*, Epoch V, pages 246-247.

drink the cup of sorrow to the days. The whole country around my home is entirely changed; fences burnt, trees cut down and devastation is everywhere visible. Judge Humphrey's beautiful house is ruined forever, no trees left and that was the beauty of the place.

Saturday, April 18th/63.

I rose this morning very early and after eating I employed the time in marking my skirt. Cousin Jane and Kate came over this morning intending to start to Franklin but owing to the Hillsborough heavy pickets, this visit was postponed. The day has been clear and delightful. Looked for Mollie Berry all day but she frustrated me in some way.

Sunday, April 19th/63.

I rose early. Cousin Jane and Kate returned home this morning. After dinner, I heard Mattie's hymns, catechism, &c. I then reviewed mine. Clear and delightful. Last night we had a hard rain, thunder and lightning.

Monday, April 20th/63.

I rose early this morning. Heard Mattie's hymns and then employed the remainder of the day sewing, practicing, &c. Pa went over to Mr. Berry's this evening and there learned "they" were pressing all the horses in town and arrests were still going on. This is truly "the reign of terror!"[119] The day has been clear and delightful but I could enjoy nothing while our once happy and peaceful country is in such a dreadful condition. When will this terrible war cease and peace reign in our midst!

Tuesday, April 21st.

I rose very early this morning. Spent the day very usefully. Clear and cool.

Wednesday, April 22nd.

Up early this morning. Pa met with great difficulty in getting out as "permits" are required for everything that is brought out. These are trying times but I trust we will yet enjoy freedom.

---

[119] The times are likened to the French Revolution, its "Reign of Terror", and the subsequent rise of Napoleon Bonaparte. See the March 13, 1862 journal entry.

Thursday, April 23rd 63.

Rose early this morning. Several Federal soldiers came to press horses but upon Pa's showing them a "certificate" they went off. Spent the day sewing, &c. Passed a pleasant evening with Mrs. Blunkhall.

Friday, April 24th.

I rose this morning very early. Spent the morning very pleasantly with Roberta Armistead. Afterward we walked to Dr. Berry's and stayed a short time as Mrs. Berry was going in to bring out Mollie. The latter staid all night. I always have loved her, but now that she has found the Christian land, she is dearer to me than ever. We had a long talk last night after the family had retired, and it now seems as if we had begun life again. May we ever encourage each other in the path of life and be the sharer of each other's joy and sorrow. Oh! that every friend I fondly have would join the happiness of which we are members.

Saturday, April 25th.

Up early this morning notwithstanding Mollie and I lay awake talking until 1 or 2 o'clock. Spent the time before breakfast in reading our Bibles. Clear and very warm. Pa went in to day. Still pressing horses in town.

Sunday, April 26th.

Two years ago to-day I commenced my journal. I have much to be thankful for and many sins to mourn. Employed the morning reading my Bible hymns, catechisms, &c. Mollie and her Pa came over this evening. Bless her heart! How dear she is to me now that she has become my sister in Christ. To-day I finished copying the "Self Examination" in a book[120] and as it has proved invaluable to me in assisting me in my heavenly course I lent it to Mollie and I trust she too may be encouraged to cling closely to the cross. Intend spending the day with her on Thursday and I looked forward to it with great pleasures.

---

[120] The book *Self Examination* is identified in Volume Two of Maggie's journal. While writing her daily entries in Volume One, Maggie was using the beginning pages of the second for copying "Rules and Regulations" and other articles which she used to guide her daily life. These copied articles can be found in the appendix of this book.

April 27th/63.

I rose this morning quite early. Spent the morning sewing, practicing, hearing Mat's and sister's lessons and renewing my long neglected tasks. I have lost so much valuable time at school I fear it never can be regained! Cloudy and warm and it has now the appearance of rain. I have to answer for many sins to-day but I hope to overcome them all by the aid of my heavenly Father. Wrote a long letter to Queeny Humphrey begging her to become a member of our little band that has chosen the Saviour for our leader.

Wednesday, April 29th/63.

I rose very early and spent the time before breakfast in reading my Bible, &c. A real April day! Pa went in town to-day; all of our most influential men have been arrested, some sent North and other's South. Oh! what a dreadful state of things.

Thursday, April 30th.

I rose this morning early. Performed my devotions before breakfast. Passed the day sewing and reading a very instructive letter work entitled "Heart and Hand." Clear and delightful! The oath of allegiance was administered to Grandma who is now 83 years old.

Friday, May 1st/63.

I rose this morning very early. Spent the day with Mollie. Nothing of interest.

Sunday, May 3rd/63.

I rose this morning very early. Spent the time before breakfast in reading my Bible, getting my hymns and my other duties which I now take a great interest in. Read a very instructive work "Home Influence." Clear, at times and then April showers.

Monday, May 4th.

I rose early this morning. Nothing of interest.

Tuesday, May 5th.

Very early when I got up this morning. Have felt very unwell all day with a severe headache. Spent the evening very quietly with Ma sewing. Charley Percy came out to-day.

Wednesday 6th.

Cold, wet and gloomy, and it is still raining. Spent the day reading, sewing and many other occupations.

Thursday, May 7th/63.

I rose this morning very early. Raining all day and it seems as if the flood gates of Heaven were opened. There is nothing of interest to write.

Friday, May 8th 63.

I rose this morning very early and spent the morning in making tape trimmings. Cleared off beautifully after breakfast and I hope we will have good weather for some time to come. Given away to my temper this morning and of course have felt very unhappy! Mr. and Mrs. James Woods spent the evening with us. There has been heavy fighting at glorious Fredericksburg[121] and how fervently <u>do</u> I <u>pray</u> that our noble Lee and Jackson has again repulsed the Vandal horde. Very much in hopes Mollie will come over to-morrow. How I regret we have to be separated so much, but I trust it will not always be so!

Saturday, May 9th/63

I rose this morning very late, not ready for breakfast. Clear and delightful. Ma and sister went over to see Mrs. Joe Woods who intends leaving for Shelbyville in a few days to remain four years. She has kindly offered to take some things for Ma to Brother Joe. She leaves on Wednesday. Several of our citizens intend going to the happy land of "Dixie." We have again beaten the Federals at Fredericksburg and the whole of Hooker's army is now at Falmouth, [Virginia].

Sunday, May 10th.

I rose very early this morning. Performed my accustomed duties very <u>imperfectly</u> and am therefore very far from feeling happy. Oh! can I ever expect to <u>become</u> an <u>earnest</u> <u>Christian</u>! Oh! my Heavenly Father look down on thy unworthy servant, cleanse his sinful soul from all guilt, and though his sins be as scarlet may they become like wool in the blood of thy crucified Son.

---

[121] This reference is to a series of skirmishes leading up to the Battle of Chancellorsville which was fought between April 29 and May 5, 1863. This Confederate victory was not without cost, for General Thomas "Stonewall" Jackson was accidently shot by his own men, first losing an arm and then his life. [Barnes, *A Brief History of the United States*, Epoch V, page 250.]

Monday, May 11th.

I rose this morning early. Spent the day mending my clothes, reading, &c. Ma and sister went in this morning. It is generally believed Van Dorn[122] is killed, by a man in Maury county. Nothing more of interest.

Thursday, May 14th/63.

I rose this morning early. Spent the day sewing and many other useful employments. Clear and delightful. Packed Brother's carpet bag as we think we may have a safe opportunity of sending it ere long; Mr. Joe Woods and family went south.

Friday, May 15th 1863.

I rose early this morning. Spent the morning very pleasantly with Ma talking over future projects. Sister and Mattie went to see Mrs. Cantrell. Mollie Berry staid over night with me.

Saturday, May 16th.

I rose this morning very late as a matter of course when Mollie stays with me. Clear and warm. Spent the day making my dress as I am anxious to become an accomplished seamstress. No news to-day.

Sunday, May 17th.

I rose this morning very early to take a dose of medicine. Spent the day very quietly reading the blessed Word of God.

Monday, May 18th.

I rose early this morning. Spent the day very pleasantly sewing, reading and practicing. Roberta and Mrs. Armistead spent the evening with us.

---

[122] Major General Earl Van Dorn CSA, died in May 1863, not by a Union bullet but by a jealous husband. Dr. James Peters shot the general at the army's Spring Hill headquarters over an affair with the doctor's wife. The doctor was arrested but never tried. His defense was that the general had "violated the sanctity of his home."

Tuesday, May 19th 63.

I rose this morning very early as Ma and I went in town. There learnt a very distressing piece of news, the taking prisoner of Pillow Humphrey's. The day has been very warm and disagreeable. It is reported Jackson Mississippi has fallen into the hands of the enemy. Dark clouds are now hovering over our ill fated South, but I put my trust in our ruling Providence, and pray that He may ordain all things for the best.

Wednesday, May 20th/63.

I rose this morning very early. Spent the morning in making my dress and assisting Mama in making straw-berry preserves.

Friday, May 21st.[123]

I rose this morning early. Ma went to town this morning. Very warm to-day and the consequence is I have been very lazy. Dr. Berry came over this evening but there is no news.

Saturday, May 22nd.

I rose this morning very early. Spent a very pleasant day with Mollie. Clear and very warm; a rain would be of great advantage now, as the dust is almost intolerable.

Sunday, May 23 24th 1863.

I rose this morning very early and had a delightful day for prayer and meditation. My hymns and verses received better care than ever before.

Monday, May 24 25th 1863.

I rose this morning early and went to town with Ma. Vallandigham[124] passed through the city yesterday en route for Dixie. Lieutenant [William] Van Dorn[125] of the gun boat

---

[123] No journal entry for Thursday May 21st. Note that the journal dates for the following two days are off. She gets back on track on Sunday. The original journal entries show scratch-outs in correcting the Sunday 24th date.

[124] Clement Vallandigham, a pro-south Ohio political leader banished and sent south under armed guard and would eventually by way of blockade runner, make his way to Canada. Walter Durham, *Nashville, the Occupied City*, pages 261-262 (Knoxville, The University of Tennessee Press).

[125] Infantry commander of the Union gunboat W.H. Sidell, a boat fitted to provide cover for cargo along the Cumberland River between Harpeth Shoals and Nashville.

notoriety is now in town. He speaks in the highest terms of the Southern people and very particularly of Brother, styles him a "prince of a fellow." Miserable, and unhappy all day. Oh! how imprudent I am! Can I ever be a true and good woman? I fear not until I put my whole trust in God for he alone can work this mighty change.

Tuesday, May 26th.

I rose this morning rather late as I lay awake a greater part of the night. My efforts to bring myself nearer to my God have been attended with no success; indulged in my temper and other sinful passions.

Wednesday, May 27th.

I rose this morning early. Very warm and sultry all day but it rained a little in the evening which cooled the atmosphere. Spent the day sewing. Finished writing a letter to dear Brother Joe this evening.

Thursday, May 28th/63.

I rose this morning very early. Mrs. Bluckhall went over to the Hillsboro pike and took a carpet bag for Brother Joe. I trust he will get it. The paper state the capture of Vicksburg, but as there is no official dispatches, I trust it is not so. Cloudy and a little rain.

Friday, May 29th/63.

I rose this morning very early. Raining all day but it now looks as if it might clear as it has turned quite cool.

Saturday, May 30th/63.

I rose this morning very early and assisted Ma in her household affairs. Cloudy and raining at intervals but is very cool and clear. Mrs. Blunkhall came down this evening and gave us the welcome intelligence that "the carpet bag" reached Hillsboro in safety, and the lady to whom she gave it was just about starting to Columbia to see her husband and the latter would forward or take them himself to Shelbyville. I trust Brother Joe may at some future day have it in his power to return this favor. Hemmed a great deal on my skirt as I am tired looking at it and am determined to finish it.

Sunday, May 31st.

I rose this morning early. Spent the morning studying my Bible, hymns and the remainder of the day reading "Dagg's Moral Science" and talking to my kind good mother. I feel that I am far from loving her enough! Had a severe thunderstorm.

Monday, June 1st.

I rose this morning very early and went to town with Ma. There are many sins to mourn to-day and I fear that I will ever be the thoughtless girl I am now. I say so many imprudent things, and my thoughts are very wicked.

Tuesday, June 2nd/63.

I rose this morning early. Cloudy and cool to-day with a little rain.

Wednesday, June 3rd.

I rose this morning early. Clear and cool to day. My actions are much improved, but my thoughts are sinful in the extreme. Let the words of my mouth be medication of my heart, be acceptable in thy sight oh! my Heavenly Father.

Thursday, June 4th.

I rose this morning very late, why I cannot tell. Cloudy and has very much the appearance of rain. Heard heavy firing all day in the direction of Franklin, but have yet learn nothing definite. Employed the morning hearing Mattie's lessons and practicing. Have said nothing that is wrong but am not as lively in secret prayer as I would like. How I would like to see Mollie, how many encouraging words she could give me. One thing, which causes me much regret is that I am not as open and ready to lay bare my heart to Ma and ask her assistance in this great work of bringing myself nearer to my God! It is no use making resolutions, for I have not the firmness to keep them.

Friday, June 5th/63

I rose this morning very early. The day has been cold, wet and gloomy and it is now raining quite hard. Spent the morning sewing, reading, &c. Pa went in town today. Quite a fight occurred at Franklin[126] yesterday. Our forces succeeding in routing the Federals and driving them from that

---

[126] This skirmish is commonly referred as the First Battle of Franklin.

place; a portion of the town is reported as being burnt, Genl. [Bauch] and his division taken. I trust it is so. In regard to my conduct, I have to acknowledge many sad failings!

Saturday, June 6th/63.

I rose this morning very late. Spent the day helping Ma about her household affairs. Clear and a delightful day. No news to-day. My temper has been pretty good but it needs to be guarded very closely.

Sunday, June 7th/63.

I rose this morning early. Spent the morning reading my Bible, performing my other duties. Finished reading the "Mother's Recompense" to the children. Cloudy but cool.

Monday, June 8th/63

I rose this morning with the sun. I am sorry to confess I did not spend those hours in prayer and would that I had! I think that it would have spared me many hours of bitterness that I have this day experienced. Yes! This has been truly a day of bitterness to me; and I can scarcely ask my God to pardon my many sins.

Tuesday, June 9th/63.

I rose this morning early. Spent the day in variety of ways.

Wednesday, June 10th 63.

I rose this morning very early. Raining at intervals, but cool. Quite happy to-day. Wrote several letters for Dixie.

Thursday, June 11th/63

I rose this morning early and finished my letters to dear Brother. Have been very ill natured to-day, but I can expect nothing better as I did not commence the day as I should, by imploring the divine assistance of my Heavenly Father! I will hence forward commence a daily routine of devotion hoping that God will give me grace to persevere and overcome <u>all</u> <u>obstacles</u>.

Friday, June 12th/63.

I rose this morning very early and went to town with Ma and Sister. The latter staid all night with Hettie. Heard joyful news to day! There will be preaching at the little school house every Sunday by Mr. Philip Fall. Oh! how glad I am, for I now hope to have more intercourse with my Heavenly Father.

Saturday June 13th 63.

I rose this morning very early. Spent the day as Saturday's generally are, cleaning, sweeping, &c. Very warm all day. Heard nothing more of the preaching at the school house. I hope [nothing] has prevented Mr. Fall from fulfilling his engagement.

Sunday, June 14th.

I rose this morning early. Performed my devotions most imperfectly. After breakfast we walked to the little school house and heard a very good sermon from Mr. James Fall. Mollie spent the evening with me. Spent the day very profitable reading our Bibles, &c.

Monday, June 15th/63.

I rose this morning very early. Very warm all day. Been busily employed assisting Ma [with] making my dress. There are many sinful thoughts to mourn to-day.

Tuesday, June 16th/63.

I rose this morning early. Went in town and there learnt some excellent news from Genl. Lee's army. Pennsylvania and Maryland[127] are again invaded. Genl. Forrest is reported wounded by one of his Lieutenants. Don't know what to believe these days.

Wednesday, June 17th/63.

I was very late rising not feeling at all well. Very warm and sultry to-day. Had a very pleasant visit from some friends, one I had not seen [since] the day before the memorable stampede.[128] Had a very hard and refreshing rain in the evening, with a great deal of thunder and lightning.

---

[127] After the victory at Chancellorsville, General Robert E. Lee moved his Army of Northern Virginia to take the offensive in Maryland and Pennsylvania. The Battle of Gettysburg would be fought in early July 1863, with Lee being opposed by General Joseph Hooker and later General George C. Meade. The Confederate army would be defeated but allowed to escape back into Virginia. Barnes, *A Brief History of the United States*, Epoch V, pages 251-254.

[128] The memorable stampede is a reference to the "Great Panic." In his 1862 book, "The Great Panic," John Miller McKee used the term grand stampede in referring to the same event. The one noted friend is Sallie House; see the February 15-16 1862 journal entries.

Thursday, June 18th/63.

I rose this morning very early. Spent the day sewing, practicing and hearing Mattie's lessons. Charlie Percy came out this evening. Very warm all day.

Saturday, June 20th.

I rose this morning with a bad cold and headache. Spent the day very profitably sewing and doing my usual Saturday's tasks. Mollie staid all night with me. Cloudy but cool.

Sunday, June 21st 63.

I rose this morning very early. Mollie and I read our Bibles &c. Went to church this morning and heard a very excellent and instructive sermon from Mr. James Fall. Spent the remainder of the day reading religious works.

Monday, June 22nd/63.

I rose this morning quite late. Went to town to day. I was very much surprised to hear of the marriage of a friend of mine. Mary Nicholas in New Orleans.

Tuesday 23rd.

I rose this morning early. Assisted Ma in packing the winter clothes. Very warm and sultry all evening. No news. Given way to many sinful passions.

Wednesday, 24th/63.

I rose rather late as it was an excellent morning for sleeping. After breakfast, I spent some time in prayer, beseeching my Heavenly Father to assist me in overcoming the many sins and obstacles that are constantly besetting me. Raining all day.

Thursday 25/63.

I rose this morning very early. After breakfast I spent a short time in prayer. Another cold, wet and gloomy day and the rain still continue to pour. Heard Mattie's lessons thoroughly and gave her a music lesson from 10:30 AM. I hope I may soon get her to take from a better teacher than I.

Friday, June 26th/63.

I rose this morning early. Heard Mattie's lessons. Raining all day. Nothing of importance.

Sunday, June 28th.

I rose this morning late and was very much disappointed to find it still raining and on that account I was compelled to be away from church. It cleared off in the evening and remained so the remainder of the day. Spent the day very profitably. After performing my duties, I read one of Dr. Foot's sermons from the text John v 4, "And ye will not come unto me that ye might have life."[129] He clearly shows us that our becoming Christians is God's work alone.

Monday, June 29th.

I rose this morning early and performed my devotion before breakfast. Clear at times. Had a hard rain and thunderstorm this evening. Ma and Mattie went in town this morning. There has been another desperate engagement beyond Murfreesboro. There is nothing definite as yet. Oh! how earnestly do I pray that the God of battles will shield and protect the dear absent ones. If any of them should fall, I trust they will go to a purer and better world.

Tuesday, June 30th/63.

I rose this morning early and spent the morning in prayer and then assisted Mattie in her lessons. Spent the day making doll clothes for her. Cloudy and warm. Had several showers. Heard nothing from the front.

Wednesday, July 1st 63.

I rose this morning very early. After Ma and Mat went to town. I retired to my room and spent an hour in prayer. Very warm. Had a hard rain this evening. No news.

Thursday, July 2nd 63.

I rose this morning early. Spent a most delightful day with my friend Mollie Berry. Many sinful thoughts have fluttered through my [head], but I lay bare this vile heart to the Great Searcher, being fully convinced he will cleanse it from all guilt. Clear and I think one of the nicest days we have had this summer. Expect Mollie over to-morrow.

Friday, July 3rd/63.

I rose this morning very early. Mollie spent the day with me. Cloudy and cooler than yesterday. I hope it won't rain as I am <u>so anxious</u> to attend church on Sunday.

---

[129] John 5:40

Saturday 4th.

I rose this morning very early. Spent the day sewing, reading, &c. Very warm, frequent showers. Cleared off in the evening so I have a prospect of attending church to-morrow.

Sunday, July 5th/63.

I rose this morning early. A very dense fog but it cleared off in time for church. Mr. Fall was prevented from preaching from some cause. Have spent the day by no means properly. Had a very hard rain with thunder and lightning.

Monday, July 6th 63.

I rose this morning early and spent the morning hearing Mattie's lessons which occupied me until 11 o'clock. Failed to perform my devotions to-day. Cousin Sam and Ella came by this evening from Triune. Cloudy.

Tuesday, July 7th 63.

I rose this morning early. Performed my duties very imperfectly and the consequence of I have had many sad failures. Raining all day. 10 inches of rain fell during the month of June.

Wednesday, July 8th 63.

I rose very early. Unhappy all day on account of my temper. Had a little shower. Cleared off and remained so the rest of the day.

Thursday, July 9th 63.

I rose this morning quite early. Have had a very quiet day as Ma and sisters went to town. In the afternoon, Mollie and I spent a very delightful evening with Mrs. Thompson as Sallie was not at home.

Friday, July 10.

I rose early. Spent the day with Mollie. Very warm and smoky, the most irregular weather I have ever seen. It is really a phenomenon.

Saturday, July 11th 63.

I rose early this morning. Still smoky and warm. There will be preaching at the school house. Very, very unhappy all day. I am again a wandering sheep from the fold of Christ.

Sunday, July 12th 63.

I rose this morning very early and much to my disappointment found it cloudy and smoky, but that did not prevent me from me going to church and heard a most excellent sermon from Mr. Fall. I fear this will be our last opportunity we will have, but I hope some of our neighbors will make arrangements for some minister to instruct us every Sabbath. A great many of our citizens believe our little Vicksburg[130] has succumbed to our [enemy] on the 4th, but as there is yet no official report from Genl. Grant. I live in hopes it is not so.

Monday, July 13th 63.

I rose this morning very early. Spent the day sewing, reading, &c. Raining all day. Ma went in. No one believes Vicksburg has been taken as there is no mention of it in Northern journals or in the extract from Southern papers. What a blessed thing is hope!

Tuesday, July 14th 63.

I rose this morning very early. Spent the day sewing and reading. Raining all day!

Wednesday, July 15th/63.

I rose this morning very early. Mollie came over and spent the day with me. Clear but warm and looks as if it might rain.

Thursday, July 16th/63.

I rose this morning early. Sister and I went over to see Sallie and Liza Branch but found them not at home. Vicksburg has undoubtedly fallen! A gloomy picture for the South.

Friday, July 17th/63.

I rose this morning very early. Went in and spent a most delightful day with Lizzie and Ellen Fall. Clear and cool. Rather unhappy all day. When will I ever be a Christian?

Saturday, July 18th/63.

I rose this morning very early. Been very busy all day. Clear and cool. It is rumored that Charleston [South Carolina] is taken.

---

[130] The surrender of Vicksburg occurred on July 4, 1863. The Union Army of the Tennessee, under Major General Ulysses S. Grant, gained control of the Mississippi by defeating the rebel army commanded by Lt. General John C. Pemberton. Barnes, *A Brief History of the United States*, Epoch V, pages 244-245.

Sunday, July 19th/63.

I rose this [morning] very early. We had no preaching and the day has been very long; but I endeavored to spend the day in such a way as to be profitable to my immortal soul. Raining at times but cleared off in the evening.

Monday, July 20th/63.

I rose this morning <u>very</u> late. Warm and sultry all day. Commenced the day by retiring and spending some time in prayer. Heard Mattie's lessons and assisted thoroughly and without giving way to my temper.

Tuesday, July 21st 63.

I rose this morning again late. Everything has gone wrong with me, and no wonder! Did I begin the day by beseeching that Aid, without which I can do nothing? Oh! that I had, how differently would be my record!

Wednesday, July 22nd/63.

I rose this morning very early. Spent the day with Cousin Jane Morgan. Kate saw more of our boys but heard through persons coming from Shelbyville they were well. Performed my duties but I have many important things to-morrow.

Thursday, July 23rd/63.

I rose this morning very early. Neglected my prayers. Clear and very warm. Been busy all day pasting in my book.

Friday, July 24th/63.

I rose this morning very early. Spent the day with my dear Mollie. Our conversation was at times very worldly; it is hard for me to speak of religion as to be profitable to us both. Clear and warm.

Saturday, July 25th/63.

I rose this morning very early. Neglected my prayers and everything is wrong. Raining most of the day.

Sunday, July 26th/63.

I rose this morning very early. Attended church and heard a most excellent sermon from Dr. Wharton and I am most happy to learn, he will be able to instruct us every Sabbath. Clear and warm. Have spent the day by <u>no means</u> properly. Oh! how I lack firmness to put into effect my <u>many</u> resolutions. Will I ever overcome my weakness!

Monday, July 27th/63.

I rose this morning quite late. Been very busy to-day sewing and airing my drawers and assisting Ma in her duties. John H. Morgan[131] is captured.

Tuesday, July 28th/63.

I rose this morning early. Performed my devotions but have been <u>hasty</u> several times. Clear and quite cool. Spent the day altering my dresses and practicing. Look for Mollie a little tomorrow.

Wednesday, July 29th 63.

I rose this morning rather late. Heard Mattie's lessons and gave way to a <u>little temper</u>. Very warm all day but had quite a hard rain which cooled the atmosphere. Never saw the trees and grass look so green and beautiful at this time of the year, it seems more like May than the latter part of July!

Thursday, July 30th.

I rose this morning rather late. <u>Have performed none of my devotions</u>. Heard Mattie's lessons and music lessons. <u>Rained all night</u> and the whole morning.

Friday, July 31st/63.

I rose this morning early. Disappointed in not going to town and displayed a little temper on that account. Cloudy and raining at times. Why <u>don't</u> Mollie come over! Not happy to-day.

---

[131] On July 26, 1863, Confederate general and cavalry officer John Hunt Morgan was captured during a raid into Ohio. He was able to escape in late November, but he was later killed during a September 4, 1864 raid on Greeneville, TN.

Saturday, Aug 1st/63.

I rose this morning very early. Mollie spent the day with me. Oh! how bright and frivolous our conservation has been! How unlike the children of God. There will be preaching at the school house tomorrow and I trust my mind will be in a Sabbath frame. Cloudy and very warm!

Maggie closes Volume One of her journals with the Saturday August 1st, 1863 entry. The inside back cover of the first journal contains a short list of important dates:

Important Dates

April 26th 1861, commenced my religious life![132]
February 16th 1862, the surrender of Nashville.
July 1st 1861, the battle of Manassas.
April 15th 1861, war declared between the North and South.
April 13th 1861, the fall of Fort Sumpter.
February 16th 1862, the fall of Fort Donelson.
April 10th 1862, the battle of Shiloh.
December 13th 1862, the battle of Fredericksburg.

---

[132] Note that this is also the date she commenced writing her journals.

Chapter Nine
Volume Two

"I have commenced the second volume of my journal and I trust that when it is finished that I will find less sad failures recorded."

Volume Two of the journal begins with daily rules and resolutions, and Maggie records the words of the epic poem "My Maryland." Maggie also lists four pages of important war dates. Maggie titles the listed dates as the "War for Southern Independence." This poem and the recording of dates may very well illustrate the significance the war has taken on her life now as opposed to times at the beginning of Volume One.[133]

Vol. II. Home - Sunday August 2, 1863.

Home, Sunday, August 2nd 1863.

I rose this morning quite early and took a refreshing bath. I performed my devotions and I trust my prayers were heard by my kind and much loving Father. Attended church and heard a most excellent sermon from our present pastor Dr. Wharton. After dinner I wrote a letter to my friend Mrs. Sion and then spent the remainder of the day profitably reading "Scott's Family Bible." Clear but warm. I have commenced the second volume of my journal and I trust that when it is finished that I will find less sad failures recorded. I wish that I could prevail upon Mollie to commence one; she would find it to be of the greatest assistance and pleasure to her, in her journey to heaven. I regret so much that I did not commence my sooner.

Monday, Aug 3rd 1863.

I rose this morning rather late. Went to town this morning. Performed my devotions and I am most thankful to record a perfect account of myself. Had a hard rain but is clear as I now

---

[133] Refer to appendix for the full poem "My Maryland" and Maggie's listing of Dates for Southern Independence.

write. Mattie staid in town all night. A federal officer acknowledged that they had been terribly repulsed at Charleston.

Tuesday, Aug 4th 1863.

I rose this morning very early. Spent the greater part of the day pasting my Scrap book. Cloudy and very warm, with a little rain. Mattie returned home but sister staid with Hettie. Again my Heavenly Father has enabled me to resist temptation! Oh! that it may ever be so.

Wednesday, Aug 5th/63.

I rose this morning very late. Performed my devotions after breakfast. Mat and I spent the day with Mollie. Once or twice I have been imprudent, but otherwise my conduct is proper.

Thursday, Aug 6th/63.

I rose this morning very late. Cloudy in the morning but a little clear now. Had a very pleasant visit from Mrs. Holcombe this evening. Mat and sister went to the "tableaux" at Mrs. Armistead's. Performed my devotions, but have many sins to pardon.

Friday, Aug 7th/63.

I rose this morning very early – before sunrise and had an hour of quiet for my devotions before breakfast. Ma and Mattie went to town. Had two hard rains, but it is now quite clear. Pa has been quite unwell for several days with the gout, but is now much better.

Saturday, Aug 8th/63.

I rose this morning quite early. Spent the day very busily. Mrs. Jones little children came over and spent the day. Clear but very warm. Looked for Mollie over to stay all night but from some cause she disappointed me.

Sunday, Aug 9th/63.

I rose this morning early. Spent the time before going to church in reading my Bible, and trying to get my mind fixed on God's Holy Word. Attended worship and heard a very excellent discourse from Dr. Wharton. Mollie is quite sick with an attack of bilious fever.[134] I hope she will soon be well. Cloudy, but cleared off in the evening. Very warm all day.

---

[134] Bilious fever is a medical condition caused by liver dysfunction.

Monday, Aug 10th.

What a miserable day I have spent! Everything went wrong with me. Will I ever overcome my vile temper. Clear but very warm.

Tuesday, Aug 11th.

I rose this morning rather late as I had to be up in the night with sister who is rather unwell. My conduct is not such as I would like to record. The warmest day we have had. A hard rain with some thunder and lightning.

Maggie records examples of obtaining war news in town. After one visit, she records that Union General Rosecrans had ordered seventeen days' worth of rations to be cooked so troops could head to East Tennessee. This action is a prelude to the great battles around Knoxville and Chattanooga.

Wednesday, August 12th 1863.

I rose this morning early. Performed my devotions. Clear but not so warm as yesterday. Went to town but there is nothing but bad news. Rosecrans has ordered seventeen days rations to be cooked and is marching over the mountains into East Tennessee. When will this miserable war cease! I just feel as if I want to sleep until it is all over.

Thursday, Aug 13th.

I rose this morning rather late as it seemed almost impossible for me to get to sleep. Gave way to my terrible temper this morning and am consequently far from feeling happy! Clear but very warm. Busy all day sewing. No news.

Friday, Aug 14th.

I rose this morning early, cleaned up my room and heard Mattie's lessons before breakfast. Went to town this morning with Mama. Very warm and a little cloudy. Why doesn't Mollie come over? I wonder if she can still be sick.

Saturday, Aug. 15th.

I rose this morning quite late. Very busy all day cleaning and arranging our room. Very warm and cloudy and looks very much like rain. Neglected my Heavenly Father. Can I ever become a consistent Christian. Oh! how I ardently long to be entirely God's! Another week has commenced and oh my Heavenly Father will thou enable me to observe strictly Thy Holy Laws and may I look back upon the expired time with joy and may it serve to convince me that with thy Holy Aid I can overcome every obstacle, however besetting it may be. Looked for Mollie all day but she disappointed me. I hope to see her tomorrow, and she may look out for a scolding.

Sunday, Aug 16th.
I rose this morning quite late, but had time enough for my devotions before breakfast. Went to the little church and heard an excellent sermon. Passed the day profitably. Very warm. Mollie is still very unwell.

Monday, Aug 17th.
I rose this morning very early. Neglected my God. A poor beginning for this week! Oh! that I had firmness, to put into execution my many resolutions. I must not despair for my Saviour is only testing my faith. Went to town this morning with Mama. A wagon train and several negroes were captured by the Confederates near Brentwood, and one also at La Vergne.

Tuesday, Aug 18th/63.
I rose very late this morning. Performed my devotions after breakfast. Busy all day sewing for Ma and trying to assist her in every way I could. Very warm, but clear. Mrs. Montgomery's elegant residence burned last night, by Yankees and negroes. I feel very sorry for her although a woman of many peculiarities.

Wednesday, Aug 19th.
I rose this morning early. Performed my devotions and commenced to hear Mat's lessons, but we concluded to take a holiday and spend it with Mollie. Of course it was a most delightful one and when I review the past day, I find "all is well." A little cloudy and warm!

Thursday, Aug 20th.
I was remarkably lazy this morning in getting up, and can give no reasons for it. A great many troops went out this morning to Columbia and among them were several <u>negro regiments</u> fully armed and equipped. How humiliating a condition the South is in! Busy all day sewing.

Friday, August 21st/63.

I rose this morning early. Spent the day visiting some friends with Mollie. She returned with me and staid all evening. Imprudent at times. Very cloudy and warm.

Saturday, August 22nd 1863.

I was up this morning early. Busy all day as a general thing on Saturday. Clear but warm. Mollie staid all night with me.

Sunday, Aug 23rd.

Mollie and I rose this morning early, but we were so slow in dressing, the breakfast bell rang, before our toilets were completed. Went to church and heard an excellent sermon from Dr. Wharton. Spent the day properly. Clear but very warm. Dr. Berry came over and staid all evening.

Monday, Aug 24th.

I rose very late this morning as I lost a great deal of sleep last night. Sallie Branch spent the day with us and I was very much disappointed because Liza did not come. Cloudy all day and I hope it will rain, as it is very dusty. Performed my devotions this morning.

Tuesday, Aug 25th.

I rose this morning early. Performed my devotions and heard Mattie's lessons without giving way to my temper. Very cool and cloudy, quite a change as it has been intensely hot for several days.

Wednesday, Aug 26th.

I rose this morning early. Spent a most delightful day with Mollie. Very cool and clear. A fire was very comfortable. Performed my devotions and I lay bare my heart to my Heavenly Father's inspection.

Thursday, Aug 27th.

I rose this morning early. Performed my devotions and then gave Mattie a music lesson before she went to see Mrs. Jones's little children. Quite cool, but moderating.

Friday, Aug 28th.

I was up this morning quite late. Cloudy and rainy a part of the day. Busy all day helping Ma in various ways. Mattie and Sister spent the day with Sallie Branch.

Saturday, Aug 29th/63.

I rose this morning very early. Busy all day cleaning and arranging some drawers for Ma. Very cool and clear.

Sunday, Aug 30th/63.

I rose this morning early with a severe headache, but after washing and dressing I felt relieved. Quite a frost this morning. Went to church and heard an excellent sermon from Dr. Wharton who returned and took dinner with us. Clear and still cool. Thermometer at 30 deg. Spent the day properly.

Monday, Aug 31st.

I rose this morning very late. Performed my devotions. Mollie came to spend the day with me, but owing to some of her relations coming down from Franklin, she was compelled to return home. Clear, but much warmer than yesterday.

Chapter Ten
Homesick at South Side Institute, 1863

"Day after tomorrow is Friday!"

This school year finds Maggie and Sister Kate boarding at Mrs. Holcombe's South Side Institute. This is due to the Federal pickets which are set up on the Franklin pike to protect the entrance to Nashville. They are picked up by their parents each Friday and returned on Monday. Younger sister Mattie is being home-schooled at this time. Maggie's journal entries will clearly show her homesickness, and she noticeably lives for Fridays.

Tuesday, September 1st, 1863.
I rose this morning very early and heard Mattie's most difficult lesson's before breakfast. Went to town to see Mrs. Holcombe about my boarding with her, as I am determined to pass the next year at hard study. Clear and very warm.

Wed. Sept. 2nd.
I rose this morning early. Performed my devotions. Spent a most delightful day with my dear Mollie. Hazy and warm.

Thursday, Sept. 3rd 1863.
I rose this morning very late, though in time for breakfast. Cloudy and quite cool. Performed my devotions, though imperfectly. Busy all day arranging pieces for my scrap-book.

Friday, Sept. 4th.
I rose this morning early. Heard Mattie's lessons and was very busy all day doing little jobs for Ma. Cloudy, but warm.

Saturday, Sept. 5th.
I rose this morning very late and took breakfast at 10 o'clock. Sewing all day. Clear and very warm. Mollie again disappointed me.

Sunday, Sept. 6th.

I rose this morning quite early. Performed my devotions imperfectly. Went to church and heard an excellent sermon from Dr. Wharton. Cloudy with a little rain but as now clear and very warm.

Life goes on: Maggie's last year of school begins, and there are music lessons, church, and family separations as the war continue. The following announcement appeared in the *Nashville Daily Press* regarding her school.

September 7, 1863 - South Side Institute

The annual session of this excellent school will begin this morning. Mrs. Emma Holcombe, the Principal is well known as one of the most successful teachers and disciplinarians in the country, and the Institute has every other attraction to commend it to a liberal support. We are informed that the accomplished artiste and teacher of the Piano, Miss Panelle,[135] whose services have been engaged, is expected here in the course of the present month, she being unavoidably detained on account of illness.

Nashville Daily Press, **September 7, 1863**

Monday, Sept. 7th/1863

I rose early this morning. Busy all day making preparation to start school tomorrow. Clear and very warm.

Tuesday, Sept. 8th.

I rose this morning early and after breakfast I got ready for starting to school. Clear as there is no chance of rain. Studied a few of my lessons.

Wednesday, South Side Institute, Sep. 9.

I rose this morning early at 5:30 o'clock and ate breakfast at six. Knew some of my lessons, as it is very difficult to get into a regular way of studying.

---

[135] The 1860 United States Federal Census lists Miss Elise Panelle, age 22, as teacher of music and household member of Mrs. Holcombe.

Thursday, South Side Institute, Sept. 10ᵗʰ.

I rose this morning at my accustomed hour and I am sorry to record I am again growing negligent in my prayers to my God, can I expect to be successful in my studies, without not first imploring his aid and assistance. O! may I by my example be the means of bringing others to their God. Homesick!

Living for Friday

Friday, South Side Inst. 11ᵗʰ.

I rose this morning early, with a very bad ache, but it was relieved by taking a walk on the piazza. Going home this evening.

Saturday, Home Sep. 12th.

I rose this morning very late to make up for the last week. Studied my lessons well and wrote six Latin exercises. Had a severe thunder storm, which cooled the air, but had no rain.

Sunday, Home Sep. 13th.

I rose this morning early. Cloudy and cool, with a prospect of clearing off. Went to our dear little church and heard a most excellent sermon from Dr. Wharton. Saw Mollie.

Monday Eve, South Side Inst. Sep 14.

I rose this morning very early. Had a delightful ride in. Another long week has commenced. Studied my lessons faithfully, but it is doubtful about my knowing them. Clear and cool.

Tuesday, South Side Inst. Sep 15th/63.

I rose this morning very early. Again have I neglected my Heavenly Father. Cloudy and excessively warm. Knew my lessons. Practiced a good hour.

Wednesday, South Side Institute, Sep 16th/63.

I rose this morning very early. Had a most terrific thunder-storm last night which kept us awake during the whole night. Raining.

Thursday, South Side Institute, Sept 17th/63.

I rose this morning early. Moved into Miss Christon's room and think I shall find it far more agreeable as I will now have more quiet for my devotions. Took a long walk and was unfortunate enough to be caught in a hard rain.

Friday, South Side Inst. Sept 18th/63.

I rose this morning early and studied my lessons over. Cloudy now and cool. Ma came for us late this evening. I had given her out.

Saturday, Home, Sept 19th.

I rose this morning late. Busy studying all day and hearing Sissie's lessons. Ma and Pa went in to see about putting me to singing with Mr. Weber. Clear, with a white frost.

Sunday, Home Sept 20th.

I rose this morning late. Went to church and heard a good sermon from Dr. Wharton. Clear with another white frost.

Monday, South Side Inst. Sept 21st.

I rose early this morning. Home sick, terrible homesick. Took my first singing lesson under Mr. Weber and hope to make a good singer as Pa is so anxious for me to learn. Knew my lessons very well, but I think it is doubtful about my knowing them tomorrow.

Tuesday, South Side Inst. Sept. 22nd.

I rose this morning early. Studied my lessons and knew some of them. Practiced my music for two hours. Clear and quite cool.

Wednesday, South Side Institute, Sept 23rd 1863.

I rose this morning early. Took another music lesson. Knew some of my lessons. Another bloody engagement has taken place this side of Chattanooga, and oh! how anxiously do I await the tidings of my dear absent brother. Oh! my Heavenly Father will thou protect him during the hour of battle! It is reported that the bridge at Bridgeport is burnt by the Confederates.

In October General Grant was appointed successor to Rosecrans and immediately hastened to Chattanooga. Affairs soon wore a different look. Hooker came with two corps from the Army of the Potomac; and Sherman hastened by forced marches from Iuka, two hundred miles away. Thomas held command after Rosecrans left, and Grant was afraid he might surrender before reinforcements could reach him, and therefore telegraphed him to hold fast. The characteristic reply was, "I will stay till I starve." Communications were re-established. Thomas made a dash and seized Orchard Knob on November 23. The following day Hooker charged the fortifications on top of Lookout Mountain, His troops had been ordered to stop on the high ground, but, carried away by the ardor of the attack; they swept over the crest, driving the enemy before them.

The first day the Confederate left rested on Lookout Mountain, there two thousand four hundred feet high; the right, along Missionary Ridge-so called because, many years ago, Catholic missionaries had Indian schools upon it; and the centre, in the valley between. The second day their army simply occupied Missionary Ridge, in the centre of their former line, in front of Grant at Orchard Knob. On Lookout Mountain, Hooker met with so feeble a resistance, that Grant is reported to have declared the so-called "battle above the clouds" to be "all poetry, there having been no action there worthy the name of battle." Through the mist that filled the valley, the anxious watchers below caught only glimpses of this far-famed "battle above the clouds." The next morning Hooker advanced on the south of Missionary Ridge. Sherman during the whole time had been heavily pounding away on the northern flank. Grant, from his position on Orchard Knob, perceiving that the Confederate line in front of him was being weakened to repel these attacks on the flanks, saw that the critical moment had come, and launched Thomas's corps on its centre. The orders were to take the rifle-pits at the foot of Missionary Ridge, then halt and re-form; but the men forgot them all, carried the works at the base, and then swept on up the ascent. Grant caught the inspiration, and ordered a grand charge along the whole front. Up they went, over rocks and chasms, all lines broken, the flags far ahead, each surrounded by a group of the bravest. Without firing a shot, and heedless of the tempest hurled upon them, they surmounted the crest, captured the guns, and turned them on the retreating foe. That night the Union camp-fires, glistening along the heights about Chattanooga, proclaimed the success of this, the most brilliant of Grant's achievements and the most picturesque of all the battles of the war.

The Battle of Missionary Ridge

The effects of this campaign were the utter rout of Bragg's army, the resignation of that general on November 30, and the possession of Chattanooga by the Union forces. This post gave control of East Tennessee, and opened the way to the heart of the

Confederacy. It became the doorway by which the Union army gained easy access to Virginia, North and South Carolina, Georgia, and Alabama. [136]

Thursday, South Side Institute, Sep 24th.

I rose this morning early. Practiced two good hours. Knew all of my lessons. Tomorrow is Friday and how glad I am!

Friday, South Side Inst. Sep 25th.

I rose this morning early. Took a music and singing lesson. Knew my lessons. Ma came for us this evening. Cloudy and cool but cleared off.

Home, Saturday 26th/63.

I rose this morning late. Studied my lessons hard all day and at last did not get through with them. Clear and quite cool. Have felt very unwell all day; think I must have taken cold.

Home, Sep. 27th/63.

I rose this morning early. I was compelled to write my composition to-day, and I hope it will be the last time. Did not go to church to-day on account of having such a bad cold. Lovely day.

South Side Inst. Monday 28th.

I rose this morning early. Very unwell, but could not stay at home as my time is too precious to lose. Knew my lessons.

South Side Institute, Tuesday Sep 29th.

I rose this morning early. Took my music lesson. Very unwell with such a cold. Cloudy and a little warm.

South Side Inst. Wed. Sep 30th.

I rose this morning early. Took another music lesson. Cloudy and raining all evening. Very homesick.

---

[136] Barnes, *A Brief History of the United States*, Epoch V, pages 246-250.

South Side Institute, Thursday Oct 1st/63.

I rose this morning early. Practiced two hours. Raining all day. Going home tomorrow.

South Side Institute, Friday Oct 2nd.

I rose this morning early. Took a music lesson. Clear and cold. Went home this evening. Copied my composition.

Mount Alban, Oct. 3rd 63.

I rose this morning late. Busy all day studying. Practiced two hours at night.

Home, Sunday 4th.

I rose late this morning. Pa and I went to church and heard a very excellent sermon from Dr. Wharton. Cloudy and cool with an appearance of snow.

South Side Institute, Oct 5th.

I rose this morning early. Knew all my lessons. Had a short visit from Ida Hamilton. Studying all evening.

South Side Institute, Oct 6th.

I rose this morning early. Looked over my lessons and hope to know them.

South Side Inst. Wed. 7th 63.

I rose this morning early. Took a music lesson this morning. Raining all day and very cool. Knew my lessons.

South Side Inst. Thursday, Oct 8th 63.

I rose this morning early. Knew some of my lessons. Clear and cool. Took a walk this evening and on returning met some Confederate prisoners, who cheered us most lustily, but <u>we poor slaves</u> could make no demonstration, for fear of being arrested. I hope the <u>day of redemption</u> is near, such <u>tyranny</u> cannot last always.

South Side Inst. Friday, Oct 9th 63.

I rose this morning early. Knew all my lessons. Ma came after us this evening. Clear and very cool.

Home, Sat. 10th/63.

I rose this morning late. Studying all day and practiced at night. I will be compelled to write my composition tomorrow.

Home, Sunday Oct 11th/63.

I rose early. Compelled to stay home from church, on account of my school duties. Cloudy.

South Side Inst. Monday, Oct. 12th.

I rose this morning early. Left my dear home for another long week of school. Took a music lesson. Mr. Weber was exceedingly cross and ill natured and on that account I have spent a very miserable day. Raining all day.

South Side Inst. Tuesday, Oct 13th/63.

I rose this morning early. Practiced for two hours faithfully; as I am determined Mr. Weber shall never scold me as he did and it happened I was so much confused and this was the cause of my trouble. Knew my lessons. Raining all day.

South Side Inst. Oct 14th/63.

I rose this morning early. Took a music lesson. Raining all day. Knew all my lessons.

South Side Inst. Thursday, Oct 15th.

I rose this morning early. Practiced two good hours. Still raining and I am very much afraid it will be inclement weather tomorrow and thus I will be prevented going to my dear home.

South Side Inst. Friday, Oct 16th.

I rose this morning early. Cleared off and of _course_ I went home.

Home Oct. 17th.

I rose this morning early. Studying all day. Nothing of importance.

Home, Oct. 18th/63.

I rose early this morning. Again, compelled to remain at home from church, on account of the many duties I have to perform.

Monday, Oct 19th.

Again at school for another <u>long</u> week. Knew my lessons.

Friday, Oct 23rd.

I rose this morning early. What was my disappointment at finding it pouring down rain! Oh! I hope <u>I can get home</u>. Mr. Weber did come to-day. <u>Dear Ma</u> came for us.

Saturday, Oct. 24th.

I rose this morning late. Studying all day and will be compelled to write my composition tomorrow. Clear and a little ice this morning.

Sunday, Oct 25th 1863.

I rose this morning early. Clear and cold. Mollie spent the evening with me.

South Side Inst. Oct 26th.

I rose this morning early. O! how I hated to come from my dear parents home. Pa has very serious notions of coming to town, and I sincerely hope he will, not only <u>on our own</u> account, but for various reasons too numerous to mention.

South Side Inst. Oct 27th.

I rose this morning early. Studied my lessons faithfully. Clear. Nothing of interest.

South Side Inst. Oct 28th/63.

I rose this morning early. Took a music lesson this morning. Cloudy and cool. I hope it will not rain. On account of talking I was compelled to remain in after school and I trust it will be the last time.

South Side Inst. Oct 29th. (Thursday).

I rose this morning early. Practiced for two hours. Knew my lessons. Clear. Tomorrow is Friday.

South Side Inst. Oct 30th/63.

I rose this morning early. Raining, raining. Mr. Weber was again cross. Went home.

Home, Saturday 31st 1863.

I rose this morning early. Studying all day. Clear and cold.

Home, Sunday Nov. 1st.

I rose this morning early. There was no preaching at the school house. Cloudy.

Wednesday, South Side Inst. Nov 4th.

I rose this morning early. Took a music lesson. Mr. Weber was remarkably good. Clear. Day after tomorrow is Friday!

Thursday, South Side Inst. Nov 5th.

A year ago to-day the attack on Nashville was made. How many changes have occurred since that time! Many of the dear ones that were then alive have been gathered around the throne of God. Raining and from appearance I think it is fixing for another gloomy Friday.

Friday, South Side Inst. Nov 6th.

I rose this morning very early and was delighted to find it perfectly clear. Took a music lesson.

Home, Nov 7th 1863.

I rose this morning early. Studying all day and wrote my composition, so there will be some chance of my going to church to-morrow. Clear and cold.

Home, Sunday Nov. 8th.

I rose this morning early. Went to church and heard a most excellent sermon from Dr. Wharton. 10th chapter Hebrews.

Monday, Nov 9th.

I rose early this morning. Practiced two [hours] before breakfast. Knew my lessons. Clear and cold.

South Side Inst. Nov 10th 1863.

I rose this morning early. Studied hard before breakfast. Knew my lessons and I am happy to say I am getting in to the old way of studying. Clear.

South Side Inst. Nov 11th (Wed).

I rose this morning early. Took a music lesson from 8-9, and commenced a very difficult piece "Murmuring in the Trees" by Wallace. Knew my lessons.

South Side Institute, November 12th. Thursday

I rose this morning at 4 o'clock through mistake thinking as the fire was made the 6 o'clock bell had struck. Took a music lesson. Tomorrow is Friday! Clear.

South Side Institute, November 13th, 1863

Rose early. Went home!

Monday, November 16th, 1863

I rose very early this morning. O! how I hated to leave my home for another long week of school.

Tuesday, Nov 17th 1863.

I rose early this morning. Knew all my lessons. Clear and warm.

Wednesday, Nov 18th 1863.

I rose this morning early. Took a music lesson from 8-9. Mr. Weber was in a very good humor, and I think indulged in flattery.

Thursday, Nov. 19th.

I rose this morning early. Took a music lesson. Mr. Weber was in a bad humor. Clear. Pa came to see me and brought me a very handsome cloak. Do I love my kind father enough?

Friday, Nov 20th/63.

I rose early this morning and found it raining good fashion, but our good, kind Pa came for us and was so sorry to learn that Ma was still suffering with her tooth.

Home, Nov. 21st/63.

I rose early this morning. Practiced an hour and then studied hard the rest of the day. Cleared off and very cold.

Home, Sunday, Nov 22nd.

I rose early. Wrote my composition and then relieved Ma of many of her duties as she is still suffering with her tooth. Clear and cold with a white frost.

Home, Sat 19th/63. (December)

I rose early this morning. Studied hard all day and strange to say I finished before night. I have been so busy for the past two weeks that I have had no time for writing in my journal. Clear and very cold.

Home, Sunday, December 20th 1863.

I rose this morning rather late. Attended church and heard a very excellent sermon from Dr. Wharton. Agreeably surprised to see an old friend, Montgomery Baxter,[137] who has been discharged from the C.S.A. Poor fellow! I fear he is a victim of this cruel war. Clear and very cold.

Home, Wednesday Eve. Dec 23rd/63.

Came home this evening for the week [has] a holiday. Cloudy but cold.

Home, Thursday, Dec 24th/63.

I rose this morning late. Studied my lesson for Monday. Clear. Busy knitting all day. Charlie Percy came out this evening. Have felt so sad to-day! Poor Annie Moore is now lying at the point of death, pneumonia. I expected to spend a happy Christmas with her, but our Heavenly Father has ordained it otherwise. How fervently do I pray that He may spare her to her family and friends.

Friday, Dec 25th 1863.

I rose this morning early. Spent the day knitting little Mamie a pair of stockings. Went over to Liza Branch's for entertainment and sat up until 5 o'clock.

---

[137] Baxter was an early childhood friend of Maggie. He was the second son of Judge Nathaniel Baxter and the half brother to Capt. Edmund Baxter, who organized and commanded an artillery unit which bore his name. In later life, Baxter would become a physician and appear in the 1880 Nashville City Directory as the chief physician at Nashville's City Hospital.

Saturday, December 26th.

I rose this morning at 10 o'clock and after breakfast I went over and spent the day with Mollie. Cloudy and raining.

Sunday, Dec 27th/63.

I rose this morning late. On account of rain, I was prevented from going to church.

Monday, Dec 28th.

I rose this morning early feeling very unwell. Mollie and Nannie White spent the day with me. Had a hard chill.

Wednesday, Dec 30th.

I rose early this morning and felt so much better I concluded to spend the day with Lizzie Fall. Spent a delightful day. Sister Kate staid all night with Liza Branch.

Thursday, Dec 31st.

I rose rather late this morning. Spent the last day of the year with Mollie. Raining all day but turned intensely cold about night with sleet and snow.

The close of the third year of war found the following results. The Confederates had gained the great battles of Chickamauga and Chancellorsville, seized Galveston, and successfully resisted every attack on Charleston. The Federals had gained the battles before Vicksburg, and at Chattanooga and Gettysburg. They had captured the garrisons of Vicksburg and Port Hudson. The Mississippi was patrolled by gunboats, and the supplies from the West were entirely cut off from the Confederate army. Arkansas, East Tennessee, and large portions of Louisiana, Mississippi and Texas, had been won for the Union. The main opposing forces had Grant opposite Lee in Virginia and Sherman facing Johnston in the South. A brief respite would occur with action to begin in early spring.[138]

---

[138] Barnes, *A Brief History of the United States*, Epoch V, page 255.

Maggie ended the year of 1863 with the following quote.

Beauty and Piety

"The rose is sweetest when it first opens, and the spikenard root when it dies. Beauty belongs to youth and dies with it; but the odor of piety revives death and perfumes the tomb."

The journal entry for the 1864 New Year opens with, "1864, New Year! 1864!"

Home, January 1st 1864. (Friday)

Another sad New Year! Clear but <u>intensely</u> cold. Invited to a "storm-party" but on account of receiving my invitation so late, I was compelled to decline the invitation. Another year of war's bloodshed has commenced, but we must put our trust in God and leave the issue in His hands. Wrote a letter to Brother Joe to send via Fortress Monroe. Our "kind friends" only permits us to write a page!

Home, January 2nd 1864.

I rose this morning late. Cloudy and cold and has the appearance of snow. Looked for Mollie to-day but she disappointed me. Heard that Annie Moore was improving and I trust she may soon be well. She is a firm disciple of Jesus Christ and a dear friend of mine.

Home, January 3rd 1864.

I rose early this morning and was so disappointed at finding it snowing and consequently I was deprived of the pleasure of attending church but I endeavored to spend the day profitably. A dreary day.

Home, Jan. 4th 1864.

I rose this morning early. Another disagreeable day. Busy all day sewing. Have felt so unhappy, thinking of this miserable war, which seems as if it is never to end. Another subject of regret is that I am now a lonely wanderer from the fold of Jesus Christ, Oh! I must love my Heavenly Father more and serve Him more faithfully! O! the vileness of this sinful heart.

Home, January 5th

I rose early. Snowing and raining all day. O! such disagreeable weather.

Home, Wednesday, Jan 6th 1864.

I rose this morning late as the fire seemed determined not to burn. Cleared off, but is bitter cold. Very low-spirited to-day as is always the case whenever I try to penetrate the future, everything is so dark and dreary. What a support and solace our Heavenly Father is in these trying times.

Home, Thursday, Jan 7th 1864.

I rose this morning early. Cloudy and cold and snowing all day. Invited to a "storm-party" at Capt. Collier's but it is so cold and disagreeable I shall be compelled to decline the invitation.

Home, Friday, Jan 8th /64.

I rose this morning early. Busy all day knitting a pair of socks for Frank, which will be received with much thanks. Clear, but bitter cold. I am so anxious to see Mollie!

Home, Saturday, Jan 9th 1864.

I rose this morning early and as Sister and I anticipated spending a pleasant day at "Elm Wood," but we were doomed to be disappointed as Mrs. Berry wrote us word that on account of the bad roads she was prevented from going in for dear [Mollie]. Clear but moderating. Papa went in and says the roads are almost impassable!

Home, Sunday, Jan 10th 1864.

Again compelled to remain at home from church but Dr. Wharton hardly came out as it indicated snow early in the morning. Spent the day profitably.

Home, Monday, Jan 11th

I rose early this morning. Busy today studying lessons and I hope by next week we can attend school as we are losing precious time which can never be regained.

Home, Tuesday, Jan 12th/64.

I rose this morning early. Pa is quite sick having taken cold on Saturday, but I hope he will soon be well. Dr. Kelly, who is staying at Greenfield's came over to see him. Great deal warmer.

Wednesday, January 13th/64.

I rose this morning late, just ready in time for breakfast. Clear but much warmer. Pa is still very unwell. Busy all day sewing and knitting.

Thursday, Jan 14th 1864.

I rose this morning early. Dr. Bowling came out to see Pa and pronounced his case to be an attack of bilious fever! Heard that Mrs. Foster had returned from Dixie. I hope she brings us cheering news from our friends in the C.S.A. Cloudy and warmer!

Friday, Jan 15th 1864.

I rose this morning early. Busy pasting in my "scrap-book" and knitting. Invited to a "storm-party" at Mrs. James Wood's but as Pa is so unwell, I shall decline the invitation. Cloudy and much colder and looks as if it might clear off.

Saturday, Jan 16th 1864.

I rose this morning early. Spent a pleasant day with Mollie. Preaching at the church tomorrow.

Sunday, Jan 17th 1864.

I rose this morning quite early and was sorely disappointed to find it raining. Have spent the day by no means properly.

Monday, Jan 18th 1864.

I rose early this morning. Ma and sister went in to bring out some meat. Snowing all day. Spent the day knitting socks hoping to have an opportunity of sending them to my dear brother. Commenced an "umbra" for Cousin Sam Perkins who has been so kind and good to us all. Cousin Ella is now in town.

Tuesday, Jany 19th/64.

I rose this morning quite late as I sat up until 11 o'clock knitting. Clear and much warmer. Dr. Bowling came out and pronounces both Pa and Henry[139] better.

Wednesday, Jany 20th 1864.

I rose early this morning. Busy all day knitting. Clear and much warmer.

---

[139] Henry was a family servant who would assume the Vaulx family name after the war. He is listed in the 1880 Nashville City directory and the federal census as Henry Vaulx.

Friday, Jany 22nd/64.

I rose very early and knit a great deal before breakfast. Went to a "Storm- party" at Mr. Duncan's. Enjoyed it as much as I could during these war years. Mollie staid all night with me.

Saturday, January 23rd 1864.

Of course I rose late after sitting up so late. Mollie and Montgomery Baxter spent the day with me!

Sunday, January 24th/64.

I rose quite early. Attended church for the first time in four weeks. I hope the weather will continue good. Clear and very warm!

Monday, January 25th 1864.

I rose this morning early and concluded not to go to school until next Monday as the session is so near out. Have felt uncommonly sad and low spirited to-day. I feel as if something dreadful is to happen. O! how I wish this dreadful war would cease and our dear friends and relatives return to their desolate homes. Clear and delightful out!

Home, Tues. January 26th 1864.

I rose this morning early. Sister and I spent the day visiting friends as the weather is still delightful and there is no telling how long it will last. Mrs. Foster had no news whatever from my dear brother! Strange, I think.

Home, Wednesday, January 27th/64.

I rose this morning late as I felt tired from my walk. Heard Mattie's lessons and then spent the day with Mrs. James Woods. Clear and delightful out.

Home, Thursday, January 28th /64.

I rose this morning early. Spent another pleasant day with Mrs. Cantrell as I am determined "to make hay while the sun shines."

Home, Friday 29th

I rose early this morning. Went in town to see Cousin Ella as I have so little time to go to see her when I am at school. Clear, but warm!

Home, Saturday, January 30th

I rose this morning late. Went to see Mollie but her not being at home I concluded to pay a visit to Sallie House. Raining all morning, but cleared off, so I hope we shall have a pretty day tomorrow.

Home, Sunday, January 31st

I rose this morning early. Attended church and heard a very excellent sermon from Dr. Wharton. Raining all morning, but stopped in time for church.

South Side Institute, February 1st, 1864.

I rose this morning very early. Started to school after a long absence of four weeks! Many sad changes have taken place since I was last at the dear old Institute. Dear Annie Moore still lingers, but her constitution is so shattered, she will never regain her former health. Addie Read (now Mrs. Sealy) has bid farewell to her school-girl days!

Home, Saturday, February 6th 1864.

I rose this morning late. Mat and I attended church and heard an excellent sermon from our kind good friend Dr. Wharton. Montgomery Baxter and Willie Goodwin returned and spent the evening with me. Clear and cold!

Home, Feby 13th 1864.

I rose rather late as we are compelled to get up at six o'clock through the week. Studying all day. Cloudy. I hope it will be a good day tomorrow. Ellen Fall and Irene Watkins and several other Nashville girls intend leaving for "Dixie" next week. I hope some of them will take a letter for me to my dear brother. Looked for Mollie, but she disappointed me!

Feby. 19th/64. (Home)

I rose very early. Studied hard before breakfast. Bobbie Armistead and Yeatman Hardcastle came to see us to-night. Ma saw Montgomery Baxter in town who told her he had an opportunity to send a letter to Dixie and kindly offered to send one for me. Ellen Fall and Irene Watkins are so uncertain about going. I shall avail myself of this opportunity. Clear and cold.

Home, Feby 20th 1864.

I was late in rising this morning and had scarcely got settled at my studies when Montgomery Baxter came for my letter and staid until 1 o'clock, which threw me back considerably.

Home, Feby 21st 1864.

I rose very late. Went to church and heard a very excellent sermon from Dr. Wharton. Dr. Ford will preach to us next Lord's Day.

South Side Institute, Feby 24th (Wednesday)

I rose very early. Took a music lesson. Dear Annie Moore came to see us to-day. She is very weak but expects to start to school in April. Went out to see Addie Sealy who is now keeping house on Summer Street.[140]

Home, Feby 27th (Saturday).

I rose very early and studied very hard before breakfast and finished about 2 o'clock. Sister and I went over to Mollie's and spent the evening. She returned and staid all night.

Home, Feby 28th

Very late in rising this morning. No church at the school-house and therefore the day has been a very long one. Cloudy and looks very much like rain. Mollie returned home this morning, but intends going in as Liza Branch expects to join the church tonight.

Home, Feby 29th 1864.

I rose early this morning and studied my lessons but on account of rain was compelled to remain at home. All the trees are now covered with ice. Made a needle-book for my friend Montgomery Baxter.

In March 1864, General Grant was made Lieutenant-General in command of all the forces of the United States. Heretofore, the different union armies had acted independently. They were now to move in concert, and thus prevent the Confederate forces from aiding each other. The strength of the South lay in the armies of Lee in Virginia, and Joseph E. Johnston in Georgia. Grant was to attack the former, Sherman the latter, and both were to keep at work, regardless of season or weather. On May 4, while the Army of the Potomac

---

[140] Today in Nashville, this is 5th Avenue.

was crossing the Rapidan River to begin the Wilderness campaign, Grant, seated on a log by the road-side, penciled a telegram to Sherman to start his advance upon Atlanta. This last full year of war was about to heat up. Sherman, with one hundred thousand men, now moved upon Johnston, who, with nearly fifty thousand, was stationed at Dalton, Ga. The Confederate commander, foreseeing this advance, had selected a series of almost impregnable positions, one behind the other, all the way to Atlanta. For one hundred miles there was continued skirmishing among mountains and woods, which presented every opportunity for such warfare. Both armies were led by profound strategists. Sherman would drive Johnston into a stronghold, and then with consummate skill outflank him, when Johnston with equal skill would retreat to a new post and prepare to meet his opponent again. In July, President Jefferson Davis, being dissatisfied with this cautious policy, put General John Bell Hood in command. He attacked the Union army three times with tremendous energy, but was repulsed with great slaughter.[141]

This campaign during four months of fighting and marching, day and night, in its ten pitched battles and scores of lesser engagements, cost the Union army thirty thousand men, and the Confederate, thirty-five thousand.[142]

Grant's Telegram to Sherman

---

[141] Barnes, *A Brief History of the United States*, Epoch V, pages 255-257.
[142] Barnes, *A Brief History of the United States*, Epoch V, pages 257-258.

Home, March 1ˢᵗ.

I was again compelled to be at home but I studied my lessons, practiced and wrote my "essay". Snowing fast all day and is now bitter cold.

South Side Inst. March 2ⁿᵈ

Clear and cold. Went in to school, as I hate to be absent having lost so much precious time.

Home, Friday, March 4ᵗʰ

Up at 6 this morning. Took a music lesson. Came home. Cloudy and raining, but is much cooler and I think it will be clear in the morning.

Home, Sat 5ᵗʰ 1864.

I was very lazy this morning in getting up as I sat up until 11 o'clock talking. Got through my lessons early and it was fortunate I did as Liza and Sallie Branch and Birda Armistead came over and spent the greater part of the day.

Home, March 6ᵗʰ.

I rose very late. Went to church and heard a very excellent sermon from Dr. Wharton. Very few in attendance, several girls went into town to church. Bright and a lovely day. Yeatman Hardcastle walked home from church with me.

Home, March 12ᵗʰ/64.

I rose very early this morning. Studied hard all day but finished in time to pay dear Mollie a visit. Heard there that Queeny Humphreys was at Mrs. Brown's. Spent a delightful day [and] evening. Queeny and Mollie returned and staid all night with me. O! how vividly their presence bought up old times, and the happy days we have spent at dear Ingle Side. Cloudy and rained very hard in the evening.

Home, March 13ᵗʰ.

Very lazy this morning. Went to church and heard an excellent sermon from Dr. Wharton. He is very anxious to commence a Sunday school which I hope it will succeed. Dr. Ford died last Friday. Montgomery Baxter returned and spent the evening with us.

At school, March 17th/64.

I rose very early. Took a music lesson. Mollie and Queeny came to see me and I went with them to have my photograph taken. Sallie Read and I went to see Allie Sealy this evening.

Home, Sat. March 19th/64.

I rose early this morning. Studied hard all day and finished by 12 o'clock. Clear and pleasant.

Home, Sunday, March 20th.

I rose early. No church to-day. Charlie Percy came out and spent the day. Looked for Queeny but she did not come until very late in the evening. Cloudy and has the appearance of rain.

South Side Inst. March 21st.

I rose late as Queeny and I sat up until 11 o'clock talking over old times and of the happy days we used to spend. Went in town, but did not go to school as Queeny was anxious for me to go shopping with her.

Wed. March 23rd/64.

I rose at six. Was to have taken a lesson but was compelled to remain with Sallie Read, who heard the sad news of the death of her sister! Queeny staid all evening with me and Miss Clouston and I walked out to Lizzie Fall's whom she intends staying all night.

Thursday, March 24th/64.

I rose early. Took a music lesson. Queeny came to tell me "good bye"; she leaves rather unexpectedly on account of hearing that her Grandma was not expected to live.

Home, March 26th.

I rose early. Studied my lessons faithfully and finished about 10 o'clock. Intended going over to see Liza Branch, but was prevented doing so on account of having so much to do.

Home, Sunday, March 27th 1864.

I rose early. Attended church and heard a very excellent discourse from Dr. Wharton. Mollie returned and spent the day with me.

Thursday, March 31st.
Up at six o'clock. White frost and ice this morning; took a music lesson.

Home, Sat April 2nd/64.
Very lazy this morning. Don't feel well at all to-day. Studied hard all day and did not quite finish before my friend M.B. [Montgomery Baxter] came for a document to be sent to Dixie. Clear and pleasant.

Home, Sunday, April 3rd/64.
I rose late. Walked over to the school house but there was no church. Cloudy and raining by night.

Saturday, April 9th 1864.
Very late in rising this morning as I had to be up with sister who is quite unwell. A real April day. Studying and practicing all day.

Sunday, April 10th/64
I rose very late. Started to the church but met Bob Armistead who told us there was to be no service. Clear and a lovely evening.

Saturday, April 16th 1864.
I rose late. Studying hard all day. Cool and clear. Strange weather for the middle of April. This terrible war has been raging three years to-day and from appearances there seems as if there is to be no end to all this bloodshed. O! my Heavenly Father look down in tender mercy on our bleeding South and by thy intervention stay the angry hand of war!

On April 23, 1864, there is an interesting entry in her journals. Maggie records thoughts about religion, personal traits, and her relationship with her mother and friends, but towards the end of this entry, romance comes into Maggie's life. A friend, Montgomery Baxter, professes love. "Ma will have to be consulted and I must think well upon the subject."

Home, Saturday, April 23rd 1864.
A long and unhappy week has passed and I hope I may never spend another so miserable. I have had great trouble with my music; have not taken a music lesson this week and why?

Thursday, a week ago, Mr. Weber gave me a lesson and was very cross and impatient, consequently I became very much confused, made many mistakes, which irritated him all the more and on account of his passion he concluded to give me no lesson this week; but on Friday he sent for me, made many humble apologies, complimented me very highly, knowing I would come home and make my troubles known to Ma. I am just completely discouraged and would willingly give up my instrumental music ere it not for the deep interest my dear Pa takes in my progress. I think too that music will be of but little service to me in life, as other duties will demand my attention far more than such fleeting accomplishments. I have always longed to be a steady and consistent Christian, kind and charitable to my fellow-creatures, possessing all those domestic virtues, which should gladden the fireside of every home. O! I wish I could overcome my reserve and be more open and confiding to my dear mother. It is <u>strange</u>, so <u>strange</u> that I can always be unreserved with my friends instead of making my mother the sharer of my feelings and thoughts. I wonder if other girls possess this failure! No, I know they don't for I am a strangely constituted being. Another circumstance has occurred today in which Ma is deeply concerned and I must shake off my reserve and make her the sharer of my feelings. My <u>friend</u> M.B. came to see me this evening. I have suspected his love for me; but this evening my suspicions have been fully confirmed. Ma will have to be consulted and I must think well upon the subject. The trees are beginning to be green and it is getting much warmer. So I hope that we will soon enjoy Spring. Very much surprised to find a large encampment on Dr. Berry's hill. Poor man, how I pity him!

Home, April 24th/64

I was very late in rising this morning. No preaching at the church to-day as it is now raining very hard.

The Atlanta Campaign was a series of battles fought in the Western Theater of War throughout northwest Georgia and the area around Atlanta during the summer of 1864. In May 1864, Union Major General William T. Sherman invaded Georgia from the vicinity of Chattanooga, Tennessee. He was opposed by Confederate General Joseph E. Johnston. In the face of successive flanking maneuvers, Johnston's Army of Tennessee was forced to withdraw toward Atlanta. As noted earlier, the Confederate president replaced Johnston with the more aggressive John Bell Hood, who began challenging the Union Army in a series of destructive frontal assaults. Hood's army was eventually besieged in Atlanta and the city fell on September 2, hastening the end of the war. Georgia was the workshop, storehouse, granary and arsenal of the Confederacy. At Atlanta, Rome, and the neighboring towns were manufactories, foundries, and mills, where clothing, wagons, harnesses, powder, balls, and cannon were furnished to all its armies. The south was henceforth cut off from all of its supplies. Sherman now longed to sweep through the Atlantic States. But this was impossible as long as Hood, with an army of forty thousand, was in front, while the Cavalry under Forrest was raiding along his railroad communications toward Chattanooga and Nashville. With unconcealed joy, Sherman learned that Hood was to invade Tennessee. Relieved of this anxiety, he at once began preparing his army for its infamous "March to the Sea."[143]

By May 8, two weeks have elapsed with only one journal entry. Montgomery Baxter comes back into the daily entries. After writing on April 23, Maggie consulted with mother concerning the affair of Montgomery Baxter. The answer turned out to be no; friendship it would be.

Home, Sunday, May 8th 1864.

I have been so very busy the last two weeks that I have had little time to write in my journal. I have thought long and well upon the affair of M.B. At first owning to my mind being a little agitated, I thought I could love him, but now find that I acted upon the impulse of the moment, after talking the matter over calmly with mother, I find that I can never look upon him with any other feelings than that of friendship.

Home, Monday, May 9th/64.

Spent a very pleasant day with Cousin Jane Morgan. It seemed like old times to be with them again! Our schoolmaster spent the day at the Asylum but as I had been there so often, I concluded to pass my holiday at dear old Hedge Lawn.

Home, Sat May 14th/64.

I was up very early this morning and studying hard so as to get through before the heat of the day. Invited to attend a "pic-nic" at Melrose Park but I declined, as I think it is heartless to enter into such gayety while so dreadful a battle[144] is raging. Very sorry to find an encampment in our woods.

---

[143] Barnes, *A Brief History of the United States*, Epoch V, pages 256-258.
[144] This is a reference to the Battles of the Atlanta campaign.

Home, May 15th.

I rose early this morning. Went to the church but Dr. Wharton did not come out. Clear. Bob Armistead came to see me and gave me a very graphic description of the "pic-nic". I am very glad I did not attend.

Home, May 21st

Finished my lessons very early to day. Busy sewing and practicing.

Home, May 22nd 1864.

Clear and delightful out. No church as the Yankees are still in the woods!

Home, May 27th 1864.

Up early. Took a music lesson. Very much grieved to hear of the sickness of Ma and upon returning home found her suffering with neuralgia.

Home, Sat. May 28th/64.

I rose late. After getting through my lessons, I attended to household affairs and waiting on dear Ma who has suffered a great deal with her head. Mollie Berry and Bobbie Armistead came to see me, the former staid all night. Had a fine mess of straw-berries.

Home, Sunday, May 29th

For a wonder Mollie and I rose early. Went to our dear little church and heard a fine address from Dr. Wharton. Ma is much better, though still very weak. A dreadful battle is still raging in Georgia. O! how anxiously do I fear the result.

Home, Monday, May 30th 1864.

Up early. Mattie and I went in to take our music lesson but did not go to school. Ma is much better and I hope may soon be well. Clear but very warm. No army news!

Home, Tuesday, May 31st.

Very late getting up. Busy all morning sewing, waiting on Ma, and hearing Mat's lesson. Mrs. Berry and little Emma spent the evening with us.

Home, June 1st. (Wed)

I rose early. Went in town to take my lesson. Very warm and raining by night. I see from the papers that Cheatham's Division was in the thickest of the fight at Resaca, and am very uneasy about my dear brother, but I commit the absent one to God's keeping.

Home, June 2nd/64.

I rose very late. Busy practicing, hearing Mat's lessons. Raining all day.

Home, Friday, June 3rd 1864.

Rather lazy in rising this morning. <u>Very unhappy</u> to-day. Shall I ever resist the temptation of Satan? O! I so earnestly desire to be a Christian and free from the snares of this life. How I long to be entirely God's own.

Home, Sat. June 4th 1864.

I have been very busy cleaning and arranging the house as Ma has not yet regained her strength. Cousin C. McNairy and her mother came out this evening. Pa saw Dr. Berry [wholesale druggist] on the road; according to "grape vine" an order had been sent to this place for the reception of 12,000 wounded, so I judge there has been a bloody battle in Georgia.[145] How I tremble for the fate of our dear relatives and friends, but I leave them in God's hands.

Home, Sunday, June 5th 1864.

I rose early. Clear and cool. No church. Charlie Percy and Montgomery Baxter spent the day with us.

Friday, June 10th

I rose late as I staid all night with Addie Sealy and of course sat up late. Had several hard showers. Cousin Jane Morgan and Nannie Perkins staid "all night" with us.

Saturday, June 11th/64.

Very lazy, after such an excellent night for sleeping. Cousin Jane left this morning. Studying and practicing.

---

[145] Reference to the bloody battles fought at New Hope Church, Pickett's Mill, and Dallas, GA. These battles took place northwest of Atlanta on May 27 and 28, 1864.

Sunday, June 12th/64

Up late. Went to church and heard an excellent sermon from Dr. Wharton.

Wednesday, June 15th.

I rose at six. Busy all day writing invitations for the "commencement" which comes off the 22nd and 23rd. I declined taking any part in it, as I think it is so unsuitable these times, when our dear brothers and friends are risking their lives for our country's cause. Spent a delightful evening with Bessie Thompson and staid until 11 o'clock. Mrs. Holcombe, Misses Clouston and Rogers went with us.

Thursday, June 16th 1864

Up at my accustomed time. Busy assisting the girls in writing their invitations. Had a "rehearsal" to-day. Mr. Weber seemed very much gratified with its success.

Friday, June 17th 1864.

My last day at school! How I hated to part with my dear friends, some of whom I may never see again. O! it is a sad reflection, but I am delighted to think that though death may part, we can meet in heaven where parting is known no more.

Saturday, June 18th

Lazy this morning. Having no lessons to get. I was at a loss to know what to do with myself. Clear but warm.

Sunday, June 19th

Spent the day by no means properly. No church and consequently the day has been very long.

Monday June 20th/64.

I rose very late as I have been getting up so soon for the last two months. Went to town with Ma. Another bloody battle is raging near Marietta, Oh! that this war would stop.

Chapter Eleven
Summer, 1864

"Oh! I wish I was a man and could fight the Yankees!"

Home, Tuesday, June 21st 1864.

I rose early. Busy all day arranging my Scraps for my book. Cloudy and drizzling, but is now clear. Dr. Berry brings us glorious news from our noble Lee! The Federals have sustained a loss of 8,000 men killed and wounded at Petersburg Va, and it is rumored that Burnside's whole corps is captured.[146] God grant it is so! Have been unhappy to-day! Such wicked thoughts are always in my mind! O! can I ever be entirely God's; <u>weaned</u> from the snares of this life!

Home, Wednesday, June 22nd

Lazy this morning! Went to town. Clear and warm. Our "Commencement" takes place tonight.

Home, Thursday, June 23rd

I must commence to get up early. Busy all day pasting in my "Scrap Book," as I live in hopes to see it interest dear Brother when he returns! Dear fellow! He has been absent three years and how thankful I am to my Heavenly Father for sparing his life. The "Lorrie Musicals" of the Institute comes off to- night. I wish the girls every success and they greatly deserve it, as they have practiced faithfully for the last six weeks.

Home, Sunday, June 26th

I rose pretty early. Went to church and heard a very fine address from Dr. Wharton. Ed Gale and Charlie Percy took dinner with us.

---

[146] The reference is to the infamous Battle of the Crater which took place during the Siege of Petersburg. It resulted in heavy losses for the Union army. Union General Ambrose Burnside was relieved of duty for his part in the disaster.

Home, Monday, June 27th/64

I rose early. Went to town and spent a very pleasant morning with Mollie who is now staying at Dr. Wharton's as there are so many troops on poor old Elm Wood.

Home, Tuesday, June 28th 1864.

Busy all day assisting Ma in packing the chests. Yeatman Hardcastle came to see me this morning. Very warm, but not so sultry as yesterday. I <u>feel very low spirited</u> to-day! O! can I ever pursue a steady Christian-like course? There are so many wicked thoughts in my mind.

Home, Wednesday, June 29th, 1864.

Up much early than usual. Went to town this morning. Had a very refreshing rain in town, but none out home. Capt. Gurley who killed Genl. McCook is now in the Penitentiary sentenced to be hung. He was acquitted by a court martial; some time, since, but his doom is now sealed through the hatred and influence of the McCook family. I saw Capt. Gurley when over at Cousin Jane Morgan's. He is a very gentlemanly man and entirely innocent of the charge of "bushwhacking." Poor fellow, I hope that he is prepared for his fate![147] Six confederate soldiers (guerrillas, as the Yankees call them) were hung several weeks ago for no cause whatsoever. O! when will this retaliation end? Heard from brother. God has mercifully spared his life. He is now with Genl. Johnston, six miles from Marietta. Aunt Jane heard that Bob had been slightly wounded in the thigh and is in the hospital in Atlanta. O! that they could return home and this horrid war would end!

Home, Thursday, June 30th.

Lazy this morning! Busy all day pasting my "Scrap Book." Very warm. <u>Neglected my Heavenly Father</u>.

Home, Friday, July 1st.

I rose early, not that I had any inclination to do so, but it was so warm I could not sleep. Ma and sister went to town this morning. Very warm!

---

[147] A Confederate officer falsely accused of being a bushwhacker (one who takes part in irregular guerrilla warfare) in the death of Union General Robert McCook. False charges and political influence played major roles in his subsequent guilty verdict and death sentence. After a year on death row, Gurley was accidently made part of an officer exchange. Gurley's enemies unsuccessfully hounded him for years trying to have the death sentence carried out. He died in 1920, having outlived many of the men who had sought his execution.

Home, Saturday, July 2nd.

What a busy day this has been! Towards evening it clouded up and rained all evening. Looked for Charlie Percy out, but he disappointed me.

Home, Sunday, July 3rd/64.

Up early. Raining all morning, but is now quite clear. Charlie came out. Much cooler.

Home, Monday, July 4th/64.

Up early. Another anniversary has come and still our enemies are around us. Sister and I walked to see Liza and Sallie Branch, but as they were not at home, we concluded to pay Mrs. Wood's a visit. Mrs. Kelly went in and reports the "negro soldiers" marching through the city. Montgomery Baxter came to see us.

Home, Tuesday, July 5th 1864.

Up late. Went in town this morning. Very pleasant.

Home, Wednesday, July 6th.

I rose early. Had a hard rain this evening. Mollie came out to spend several days with me. Quite clear.

Home, Thursday, July 7th 1864.

Mollie and I were lazy this morning. Busy all day cleaning some lace. Had a hard rain. Ed Gale and Montgomery Baxter spent the evening with us and staid until 11 O'clock, which is evidence that they were entertained well.

Home, Friday, July 8th.

Very lazy. Finished the lace. Clear in the morning, but raining all evening. Sewing on my quilt.

Home, Saturday, July 9th 1864.

Up early. Busy sewing on my quilt. Clear and very warm. Mollie and I took a good bath and afterwards a walk.

Home, Sunday, July 10th 1864

Up late. Attended church and heard a fine sermon from Dr. Wharton. We had scarcely reached home before a hard rain came up. Cloudy and raining all evening.

Home, Monday, July 11th

I rose early. Mollie returned home. O! how I miss her! Went to town this morning. Clear and warm.

Tuesday, July 12th

Up early. Busy all day.

Wednesday, July 13th.

I rose late. Went in town. No news. Clear and very warm. I wish we could have some rain as the corn is suffering for rain.

July 14th Thursday.

Montgomery Baxter came to visit. He handed me a "billet doux."[148] Its contents were just what I expected; every line breathed of his affection for me, but I can't return it, but I shall always look upon him as a friend, rejoice in his prosperity, and be near to him in his adversity. It makes me unhappy to think he is throwing away his affections upon one so unworthy of them.

Saturday, July 16th.

Late this morning. Busy all day cleaning up. Warm! very warm!

Sunday, July 17th.

I rose late. A <u>long, long</u> day which is always the case when we have no church.

Monday, July 18th/64.

I rose early. Nothing of importance.

---

[148] French for love letter. Refer to the September 9, 1861 and February 19, 1862 journal entries.

Billet Doux

Home, July 20th

Up late as I have felt so unwell today. Oh! I wish I was a man and could fight the Yankees! Owning to the soldiers stealing so many vegetables, Pa has been compelled to get a guard, but on account of Pa's offering him a very nice room in the carriage house thinking it would be more convenient to the garden, he became highly insulted and wrote Pa a most outrageous letter. Vile scoundrel! I trust a rebel may fix him.

Home, Thursday, July 21st.

Up late. Mattie and I rode over to see Mollie who has been staying at home on account of the illness of her mother, but I am thankful to say God has mercifully spared her life.

Home, Saturday, July 23rd.

Up late. Mollie came over to stay all night. Very warm.

Home, Sunday, July 24th/64.

Up late. Went to church and heard an excellent sermon from Dr. Wharton. No rain for two weeks.

Monday, July 25th.

Sissie went up to Triune this morning with Cousin Sam; she intends staying several weeks. Mollie returned to town this morning. Another bloody battle has been fought at Atlanta, and rumors assert that place has fallen. Genl. McPherson,[149] the Federal general is killed. How I dread to hear from our dear relatives and friends!

Wednesday, July 27th.

Up late. Ma and I attended the funeral of Bob Bradford, who died at Camp Chase, Ohio. How deeply do I sympathize with the afflicted family? Time alone can heal so deep a <u>wound</u>, and even with the flight of years, an aching void will remain which nothing earthly can ever fill. Raining all evening and I hope may continue throughout the night as the crops are suffering for the want of rain.

Friday, July 29th.

I rose early. Ma and I went in town. Cloudy and I hope it may rain. So anxious to hear from Atlanta. It is rumored that Capt. W. G. Erwin, who was wounded at one of the late battles in Ga. has since died. How many of our noble sons must fall before this cruel war is over, but they sacrifice their lives in a noble cause, and their memory will be dearly cherished by their comrades and friends.

Saturday, July 30th 1864.

Very lazy this morning. What a busy day Saturday is! Everything is in confusion and when night comes and I am completely broke down. Cloudy.

Sunday, July 31st.

Up late. Had three very hard showers. Spent the day reading the life of "Stonewall Jackson." What a great and good man he was; so devoted to the cause of his Saviour and his country.

---

[149] General James Birdseye McPherson, USA was a graduate of the 1853 West Point class and was a highly rated aide to Sherman. He was killed on July 22, 1864 during the Battle of Atlanta.

Montgomery Baxter came to see me this evening. He places no reliance in the report of Capt. Erwin's death. I hope it is not so!

Monday, August 1st, 1864.

I rose early. Busy pasting my Scrap Book. Had three very hard rains. Received a letter from Mollie. It seems strange that we should be so near and still write but we think it may be improving, as letter-writing is so important. She speaks of going North if she should find an opportunity; she is anxious for me to accompany her, but I don't think I can conclude to go.

Tuesday, August 2nd

I rose early. Ma and Mat went in for Nannie K. who intends spending a week with her. Another little lamb has been taken to the fold of him who said: "Suffer little children to come unto me, forbid them not for of such are the kingdom of Heaven." Mrs. Cantrell's youngest child died yesterday of flux [Dysentery]. Had a very hard rain last night, but the day has been clear and beautiful! Every day confirms our victory at Atlanta, and the report now is that Gens. Hardee and Wheeler having gotten in the rear of Sherman have compelled [him] to cross the river. (Chattahoochee).

Wednesday, Aug 3rd 1864.

Up early. Ma and I attended Mrs. Cantrell's baby's funeral. Dr. Wharton preached a very sweet and comforting sermon. During the service a most violent thunder-storm occurred which kept us some time. Much cooler, I think.

Thursday, Aug 4th 1864.

I rose early. Pa went to town to day for the first time in three months. Very much surprised to day to see Kate, Cousin Jane and the two babies. Very unhappy!

Friday, Aug 5th 1864.

I rose late. Cousin Jane returned this evening. Raining hard now. O! so wretched! Can I resist temptation?

Sat. Aug 6th 1864.

Up late. Busy as I am always on Saturday. Clear, but warm.

Sunday, Aug 7th 1864.

Up quite early. Clear and beautiful in the morning. Went to church this morning and heard such a sweet comforting sermon. Very warm, but had a shower which cooled the atmosphere. Passed the day profitably reading "Scott's Family Bible."

Monday, Aug 8th

Up late. Went to see Mrs. Berry who is slowly recovering from her illness. Clear but rained in the evening.

Tues. Aug 9th

I rose early. Little Mattie Duncan spent the day with the children. Busy all day sewing my "duster."

Wed. Aug 10th.

I rose early as I expected Sallie and Liza Branch to spend the day, but was very much disappointed at their not coming. Had a slight shower which laid the dust.

Thursday, Aug 11th.

I rose early with a head ache. Received a long letter from Mollie and was very much surprised to find a note from "M.B." thanking me for the <u>friendly</u> interest I now take in him. Annie and Emma spent the day with Mattie and was very glad to see Mrs. Berry. Slight showers all day. Two Yankees came to get boarding, but the house is too small. I am thankful to say to take them, and besides we are all too "rebellious." Ma had quite a dispute [with] them. Pa went to town yesterday and [that] took a great deal of exercise, and not being accustomed to it he is quite unwell. I hope he will soon be well.

Friday, Aug 12th 1864.

I rose late. Finished my corset cover and passed the remainder of the day reading my French. Cloudy and very warm.

Saturday, Aug 13th 1864

Another busy day has closed and another week has passed into eternity! Have all my actions during that time been acceptable in the sight of God? I fear not! The children spent the day at Elmwood. Mrs. Berry sent me word Mollie would be out next week to spend some days with me, I am always happy to see her!

Sunday, Aug 14th 1864.

I rose early. Wrote a letter to dear Brother and intend sending it by Fort Monroe. Spent the day properly reading an appeal to fallen man. I hope it may prove instructive to me! Raining in showers all day.

Monday, August 15th.

Up late. Busy all day making crochet trimming for my corset covers. Had two very hard showers, but it is still very sultry. Another large cavalry regiment came out this morning and is encamped on poor Elmwood. It is commanded by a son of Parson Brownlow[150] from East Tenn. What a shame for a man to fight against his own state and in such a disgraceful course, as the Yankees are now engaged in! Hurrah! for the C.S. Army!

August 16th 1864.

I was awake this morning at day light, but on account of feeling unwell I did not rise early. A beautiful morning, but is now raining. Went to town this morning. The Negroes had a large mass meeting yesterday to celebrate their day of freedom; several colored orators spoke on the occasion. Poor old Nashville what sights she is seeing!

Wednesday, Aug. 17th 1864.

Up late. Busy today making linen pillow cases. Several Federal waggons came to get our hay which is scarcely out; only gave $20.00 a ton (government price), when it is selling in Cincinnati at $60.00. A few days since they went to our neighbor J.H. Ewing and offered him $18.00 a ton and upon his refusing to sell at that price, Col. Donaldson sent an additional number of waggons and seized the whole lot! Poor encouragement for the farmer! Lovely morning but now is raining steadily. I wish Mollie would come out, for I am lonesome when sister is away.

---

[150] William G. "Parson" Brownlow was a Pro-Union Knoxville newspaper editor, minister, and politician who served as governor of the state of Tennessee from 1865 to 1869 and as a United States Senator from Tennessee from 1869 to 1875. During the war, he was often compared to the plague, held in disdain and viewed by many as a traitor of the South.

Thursday, Aug 18th 1864.

I rose early and wrote a note to Mollie, but on account of its raining so hard, I could not send it. It has indeed been a gloomy day and the rain still continues to pour. Made one pair of pillow cases, and then buried myself with my Scrap Book. Mr. Blunkhall sent us word that the troops were preparing to leave, but I fear it is <u>too</u> good to be true.

Friday, Aug 19th 1864.

I rose late. Showery all day. Rode over to "Elm Wood" in the evening for the children who spent the day with Annie. Mollie will come out tomorrow. All the troops from our woods and Mr. Wood's left for the front, but they are still encamped at Elmwood. Busy all day sewing and practicing. Received a letter from sister and was sorry to learn that she had been quite sick. I hope she will soon be at home.

Saturday, 20th 1864.

I rose quite late. Very showery, but I think it is much cooler. Busy all day mending. Mollie came out this morning to spend some days. I hope we shall have a good day to-morrow for our church.

Sunday, Aug 21st 1864.

I rose late and was sorry to find it raining, so we were prevented from going to church. Cleared up in the evening and now quite cool. Took a walk <u>to the gate,</u> our limits are very small!

Monday, Aug 22nd

I rose late. Mollie and I spent the morning sewing and practicing and after dinner we went to see Roberta Armistead. Sissie returned from Triune this morning and I was sorry to find her hand so sore. Clear and I hope the rain is over.

Tuesday, Aug 23rd

Up late. Busy all day. Walked to the lane this evening and saw Sallie and Liza Branch; they gave no definite reason for disappointing me.

Wednesday, Aug 24th

Up late as Mollie and I lay awake nearly two hours talking. She and Mammie Hickman returned home. The house seems quite lonely without them. Clear and very pleasant.

Thursday, Aug 25th.

Rose late. Busy all day finishing my "duster," which has been on hand two weeks. Very warm and cloudy.

Friday, Aug 26th

Rose early this morning. Ma and sister went to town to see Dr. Bowling. Cloudy and raining at times. Two Yankees attempted to take milk from the spring house but upon Pa's going down they desisted. Learned to make "rose tatting." Heard a very distressing piece of news to-day. Poor Annie Moore's mind is entirely wrecked! She is either to be taken to the Asylum or to Philadelphia. Dear girl, I almost wish I never knew her!

Saturday, Aug 27th

Up late and surprised to find it clear and lovely as it was raining steadily when we went to bed. As Ma was going in, I concluded to go and stay with Mollie until Monday. Spent a pleasant evening with Lizzie Fall and Anna Mayson; the former intends going North to school soon! I think it is perfectly shameful in Southern girls patronizing Yankee institutions. Clear and quite cool.

In Town. Aug 28th.

Up very early. Attended church and heard a very fine sermon from Mr. Fall. I heard a distressing piece of news, namely the sad tidings of the death of dear Tom Percy.[151] Poor fellow! I hope it is not so. Went to church at night. What a blessed privilege it is to attend church!

Home, Aug 29th

I rose early. Went down town with Miss Carrie Fall and Mollie, who are very busy getting up a box to send to Johnson Island[152] to the prisoners. We heard some time since that Capt. Gurly had been sent North, but Dr. Wharton says he is still in close confinement in the penitentiary, and sentenced to be hung. Ma came for me this evening and I was glad to receive a letter from Brother, but it contained sad news in the deaths of Tom Percy and cousin

---

[151] Thomas G. Percy, a native of Nashville. He was killed in action during the Battle of Atlanta. He was the brother to Ellen and Hettie Percy.
[152] Johnson Island was a prisoner-of-war camp for Confederate officers. It was located on Lake Erie, about 3 miles from Sandusky, Ohio.

Joe Nichol;[153] the latter was buried on the battle field on the 22nd, no other deposition could be made of his body. Tom was wounded on the 26th or 27th of July and died on the first of August. He was buried 3 miles from Atlanta and his grave marked and his address given to the owner of the place. He sleeps his last sleep far away from the aged grandmother who so anxiously watched his return, who soothed his infant wailings and looked forward with pride to his mature years to shield and protect his two orphan sisters! He was beloved by his officers and comrades and he now has laid down his life for his country. Many of his comrades went before him and many are yet to follow as his regiment (1st Tennessee) is being sadly decimated from day to day.

Tuesday, Aug 30th

I rose early. Ma and Pa went in. Poor Ellen Percy arrives from Triune full of life and fine spirits little suspecting the sad news that awaited her. May God be to her that "Friend who sticketh closer than a brother" and may she remember that He doth not willingly afflict the children of man. What a comfort and solace is our Heavenly Father under these earthly trials!

Wednesday, Aug 31st

I was very lazy in rising this morning. Busy sewing, peeling peaches and attending to other household duties. Quite cool!

Thursday, Sept 1st.

I rose late. Ma and Pa went in. There are many conflicting reports of skirmishes at or near LaVergne. An old market man was coming in this morning on the Murfreesboro pike when he was hailed by two Confederate soldiers, who proved to be John Brown and Player Martin. After talking some time, the former requested the man to bring a note in to his Ma and as good luck would have it; the man jumped at an opportunity of doing good to a rebel soldier and accordingly handed the note to Aunt Jane. He had been in several skirmishes, but had obtained a leave of absence and entreated Aunt Jane to come immediately to Triune to meet him and bring him whatever she might have in the house. Fortunately the overseer of Cousin Sam's was down and

---

[153] Josiah Henry Nichol, a native of Nashville, was born in 1831. He had survived Stones River but was killed at Atlanta while serving in the quartermaster department under General Braxton Bragg.

after sewing, shirts, drawers and &c, to her hoops and putting on a pair of boots she left about 1 o'clock. I hope she may meet with every success![154] Busy today making my winter corset cover.

The Smugglers

Friday, Sept 2nd 1864.

I rose late, but finished copying a portion of brother's letter for Ellen. Received a note from her, thanking me for the sympathy I feel for her. Heaven bless you, dear Ellen, may this severe stroke turn you to God who is ever open to the cry of the distressed. Very much surprised to see Martha Hamilton. A warm day.

---

[154] Smuggling was against federal law but a necessary way of life for the Southern cause. See Durham, *Nashville, the Occupied City, 1862-1863*, chapter 15 (Knoxville, The University of Tennessee Press).

Saturday, Sept. 3rd.

Rose early. Hard at work all day doing Saturday jobs. Very warm; thermometer 93 degrees in the shade. Atlanta has fallen!

Sunday, Sept 4th

Rose late. Attended church and heard an excellent lesson from Dr. Wharton. Aunt Jane returned from Triune to-day. She saw Bob and many others of our acquaintances. She gave a glowing description of them, says they were the fattest "starved rebels she ever saw!" John has gained quite a name, having taken a splendid stand of colors[155] at Resaca from a Ken tuck [Kentucky] regiment. Ma and I rode in with her this evening. Poor Ellen! How badly she must feel to think of the many months that have elapsed since she had seen her dear brother, and now he has forever gone, but I hope she is prepared to meet him in Heaven!

Monday, Sept 5th.

Up late. Very much disappointed about not going to Cousin Jane's. Raining all morning. Finished my corset covers.

Tuesday, Sept 6th

I rose late. Rained in the morning. Employed all day in various ways. It is reported that there has been another bloody battle beyond Atlanta.

Wednesday, Sept 7th

Up late. Busy sewing. Cloudy and warm.

Friday, Sept 9th.

Up late. Cloudy in the morning but cleared off. Busy today, as Ma is suffering with nemalgia [neuralgia]. Commenced a letter to Brother by Fort Monroe.

Saturday, Sept 10th.

Up late. Went over to Cousin Jane's after travelling over the roughest road imaginable.

---

[155] The color standard (flag) was used in battle to maintain order and communication. The loss of the flag could result in confusion and even panic during critical times of battle.

Hedge Lawn, Sept 11th

Up early. Kate and I went over to see Mr. Weaver. Squire Farmer from the Asylum spent the day with Frank. Had a delightful ride home.

Home, Sept 12th

Up late. Have felt unwell to-day. Commenced knitting Nannie Perkins some skirts. Heard the Yanks intended beginning to draft negroes and white men. In honor of the death of Genl. Morgan and the capture of Atlanta by Sherman a hundred guns were fired at the different forts and there will be an illumination to night. That's civilization.

September 13th. (Tuesday)

Up late. Reading a very interesting work "Quits." Clear and cool. Very unhappy to-day.

Sept. 14. (Wednesday)

I rose late. Wrote a long letter to Brother by Fort Monroe. Had quite a hard rain. Ma and Mattie went in. The Federals are very busy drafting all men between 18-50. Large numbers have gone to [Confederate Gen. Joe] Wheeler, who is now about Shelbyville.

Thursday, Sept 15th.

I rose early. Bob Armistead came to see us. He intends leaving for Bethany College Saturday. What will the girls do for beaux; they are either going North to school, or joining the "rebels" army. The last is by far the most praiseworthy. Finished Nannie's skirts.

Friday, Sept 16th.

I rose early. As I had several things to get, I concluded to go in. Great excitement about the draft. Clear and very cool. Very much delighted to see Mollie.

Saturday, Sept 17th.

I was very lazy this morning. Very gloomy and low spirited today. O! shall I ever become a true and consistent Christian. Mollie and I rode over to see Mrs. Berry. Cloudy but I think too cool to rain.

Sunday, Sept 18th/64.

I rose early and took a bath. Mollie and I went to our dear little church. Dr. Wharton preached a very affecting sermon intended he said for the benefit of those who had not yet acknowledged their Saviour before men. He expressed an <u>earnest</u> <u>hope</u> that I might be brought in humble repentance at the foot stool of my beloved Lord and Master. Yes! I too am anxious to become a member of the church but I have waited long in the hopes that I might be able to connect myself with the Presbyterians. Mollie went back to town as she had to be at school at 8 o'clock. Ed Gale took dinner with us.

Monday, Sept 19th.

Up early. Busy today knitting. Very cool and clear. Have felt unhappy all day. I feel as if I am the most worthless of creatures, of so little use to anyone, but we are all put here on earth by God for some useful purpose and I hope I may see at the close of my earthly career, that my <u>whole</u> life has not been a blank.[156]

Tuesday, Sept 20th.

I rose early today. Ma and sister went in as Aunt Jane expects to go to Triune and take Ellen. Hettie wishes sister to remain with her during her absence. Wrote a very long letter to brother and enclosed him $100.00. I know it will go safe. Wrote a letter to Queeny. Practiced a great deal!

Wednesday, Sept 21st 1864.

Up late. Sewing today and finished Nannie Perkins shirt. Learned a new song "Blanche Alpen." I intend giving more attention to my singing than I have done. Commenced a very interesting work, "The Initials." The author, a daughter of Lord Erskine, married a German noble and it is in that country her scene is laid.

Thursday, Sept 22nd 1864

Have had a bad head-ache to day. Practiced a great deal. Dr. Kelley and Mr. Armistead came over.

Friday, Sept 23rd/64.

I rose late with another head-ache. Ma and Mattie went in; sister came home. Raining all day in showers but is now clear.

---

[156] Refer to the journal entry on January 27, 1862.

Saturday, Sept 24th/64.

I rose late. Had a very hard rain and thunder-storm last night and it is now very cool and clear. Busy all day mending. Finished the "Initials;" perfectly charmed with it. O! how I would like to make a European tour!

Sunday, Sept. 25th/64.

Up early. A slight frost last night. Beautiful day. Pa went to see Mr. Duncan, who has just returned from the North and heard there that Mrs. Orville Ewing is lying very low with flux.

Monday, Sept. 26th/64.

I rose early this morning. Sister and I went in with Pa. Aunt Jane returned from Triune this evening. Ellen and Dellie intend returning with Cousin Sam. Cousin Ann Dunn (now Mrs. Anderson) died in Memphis a week ago of congestive chills contracted while in Arkansas. Had to have our pass renewed, the old one having lasted a year and a month. Clear and cool.

Tuesday, Sept. 27th 1864.

Up very late. Busy knitting Morgan Perkins some shirts. Ma and Mattie went in. Mrs. Orville Ewing died last night. Raining a little. Learned a new song, "The Wild Ashe Deer."

Wednesday, Sept 28th/64.

Up late. Busy knitting. Sister and I went over to Mrs. Berry's to see Nannie White. She intends leaving tomorrow. Cloudy, but is now clear. Heard that [General] Forrest is now at Pulaski.

Thursday, Sept 29th 1864.

Up late. Finished my shirt. Nannie White came over this morning. Learned how to make "clover leaf" tatting. Cloudy but no rain.

Friday, Sept 30th/64.

Up quite late. Busy making tatting. Ma and Mat went in and was much surprised to hear of Ellen Percy's return from Triune. Mrs. Judge Maney came from Atlanta and brought Pa a letter from Brother. He acknowledges the receipt of several letters from me by Fort Monroe, but complains of having no stamps. I am sure I enclose him stamps each time! Cloudy and is now raining (8 PM).

Saturday, Oct 1st 1864.

I rose early. Cloudy and raining all day. Went in town. Nothing of any importance.

Sunday, Oct 2nd 1864

I rose early. Went to church but Dr. Wharton did not come out as he forgot to have his pass renewed. Cloudy, but is now cool and clear. Several regiments of Yankees came out to encamp on poor old Elm Wood. I trust it is but a flying trip. It is rumored that Forrest is at Spring Hill.

Monday, Oct 3rd/64.

I rose early. Busy making tatting. Learned a new song, "Stonewall Jackson's Prayer." A great many troops, cavalry, artillery and infantry went out to day. I trust Forrest may fix them.

Tuesday, Oct 4th/64.

I rose late. Ma, Mattie and Sister went in so Pa and I had a great day. Raining all evening and it still continues to pour. Busy cutting "okra," practicing, &c. Have felt a little unwell.

Wednesday, Oct 5th/64.

Up early as I am anxious to finish my tatting. Raining all day, but is now so cool I think it will clear. Learned a new song, "The Lament of the Irish Emigrant." It is beautiful and portrays the feelings of an Irish peasant previous to his leaving home for America. Practiced a great deal.

Thursday, Oct 6th/64.

Got up early and heard the greater part of Mattie's lessons before breakfast. Finished my "rose tatting" and am as glad as I was heartily tired of it. Pa saw Dr. Berry on the road. It is rumored that there was heavy fighting beyond Chattanooga near Altoona and the bridges over the Chattahoochee had been washed away. I trust something may happen to check the wicked career of Sherman.[157]

---

[157] General Sherman had built up quite a reputation for "Total Destruction" (war by which the enemy's infrastructure is destroyed) in his war against the South. He would begin his infamous March to the Sea on November 15, 1864.

Friday, Oct 7th/64.

Up early. Such a bright and beautiful day I have concluded to go in. Aunt Jane expects to go to Triune tomorrow. Went to see Miss Clouston. Mrs. Holcombe takes only Federal boarders![158]

Sherman's Army on its March to the Sea

Saturday, Oct 8th/64

Up late. Made some tatting and then attended to various other duties. Commenced a new song, "Dreams." Very cool; had a fire for the first time this fall. I hate to see winter coming! Mattie spent the day with Annie. Mollie is out. I wish she would come over.

Sunday, Oct 9th/64.

Up early. The coldest day we have had this fall. A white _frost_ and _ice_. Mollie came over this evening.

---

[158] Refer to the October 5, 1862 journal entry concerning Mrs. Holcombe. There seems to be a correlation with the lady and the Rebel cause.

Monday, Oct 10th

Up late. Employed in various ways to day. Much warmer but is very pleasant.

Home, Tuesday Oct 11th/64.

Up late. Pa, Mattie and I went in. Commenced a pair of stockings for Morgan Perkins, out of coarse blue yarn. Clear and a lovely day.

Wednesday, Oct 12th/64.

Up rather early. Busy today about several things.

Thursday, Oct 13th/64.

I rose early. Pa and Mat went in. Cloudy but pleasant.

Chapter Twelve
Hood's Assault on Tennessee

"She gave us much rebel news; having seen Forrest and his whole command."

After the fall of Atlanta, Sherman prepared to take the majority of his army on a march to the Sea through Georgia. Before leaving, he detached General John Schofield's Army of the Ohio to join Major General George H. Thomas in Tennessee. Meanwhile the Confederate Army of Tennessee with an inept General John Bell Hood in command began to move west. The goal was to retake Nashville. By recovering Tennessee, it was conceived that Sherman would be compelled to go back west instead of joining up with Grant in Virginia. Furthermore, Nashville with its valuable cache of supplies would deprive Sherman and be of great value to the rebel army.[159]

Maggie makes multiple entries relating rumors of the locations of General's Hood and Forrest. Beginning in November 1864, almost daily entries are made concerning events leading up to the bloody and much ill advised Battle of Franklin and the decisive Battle of Nashville.

Friday, October 14th/64.
Up late. Pa went in. It is reported that the left wing of Hood's army is near Huntsville, Ala. Cloudy.

Saturday, Oct 15th/64.
Up late. Very much surprised to see Kate Perkins and Lucy Wilson. Raining all day. Finished the baby's stocking and commenced an "umbra"[160] for Brother, as I hear that Mr. Maney intends returning south.

---

[159] Barnes, *A Brief History of the United States*, Epoch V, pages 258-259.
[160] A type of billed hat.

Sunday, Oct 16th

Up early and surprised to find it clear. Through a mistake we did not go to church. Charlie Percy came out. Aunt Jane came down Friday. I understand that the "Sacrament" is to be administered to the members of the Presbyterian Church to-day [and again in] two weeks. Several are to join and Nannie Perkins is to be baptized. An opportunity has now arrived and I must go forward and acknowledge my Redeemer before men; "now is the accepted time, when the evil days come not."[161]

Monday, Oct 17th

I rose early. Knit on my umbra, made tatting and practice a good deal. Cloudy but I think too cool to rain.

Tuesday, Oct 18th/64.

Up late. Very much surprised and delighted to see Queeny. She gave us much rebel news; having seen Forrest and his whole command. Clear and cool.

Wednesday, Oct 19th

I rose early, expecting to go to town but was prevented on account of all the horses being in use. Finished my round tatting. Queeny returned to Columbia, she makes flying trips. Cloudy.

Thursday, Oct 20th/64.

Up soon and cleaned up our room and the parlor. Pa, Sister and myself went in. Very much surprised to find that an order had been sent to Aunt Jane on Monday to vacate the house and send the keys forthwith to Capt Miles; but Aunt Jane after much difficulty succeeded in getting it released but I fear its only temporary, as it seems they are determined to root out the people of Nashville.

Friday, Oct 21st/64.

I rose quite early. Cleaned up our room as Susan [unidentified servent] is quite sick with intermittent fever. Nearly made one corset cover. Mattie is getting better: she has been sick since last Friday. Quite cool; the leaves are falling very rapidly.

---

[161] This quote is a combination of thoughts found in 2 Cor. 6:2 and Eccles. 12:1.

Saturday, Oct 22nd/64.

I rose quite early; I hope my former old habit of rising early is again being regained. Sissie and I cleaned our room and the parlor and then attended to many other duties. Clear and quite cold, I wonder if there will be church tomorrow.

Sunday, Oct 23rd/1864.

I rose late. No church today. Read my Bible and reviewed a portion of my favorite work, "Early Piety." I always find so much comfort in its pages! Clear and windy. Dr. Berry came over, he thinks there is a prospect of the troops leaving soon.

Monday, Oct 24th 1864.

I rose early and cleaned our room and parlor. Busy knitting on Brother's umbra as I am anxious to get it done as I hear his old friend Miss Sue Bettie W. intends leaving for Dixie soon. Clear and cool.

Tues. Oct 25th 1864.

I rose early. Cloudy and much warmer. Disappointed about not going to town and displayed a little temper. When shall I ever subdue this vile enemy and learn patiently to submit to the "ups and downs" of this world. Knit on my umbra, made tatting, &c.

Wed. Oct 26th 1864

I rose early. Raining steadily all day; the leaves are beginning to fall very rapidly and the wind sighs mournfully through its leafless bough's. Made some tatting.

Thurs. Oct 27th 1864.

I rose late and found the fire almost out. Cousin Ella and the baby came down. Raining at times. Received a note from Mollie this evening saying she would be out Friday but I hope to go in and attend church in town and therefore I asked her to defer her visit until some other time. I hope she will excuse me!

Friday, Oct 28th 1864.

I rose late as it was nearly 11 o'clock before we retired and I think must have been 12 before I got to sleep. Ma and I had a good long talk to day about my joining the church. She was very <u>much pleased</u>, but advised me to delay it for reasons which were very good. Nearly finished my "Umbra" and made tatting. Clear and a lovely day.

Saturday, Oct 29th 1864.

I rose very early. Ma and sister went in to see Cousin Ellen. Busy cleaning my room and the parlor, mending clothes, and washing dishes! Cloudy and cool. Ma returned <u>very late</u>. She saw Cousin Jane in town who told her Frank and Sissie would be over tomorrow.

Sunday, Oct 30th 1864.

I rose early. Ma and Mat went in to see the baby christened. As Sissie and she would stay, I concluded to go the church. Heard a very fine sermon. Frank, Kate and the two babies spent the day with us. Mollie and Nannie White came over. Ma and I came out very late. She <u>too has</u> gone forward and acknowledged her Redeemer before man by partaking of his sacrament. I hope soon to be baptized and become a member of the church; Ellen and Hettie Percy and several of my friends have been brought to a sense of their lost condition. I fervently hope that they may be consistent Christians, not only in name but in deed and truth! Clear but cool.

Monday, Oct 31st 1864.

I rose late. Received a note from Mollie asking me to come over and spend the day as she could not go to town. Of course, I complied! Commenced a umbra for Mr. Weaver as he was so kind to us when we were away from home. Clear and a lovely day.

Tuesday, November 1st 1864.

I rose late as I felt tired from my walk yesterday. Pa and sister went in; the latter intends staying in. Busy knitting and making tatting. Received a note from Sallie Read. Cloudy and raining a little.

Wednesday, Nov. 2nd 1864.

I rose early. Another gloomy day. Making tatting and hearing Mattie's lessons and practicing have been my employment. Pa went in; there is nothing new!

Thursday, Nov 3rd 1864

Up late. Rain, rain all day but it looks something like clearing up. Heard Mattie's lessons before breakfast. Finished my tatting.

Friday, Nov 4th/64.

Up late. Heard Mattie's lessons before she went in to take her lesson. Much cooler and I think will clear off. Sissie returned home bringing sad news to me. Annie Lou Moore died at the Asylum yesterday; she was in her right mind three days before God took her to His bosom. From some cause none of her relations were with her, but she expressed an earnest wish to meet them and her friends in a better world where death is known no more! She was the pet of the household and the idol of her parents having been afflicted almost from her birth. Her funeral takes place tomorrow.

On November 5, 1864 Maggie records a confusing but interesting story concerning the plight of a young Confederate soldier, who was wounded, unfit for return to service and destined for a Northern prison.

Saturday, Nov. 5th 1864.

I rose early and Sister and I cleaned the parlor before breakfast. Ma and Mattie went in and staid until dark. We were very uneasy for fear something had happened. Old Mrs. Luter has left Mrs. Holcombe as her conduct both in private and public has disgusted that patriotic lady. About two months ago, during one of the skirmishes which occurred at Triune, a young Confederate soldier was wounded so badly he could not be carried in, so he was removed to Cousin Sam Perkins; where he improved very rapidly but the physicians pronounced him unfit for service again. His father, an honest farmer from Ky. came in and made every effort for his unconditional release but all was vain, and he accordingly was sent to the hospital. Old Mrs. Luter succeeded in getting him out, the very day he was to be sent off (Friday) to some Northern prison; there to die. He slept at Mrs. Holcombe's in one of the servant's room and the next morning by nine o'clock he was out on this road with his kind deliverer, disguised as a cow driver. They reached Mrs. and Dr. Ford's about 1 o'clock, Mr. Miller [unknown man] almost exhausted. The former agreed to take him to a certain bridge on the Nolensville pike where he knew he would meet his own brethren and once more be a free man. May God speed his way and may his kind benefactors meet with a rich reward here upon earth and in heaven. Clear and a lovely day.

Maggie's thoughts are unclear with regards to exactly what happened between Mrs. Holcombe and her housekeeper Mrs. Luter. Mrs. Holcombe was a well known and respected school mistress. Her school, South Side Institute, also boarded Union officers. She may have been in danger should she been caught harboring an escaped prisoner, even one unbeknownst to her.[162]

Sunday, Nov 6th/64.

Up late as I felt unwell having a bad cold. Warm and cloudy all day and raining hard by night.

Monday, Nov 7th 1864.

Up early. Finished my corset covers. Heard Mattie's lessons and I am sorry to say displayed my vile temper. Raining, raining!

Tuesday, Nov. 8th 1864.

I rose late. Ma, sister and Mattie went in. Raining all day and thundered at times. This day decides who is to be elected President of the United States. I hope the Northern people are fully convinced that the subjugation of the South is a thing utterly impossible and are now willing, as General Scott remarked at the commencement of the war to "let our wayward sisters depart in peace." Wrote a note to Miss Hattie Moore expressing my deep sympathy for her in this, her hour of affliction, but I trust she recognizes it as coming from the hand of God, and thus submits without a murmur. Practiced a good deal.

Wednesday, Nov 9th 1864.

I rose late. Raining hard all day, but I think will clear off as it is much cooler. Busy making Mrs. Wood's little boy "Albert Lee" a dress. She and her husband and four children were compelled to leave their home in town and have nothing to live in! O! what misery and desolations follow in the strain of war! Mrs. Blunkhall went in; there is no news about the election.

---

[162] I think perhaps the ladies may have been involved in some type of underground activity. Refer to the October 4-5, 1862 and October 7, 1864 journal entries. Miss Fannie Holcombe was a daughter of Mrs. Emma Holcombe.

Thursday, Nov. 10th/64.

Up late, busy packing Pa's chest. Clear and cold. Old Lincoln[163] is certainly elected! What is to become of us!

Friday, Nov 11

I rose early. Went in. Clear and cool.

Saturday, Nov 12th/64.

Up late. Cleaned up the parlor. Have felt very unwell, sore and ache all over. Clear and a lovely day.

Sunday, Nov 13th/64.

Sick in bed all day, but my medicine acted upon me so well I feel much better. Pa and Mat went over to the church, but was so late they missed all the sermon. Passed the day profitably reading my favorite works "Early Piety" and the life of Mrs. M. L. Duncan. O! how I long to possess her many Christian virtues! Clear and very cold.

Monday, Nov 14th 1864.

Up late, as I felt quite weak. Hemmed a pair of sheets for Ma. Much warmer. I think will rain.

The Vaulx family is devastated with the loss of a near and dear relative. Maggie records the last days of her grandmother.[164]

Tuesday, Nov. 15th 1864.

Up late, Ma and sisters went in. Very sorry to hear of Grandma's being ill. Rainy.

Wednesday, Nov 16th 1864.

I rose early. Nearly finished making the baby [a] little dress. Raining all day. I wonder how dear Grandma is?

---

[163] Lincoln won a decisive re-election victory over the challenger, retired General and Democrat George B. McClellan. Lincoln won 55% of the popular vote and carried all states except Kentucky, Delaware, and McClellan's home state, New Jersey. Andrew Johnson, the ex-military governor of Tennessee is now in Washington as Lincoln's vice president.

[164] Great-grandmother Eleanor Ryburn Nichol, 1781-1864, was one of seven founding members of Nashville's First Presbyterian Church. She is buried alongside husband Josiah Nichol, daughter Margaret Dysart, and son-in-law General Robert Armstrong in Old City cemetery, Nashville, Tennessee. Robert and Margaret Dysart were Maggie's maternal grandparents.

Thursday, Nov 17th 1864.

I rose early. Ma and Pa went in, the former staid all night. Dear Grandma is <u>gone, gone, gone</u> and how many aching hearts mourn her loss. She was a true and consistent Christian and now God has taken her home. O! well may I exclaim "May my end be like hers!" <u>Raining</u>.

Friday, Nov 18th 1864.

I rose late. A gloomy, gloomy day. Ma staid all night again.

Saturday, Nov. 19th 1864.

Up late, as it was impossible for me to get to sleep. Will I never again see my kind, good Grandma! Raining but is cold and disagreeable. Cleaned my room and tended to Ma's duties.

Sunday, November 20th 1864.

Up late. Attended dear Grandma's funeral. Dr. Howell preached a melting sermon from the 14th chapter Revelations 13th verse, "And I heard a voice from Heaven saying unto me, Write, Blessed are the dead who die in the Lord from henceforth: Yea saith the Spirit, that they may rest from their labors, and their works do follow them." He was with her during her last hours and spoke of her terrible suffering, but when asked if she were willing to go, sweetly replied; "Yes, but pray that my faith may be strengthened." He did and after exhorting her family to meet her in her heavenly home, she fell asleep with the words of the first martyr on her lips, "Lord Jesus, receive my spirit." Grandma was born in Abington [county], Washington, Va. in 1781 and was married in 1796, being then in her 15th year. She moved to Knoxville soon after and thence to Nashville where she has since resided, being one of the oldest inhabitants of the place. She has been a humble follower of our Lord Jesus Christ for fifty years having joined Dr. Blackburn's first Presbyterian Church which held its meeting in the Court House that being the first of that denomination organized in Nashville. Farewell, dear Grandma! Never more shall thy affectionate family see thy calm, gentle face so lit up with Christian resignations under every earthly trial; and in hours of prosperity her heart overflowed with thankfulness to that Source from whence all our blessings flow. Oh! My Heavenly Father prepare each and every one of us for a happy reunion beyond the tomb, where our aching hearts will never again be torn by the anguish of parting. Let us all strive to imitate her pious example and when the Bridegroom calls may we be ready to go out and meet him. Very cold and cloudy.

Monday, Nov 21st 1864.

Up late. Bitter cold and is snowing all day. Ma came home. Busy attending to household duties.

Tuesday, Nov 22nd 1864.

Up early. Knitting on Mr. Weaver's umbra. All the troops from Dr. Berry's left, having been encamped there seven months (5th Iowa cavalry). Still cold.

Wednesday, Nov 23rd 1864.

I rose early. Cloudy and cold. Commenced Ma's flannel skirt. Reading at times "MLD". There is so much information to be gained from her life, and it seems as if her faith belonged to the inspired men of God.

Thursday, Nov 24th 1864.

I rose late. Several regiments of cavalry went out to day. I was very much afraid they intended camping near us as they stopped sometime at Foster's spring. Busy making Ma's flannel skirts. O! I feel at times if I could never repay her for the kind care she has ever manifested to me, and when thinking of the bitter past, my heart throbs with anguish, for many, many have been the sad hours passed by my dear mother, all of them caused by my wayward disposition, but I trust by the goodness of God, in the future to lead a Christian's life and by so doing to gladden the hearts of my fond parents. O! my Heavenly Father assist thy sinful servant, subdue her sinful passions, and may she learn from Thee to bring in to captivity every thought to the obedience of Christ.

Friday, Nov 25th 1864.

I rose early. Went in. Cousins Ella and Sam came down. O! how I missed dear Grandma's sweet and happy voice shedding a holy calm over everything around her. She had always a cheering word for all, and no matter how much her mind was troubled, her face always seemed to say "I have long since cast my burden on the Lord." Much warmer. Many rumors are afloat today. Some say Hood's army is at Pulaski. Cousin Sam heard there was heavy fighting at Columbia and thinks it must be so as he heard firing in that direction about 4 o'clock. O! I am so anxious to see our relatives and friends, but have been disappointed so often and afraid to look for their coming.

Saturday, Nov 26th/64.

Up late. Cleaned the parlor before breakfast. A great many troops went out, and in the course of an hour they returned. Pa is quite sick, has something like "cramp colic."[165] Dr. Bowling came out. I hope he may relieve him. Raining all day.

Sunday, Nov 27th 1864.

I rose early. Sorry to find it raining as I was anxious to attend church. Read my Bible and hymns. Wrote a long letter to dear Sallie Read, and in it I urged her to pay attention to religion and "remember her Creator in the days of her youth." I hope it may have the desired effect, for I love Sallie dearly and shall ever pray for her spiritual welfare. Troops going and coming all day.

Monday, Nov 28th 1864.

Up late. Dr. Bowling came out to see Pa who has an attack of "jaundice." Large number of negroes came in today, about a thousand, some walking, some riding in army waggons and on horse-back. Poor ignorant degraded creatures; I cannot help but pity them. It is said that fifteen or twenty negroes are shot every night. Several weeks ago, Andy Johnson made a speech to them, congratulating them on having gained their freedom, when a Federal soldier cheered for McClelland,[166] where upon the negroes bayoneted him and fired at him several times. I understand his companions in arms have vowed vengeance on every negro wearing the U.S. uniform. I trust they are getting their dose of negro equality and are intent to let them remain in their time sphere of life. Cloudy and warm.

Tuesday, Nov. 29th 1864.

I rose early. Went in town. I was glad to find Aunt Jane so cheerful, notwithstanding another order has come for her to vacate the dear home of her happy childhood. Great excitement among

---

[165] Cramp colic is a health issue found in horse's small intestines. Pa was suffering from sympton s comparable to those he had seen when his horses had this condition. Strange comparison, but the family at Mount Alban had many horses.

[166] General George B. McClellan, Democratic presidential candidate in the 1864 election. He supported the war but not the policy of the Lincoln administration.

the Yankees as it is rumored that Forrest was this side of Franklin. Mrs. Hickman told me she saw a lady from Harpeth who had seen Pillow Humphreys and several others of my friends.

Wednesday, Nov. 30th 1864.

Had quite an exciting time last night. Several companies of Federal cavalry encamped at Foster's spring; three or four of the wretches came up, searched through the negro cabins, stole their sausage meat and frightened them considerably. It was quite amusing to see them running in the house with all their budgets, &c. Great excitement on the road. Large numbers of waggons are now encamped in our bottoms at the mouth of Thompson lane. Clear and a lovely day. Received a note from Mollie. O! she is such a dear girl.

Chapter Thirteen
The Battle for Nashville

"Bid farewell to my home, perhaps never again to see it!"

After Hood crossed the Tennessee River, and after a severe struggle at Franklin, he drove Schofield's army before him, shut up General George Thomas within the fortifications at Nashville. For two weeks little was done. Great disappointment was felt at the North over the retreat to Nashville, and still more at Thomas's delay in that city. Grant ordered him to move, and had actually started to take charge of his troops in person, when he learned of the splendid victory his slow but sure general had achieved.

When Thomas was fully ready, he suddenly sallied out on Hood, and in a terrible two-days battle drove the Confederate forces out of their entrenchments into headlong flight. The Union cavalry thundered upon their heels with remorseless energy. The infantry followed closely behind. The entire Confederate army, except the rear-guard, which fought bravely to the last, was dissolved into a rabble of demoralized fugitives, who at last escaped across the Tennessee. For the first time in the war an army was destroyed. The object which Sherman hoped to obtain when he moved on Atlanta was accomplished by Thomas, three hundred miles away. Sherman could now go where he pleased with little danger of meeting a foe. The war in the West, so far as any great movements were concerned, was finished.[167]

During the month of December, the Vaulx family would find themselves changing homes for safety reasons no less than five times. Each time the family moved, the battle would come to them. This brings to memory the Wilmer McLean family, who in order to escape the war, left their Manassas, Va. home after the First Battle of Bull Run, only to have the war come home to their doorstep at Appomattox.

---

[167] Barnes, *A Brief History of the United States*, Epoch V, pages 258-259.

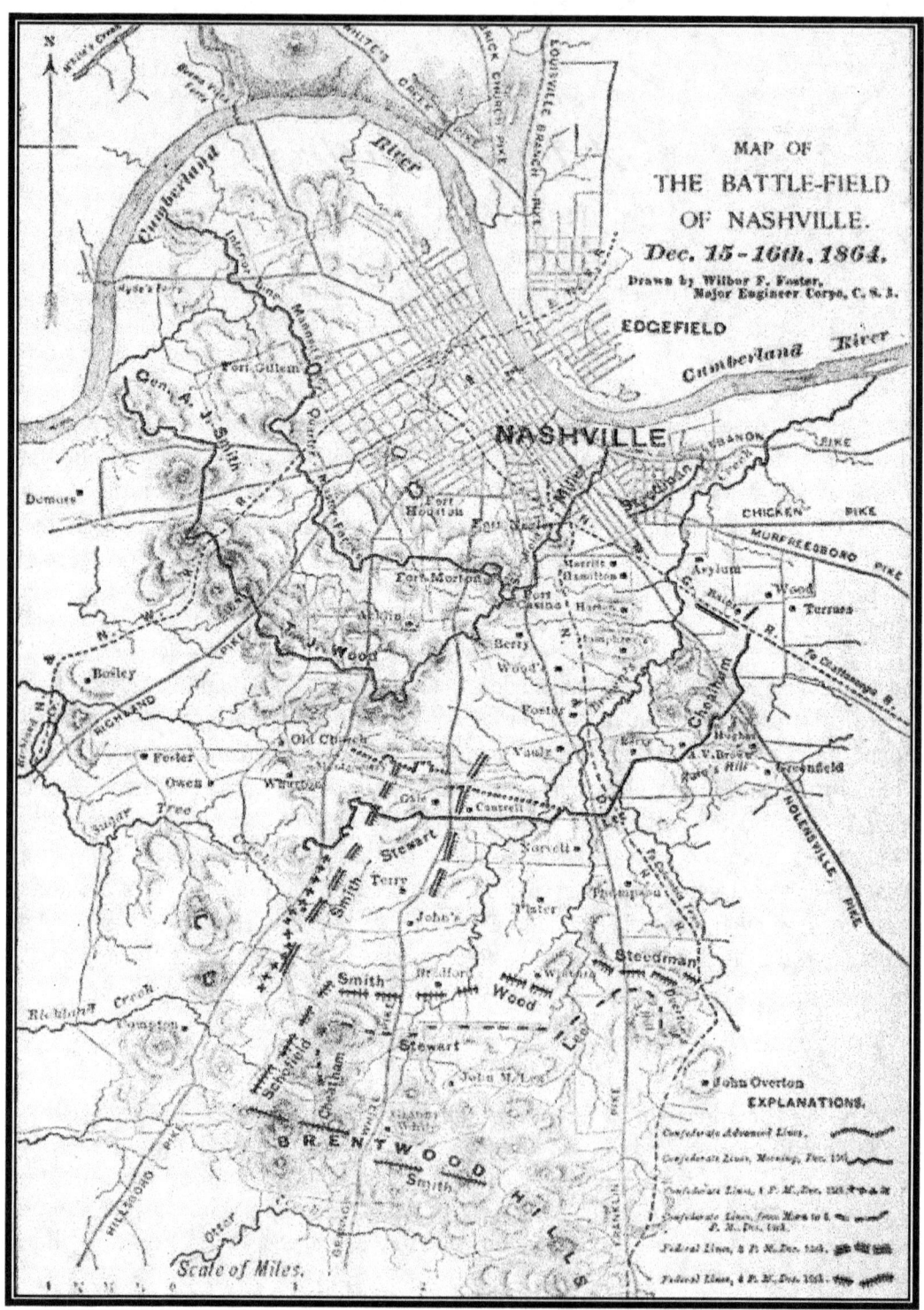

Map of the Battle of Nashville, 1864

On December 2, 1864, there are skirmishes in the area of Thompson Lane. The same day, a stray musket ball comes through Mount Alban's dining room window. Later that evening, a Federal officer invites the Vaulx family out to observe the numerous campfires in next-door neighbor John Thompson's woods. Pa wants them to go into town for safety but, due the restrictions concerning the federal line, they are compelled to remain outside Nashville.

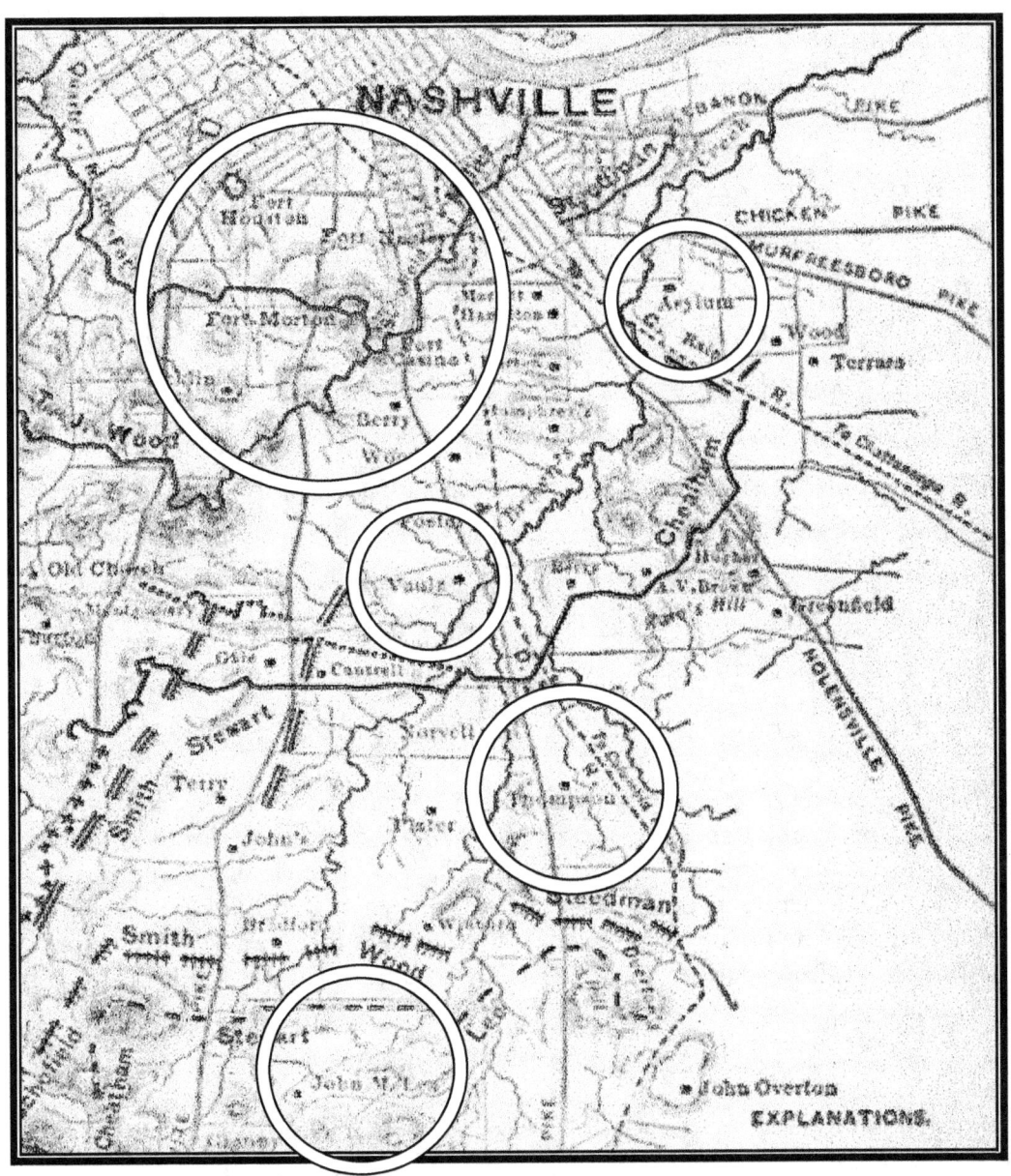

Detail of Map noting (from top) three of Nashville's seven forts, the Asylum, the Vaulx home, the Thompson home (Glen Leven), and the John M. Lee home.

Home, Thursday December 1st 1864.

I rose this morning late. All the troops from Columbia and Franklin (Schofields and Woods corps) are now here. Many think there will be a fight and others that they will go to Kentucky. The negroes became so frightened they all left, but I think it was all a premeditated thing. Sissie and I got supper and succeeded very well this being our first attempt. From all accounts there must have been desperate fighting at Franklin.[168] I understand all our neighbors have left, but I hope Pa will let us remain as I feel confident God will protect us if we put our confidence in Him and do our duty.

Friday, December 2nd 1864.

Up early. Sissie and I cleaned our room; set the table and then prepared breakfast. After getting through with the kitchen, Sissie and I ironed our clothes. Several confederates made their appearance at the mouth of Thompson lane, which caused a regiment of Yankees to go out and after going through many military evolutions they returned. There are now pickets posted at every tree in our yard and constant firing is kept up between the two parties. A ball went through the dining room window, broke the secretary glass, but did no serious damage. About dark a federal officer told Pa to come out and look at the light which shone as far as the eye could reach; it seemed as if a thousand fires were going in John Thompson woods. O! what is to become of us. Cloudy and warm. Andrew [family servant] went in as he was "afraid of the bullets." Wrote a note to Aunt Jane; Mat is still in town. Pa is anxious for us to go in, but it is impossible as no one is allowed to pass the pickets. So glad!!

The morning of December 3 finds Mount Alban still under Federal control. Just after noon, the Rebel army advances driving the Federals toward Nashville. After heavy skirmishes, the opposing forces form up their battle lines leaving Mount Alban between them. Brother Joe realizing that the home is in direct danger moves the family from harm's way to Cousin John Lea's estate, Lealand, a distance of three miles away. The family would be at Cousin John's for eleven days. The main question: would this distance offer safety from the approaching danger. Only time would tell.

---

[168] The Battle of Franklin was fought on November 30, 1864, at Franklin, TN. It would prove to be one of the worst disasters of the war for the Confederate Army. Confederate Lt. General John Bell Hood's Army of Tennessee conducted numerous frontal assaults against fortified positions occupied by the Union forces under Maj. General John M. Schofield. Hood was unable to break through or to prevent Schofield from making a planned, orderly withdrawal to Nashville.

Saturday, December 3rd 1864.

Up at daybreak expecting to hear a terrific cannonading, but all seemed quiet along the lines. Made some coffee and warmed some crackers which comprised our breakfast. Last night I pack my handsome diamond ring, valued at $600 and many other little valuables in my desk and put it in the cellar, but upon going to the porch I found the cellar full of vile Yankees, who had broken the desk open and stolen my ring, pens and &c. O' I was _so_ _mad_ I actually _cried_! Everything is in confusion and none of us know _what_ _to_ _do_. About two o' clock our skirmishes advanced driving the Yankees to James Wood's hill after having a pretty sharp fight in our woods. I can't describe my feelings after seeing our _dear_ _boys_. They all endeared us to leave as our home would be between two fires. The captain kindly offered to take a note to brother whose division is now on the Nolensville pike, Genl. Cheatham having his headquarters at Greenfield's. We immediately commenced packing our wearing apparel and bed clothes leaving many dear things to their fate. Dear Brother came over about dark. O! how I hugged and kissed him. He is very fleshly and enjoys uninterrupted health. He ordered us to leave as the Confederate lines were advancing. Orville Ewing and several officers came up. O! what a sad night this is! Brother returned about ten o'clock bringing an ambulance, two waggons and a guard composed of young [men] from his old company. Bid farewell to my home, perhaps never again to see it! Reached Cousin John Lea's about daylight, completely worn out!

Lealand, Sunday, December 4th 1864.

Brother returned to his command today, as business rendered it impossible for him to remain longer with us. All of Cheatham's staff was killed or wounded at Franklin, but himself and of course he has double duty to perform. Heard heavy firing all day. Clear and delightful out.

Lealand, Dec. 5th

I never slept as sound as I did last night. Brother brought us another wagon load of provisions and I fear this will be our last opportunity. O! I feel almost crazy. Dear Pa bears up manfully under this severe earthly trial. O! I hope God is the Friend to whom he looks.

Lealand, Dec. 6th/1864.

Up late. Bob Brown and several friends came over. O! they are so cheerful, but speak rather censuring of Hood for bringing on the fight at Franklin, which must have been a bloody engagement[169] all so unnecessary!

Lealand, Dec. 7th

Up late. Poor little Lou died last night. How distressed Mattie will be! Joe Percy came over, I fear he is doing little good! Cloudy and warm. O! how I miss my dear piano and I fear it will be destroyed or taken by the Yankees.

Lealand, Thursday Dec 8th.

Up early as the table had to be set. Joe Percy returned to camp. I am sorry to see him so trifling! Joe Gale and Amy Bradford came up. O! I feel so little inclined to entertain, but nevertheless I am glad to see them. Cloudy, but much cooler.

Lealand, Friday Dec. 9th.

Up late. Bitter cold, sleeting and snowing all day. Busy knitting. Heard a distressing piece of news, viz [namely] the burning of Judge Humphreys and Mr. James Woods houses. O! so much wanton destruction of property! Very little firing today. How I pity the poor soldier in the trenches, but they all seem perfectly contented.

Lealand, Saturday Dec. 10th.

Up early. Very cold and cloudy. Mr. Blunkhall and family came up to occupy a vacant house of Cousin John's. He had been to [our] house and says, "We would never know the place for the destruction of timber and trenches cut through the place." O! I feel as if I am houseless and at times such agony comes over me that I almost wish that I was dead!

---

[169] The Battle of Franklin was one of the bloodiest of the war. The cost to the Confederate army was staggering. Of the 27,000 rebels thrown into battle, there were 6,252 casualties; 1,750 killed, 3,800 wounded, and 702 missing in action. The military leadership was decimated, including the loss of perhaps the best division commander of either side, Confederate General Patrick Cleburne. Fourteen Confederate commanders were lost. The six generals killed or mortally wounded included Cleburne, John Carter, John Adams, Hiram Granbury, States Rights Gist, and Otho Strahl. The battle strength of the Union army was about equal with 27,000 men but the losses were much fewer with 189 killed, 1033 wounded, and 1104 missing. The Confederate loss at this battle would play a pivotal role two weeks later during the Battle of Nashville.

Lealand, Sunday Dec. 11th/1864.

What a <u>cold</u>, <u>cold</u> day this has been. Passed the day properly reading, "Sermons of Consolations." I found much information in it and hope to profit by the instructions it contains. Dear Brother came to night and staid until twelve. He was dressed in his full Confederate uniform and looks so noble. Hated to see him return to camp, but the house is so small he cannot be accommodated.

Lealand, Dec. 12th/64.

Up early. Jimmie Woods came up. He is looking well and is in fine spirits, not withstanding his dear home is in ruins. Miss Mary Hadley and Major Clare from Baltimore are to be married at Brentwood[170] today. I think that it is ridiculous for anyone to marry during such times as these. Clear and cold.

Brother Joe
Major Joseph Vaulx

Lealand, December 13th.

Up late, Dr. Elliott and Joe Wood's residences were burned last night. I expect everyday to hear that our dear home being in ashes. Cloudy and warmer. I wish I could see Mattie!

Lealand, Wednesday December 14th.

Up late. Finished my socks. Brother came tonight and then returned. Cloudy and raining. Heavy firing all day.

At daylight, on December 15, 1864, the Federal army makes its advance and the Battle of Nashville begins. By noon, the battle which had begun on the right flank, moved to the left flank, and by early afternoon, Cousin John Lea's home was in grave danger. The Vaulx family leaves during late afternoon and takes refuge along the Franklin Pike. Meanwhile, the Federals had greatly reduced the Confederate lines and both sides settled down for the night.

---

[170] The wedding took place at Traveller's Rest, the home of John Overton. Major William Clare was a member of General Hood's staff. The major would participate in the upcoming battle while his new bride would stay with the Overton family.

Lealand, Thursday Dec. 15th.

Up late. Heavy firing to day about 3 o'clock. The shells flew around the house so intensively we were compelled to leave. Went to old man Alford's. About 12 o'clock at night Cousin John sent Ma word to come over and bring our clothes away as batteries were stationed at the front gate and a bloody battle would occur in the morning. Brother took dinner with us! His command was forming their lines of battle when we left. Clear and pleasant.

By late morning of December 16, 1864, heavy fighting is again underway around Nashville. The Vaulx family having fled Cousin John Lea's home is now at the Franklin Pike home of neighbor, Robert Alford. By early afternoon of the second day, the battle lines had again shifted finding the family in its midst. Confederate and Federal forces were battling all around the Alford home. If not for Generals Knight and Hammond, the house would have been burned. It is unknown why these generals prevented the house from being destroyed. After enduring a horrendous day, the families would witness the retreat of Hood's rear guard.

Cheatham's Retreat

December, 16th 1864 Friday.

O! what a day this has been. Most terrific firing all day and many think our noble army is retreating. Our worst fears were realized. About 5 o'clock we witnessed the remnants of

Cheatham's division passed by, hotly pursuit by the vile Yankees. One Confederate was wounded; while we were all collected in one room, and the bullets were flying around, he came to the door and asked so piteously to be let in. Of course, we were compelled to refuse his urgent request, as the Yankee cavalry were all around the house plundering the smoke house. O! I shall never forget this night. Every horse, chicken was swept away like magic; and had it not been for Genl. Knight and Hammond, the house would have been burnt. Poor old Mrs. Alford how she was cursed and abused by the thieving wretches on account of her pleading for her storeroom supplies. Commence raining by night.

On December 17, 1864, Maggie laments another sad birthday. Cousin John Lea and family are now at the Alford home. Cousin John sends his foreman to check on Lealand; his return brings a sorry assessment. The house was found to be heavily pillaged. Regardless, the Lea family along with Maggie returns to Lealand.

Saturday, Dec. 17th /64.

Another sad birthday. I wish I could hear from my dear brother. Cousin John sent Mack out to Lealand who brought a sorry account of things. The home had been pillaged and everything destroyed. Raining all day. I think this is the filthiest place I ever was in and the inmates so unaccommodating! We try to make the best of it, hoping to see brighter days, although the future is veiled by <u>dark</u> hovering clouds!

"Lealand" Sunday 18th

Once more at Cousin John's and a desolate waste everything presents. Everything <u>gone</u> and many of the outhouses are almost demolished. It was really laughable to see us eating with our <u>fingers</u> and nothing to drink out of but <u>one cup</u> which was kindly left us by the Yankees. Ma and Pa remained at Mrs. Alford's to look after our plunder. Cloudy and raining.

Lealand, Monday, Dec. 19th /64.

Raining so hard today we could not send for Ma and Pa. Leut. Fielding Meigs and a squad of his negro soldiers came out for the batteries that were given up by the Confederates. O! I felt such contempt for him. Cousin John's foreman came out and brought us some provisions which were thoughtfully received. It is turning much colder.

Lealand, Tuesday, Dec. 20th/64.

Ma and Pa came over. Cousin Lizzie [Lea] went over to Mr. Overton's. Heard from home, and what a distressing account it was! The house has almost been torn to pieces by shot and shell. Mr. Woods went down and reports that the piano is still there but the cover gone. O! I hope that it may be saved. Sleeting and snowing.

Mr. James Woods, whose own home had burned during the days before the battle, is asked by Pa to occupy Mount Alban until they could return. A family servant give Maggie some bad new; he reports the piano left at Mount Alban is now gone. The July 28th 1862 Safeguard Order is still in effect but has very little results. This is a fine example of the lawlessness of battle.

Lealand, Wednesday, Dec. 21st/64.

Up late. Pa prevailed upon Mr. Woods to go down and occupy the house until some arrangements could be made. O! I hope everything can be saved! It is very cold and now snowing. Pa complains of his foot resulting from cold and exposure.

Lealand, Dec. 22nd 1864.

Andrew came up this morning and brought me a sad piece of news. My dear piano is gone and every carpet, chair, bed and bedding has been carried off! O! I felt as if my heart would break, to think of our once happy home, made desolate by the Yankees! I think that it would have been a relief to know that it is burnt, as it is impossible for us to live there again. Clear and cold. Cousin John's cook Eliza left today.

Due to the massive damage inflicted upon Mount Alban, the Vaulx family could not return home. They would be forced to move to Nashville and spend the rest of the war with Aunt Jane Ramsey Brown. Sections of Aunt Jane's house and grounds were still occupied by the Federals.

Lealand, Friday, Dec. 23rd, 1864.

Up late. Pa sent part of our things to town. Uncle William Nichol[171] sent a carriage out for us. Reached town about dark and found the two parlors occupied by Federals, and an order had been sent to vacate the two upper rooms. Clear and cold.

---

[171] William Nichol was born Feb. 12, 1800 in Abingdon, VA. He was the son of Josiah and Eleanor Ryburn Nichol. As a small boy, he came with his parents to live in Nashville. Nichol became a respected businessman and president of the Bank of Tennessee. He was an early business

Nashville, Saturday, Dec. 24th.

O! so tired and heartsick! Genl. Miller has released the house, but I fear it is only temporary as they seem determined to have the home.

Sunday, December 25th.

What a sad Christmas this is! Pa is quite sick with his foot. O! it seems as if all our troubles comes at once, but I trust we will be repaid for our troubles some day. Cousin Ella and Sam and the baby came down. Cloudy and I think will be raining soon. Charlie carried Mr. Woods some provisions to day.

Monday, December 26, 1864.

Up late and I have felt unwell. Helped Ellen clean the room. Charlie has found my piano. I immediately wrote General Miller to give me an order for it. He did so and I intend on sending it to a safe place for safekeeping. Hettie is much better. Looks like clearing off.

Tuesday, Dec. 27th 1864.

I rose late feeling very unwell. Reading a very interesting southern work ["Micaria"] O! how I long for my once happy home, rendered doubly dear to me now, as a cruel war has almost landed it in ruins. Tom came in to get medicine for the guards. Troops are now encamped in the yard to the door. Cloudy and drizzling all day.

Wednesday, December, 28th 1864.

I rose early. Pa and I went out home. Words fail to depict the desolation which meets the eye at every turn. O! it is heart-rending and time will never efface the cruel marks of war! Very cold and clear. The Federals vacated the front parlor and we hope will finally give up the whole house.

Thursday, Dec 29th 1864.

I rose early. Assisted Aunt Jane in cleaning the dining-room. Cousins Ella and Sam returned to-day. Missed dear little Nannie's loud <u>laugh</u> and her bright face so radiant with childish happiness! Hettie still continues to improve. Clear and cold.

---

partner of Joseph Vaulx, Sr. He lived with his family at BelAir on Lebanon Road from 1835 until his death and he served as Nashville mayor from 1835 to 1837. Nichol died November 23, 1878 and is buried at Mt. Olivet Cemetery.

Friday, Dec 30th 1864.

I rose late, feeling very unwell. Helped Aunt Jane in various ways and then went down town. Very much surprised to see Theora Branch who has returned from Dixie after an absence of two years. O! how changed is our once happy neighborhood! Cloudy and is now raining!

Saturday, December 31st 1864.

The last day of this sad year! How many more such will I have to record? Very much surprised to find a heavy snow, but clear and intensely cold. Leslie Nichol and Evy Bradford came to see Hettie this morning. The latter seems very cheerful, not withstanding her home is a wreck! Surely it must be artificial!

The close of the fourth year of war brought these results. The Confederates had gained the battles of Olustee, Sabine Cross Roads, the Wilderness, Bermuda Hundred, Spotsylvania, New Market, Cold Harbor, and Monocacy; had defeated the expeditions into Florida and the Red River country, the two attacks upon Petersburg, and one against Fort Fisher, and yet held Grant at bay before Richmond. They had, however, lost ground on every side. Of the States east of the Mississippi, only North and South Carolina were fully retained. Mississippi, Alabama, Tennessee, Virginia, Georgia and Florida were overrun by the Union armies. The Federals had gained the battles of Pleasant Hill, Resaca, Dallas, Kennesaw, Atlanta, Winchester, Fisher's Hill, Cedar Creek and Nashville. They had captured Fort de Russy, the forts in Mobile harbor, and Fort McAlister, and had taken Atlanta and Savannah. Sherman had swept across Georgia; Sheridan had devastated the Shenandoah, driving its defenders before him; Thomas had annihilated Hood's army; Grant held Lee firmly grasped at Richmond and the navy swept the entire coast.[172]

Maggie closes the year 1864 with the following journal entry:

1864. There is something in the very act of prayer that for a time stills the violence of passion and elevates and purifies the affections. When affliction presses hard, and the weakness of human nature looks around, in vain for support, how natural is the impulse which throws us on our knees before Him who has laid our chastening upon us! And how secure, how encouraging, is the hope that accompanies our supplication for his pity!

---

[172] Barnes, *A Brief History of the United States*, Epoch V, page 270.

Chapter Fourteen
Nashville, the Aftermath

"They are all rascals from the highest to the lowest!"

The 1865 Union campaign plan was very simple. The end of the war was clearly at hand. In the South, Sherman was to move north from Savannah against Johnston, and then join Grant in the final attack upon Lee. General Philip Sheridan, with ten thousand troopers, had swept down from the Shenandoah, cut the railroads north of Richmond, and taken his place in the Union lines before Petersburg. Wilson, with thirteen thousand horsemen, rode at large through Alabama and Georgia, and at Macon held a line of retreat from Virginia westward. General George Stoneman, with five thousand cavalry from Tennessee, poured through the passes of the Alleghenies and waited in North Carolina for the issue in Virginia. In the meantime Sherman had given his troops only a month's rest in Savannah. Early in February, they were put in motion northward. There was no waiting for roads to dry or for bridges to be built, but the troops swept on like a tornado. Rivers were waded, and one battle was fought while the water was up to the shoulders of the men. The army, sixty thousand strong, moved in four columns, with a front of more than fifty miles. Cavalry and foragers swarmed on the flanks. Before them was terror; behind them were ashes.[173]

The New Year of 1865 continues to be a time of family hardship. Joseph Vaulx spends much time trying to recover family items lost during the Federal occupation of Mount Alban. The family stays in Nashville. The Vaulxs' beloved Mount Alban has suffered significant damage during the late Battle of Nashville. General Thomas, the Rock of Chickamauga, has stood again. General Hood's debacle at Franklin, along with his misguided stand at Nashville, results in his army's decimation. The dreams of taking Nashville and victory in the Western theater of war are gone.

Maggie's journal entry for the 1865 New Year opens with, *"New Year! 1865!!"*

---

[173] Barnes, *A Brief History of the United States*, Epoch V, pages 270-272.

Nashville, Sunday, January 1st 1865.

Up late as it was so bitter cold to leave our warm beds! The New Year is again upon us and oh! how many happy friends are made desolate, that was once the scenes of joy and gladness on such occasions as this. O! will it always continue thus? I put my trust on God knowing that He can still the angry hands of war! The coldest day we have had this winter. How many poor creatures are suffering for food or raiment and when I compare my lot to theirs I feel that I am truly blessed and my gratitude to God who is the giver of all good is beyond expression. Passed the day profitably reading the Scriptures.

Monday, Jan. 2nd 1865.

Up late. Frank Morgan came to see us and was anxious for Sister and me to go out and stay. O! how thankful I am that I have so many kind relatives and friends to care for us now! Much warmer and cloudy.

Tuesday, Jan. 3rd 1865.

I rose late! Busy mending stockings which has been sadly neglected for several weeks. Pa still continues his endeavors to find our <u>stolen property</u>, but he meets with but little success. O! what trying times these are, but is all ordained by God for some wise purpose. Mr. Wood came to tell us the Federals (I mean the Yankees) are cutting all the wood left by the Confederates on our place. Cloudy.

Wednesday, January 4th 1865.

Up early. Ellen and I paid a visit to Ellen Fall and Aunt Sallie. Very pleasant out yet the mud is almost intolerable. Pa is still trying to gather up the fragments, but his efforts meet with little success. O! the vileness that exists in this army. They are <u>all</u> rascals from the highest to the lowest!

Thursday, January 5th/ 65.

Up late as my sleep were disturbed by unhappy dreams. Busy mending my dresses and trying to get our clothes in order. Clear but much warmer.

Friday, January 6th 1865.

Up late. I wonder where <u>dear brother</u> is. My love for him increases each day and many are the fervent prayers I offer for his safe return. Raining all day and now is cold and snowing. When will this horrid weather break up? It throws a gloom over everything! I try to look on the bright side of this gloomy picture and I hope ere long to be happy with the dear absent ones of our already afflicted family.

Saturday, January 7th 1865.

I rose early, sorry to find the ground covered with snow. Kate Perkins came to see me and insisted upon my going out, but my clothes are in such a condition I could not accept her invitation. Clear and cold.

Sunday, January 8th, 1865.

Up late. Ellen and I attended the Episcopal Church. Very muddy and disagreeable. Spent the day very profitably.

Monday, January 9th, 1865.

I rose early. Busy knitting Pa's socks. Raining all day. Gloomy and despondent!

Tuesday, January 10th, 1865.

Up late. Ellen and I cleaned our room. Nothing of interest. Snowing at times! Unwell.

Wednesday, January 11th, 1865.

I can scarcely sit up to write, as I have a severe, throbbing headache. Nothing new. Frank again came in to day to take us out. How kind they all are!

Maggie is back at Hedge Lawn spending some time with the Morgans. The editorial page of the *Daily Times and True Union*, a pro-Union Nashville newspaper, made her the object of publication during the first month of the new year.

The January 14, 1865 edition published a letter from one of Maggie's friends to her. Maggie recorded the following, "*Letter from <u>Queeny</u> to me being published in the <u>Times</u> edited by <u>Mercer</u>, and he threatens to publish more. I now remember of having left my portfolio of old letters at <u>home</u> and they are now in the hands of that vile scoundrel.*"

Apparently Samuel C. Mercer, the *Daily Times and True Union* editor took exception to Queeny's reference to "Mercer Hall" and threatened legal action. The *Times* publication also reveals why some Southern people had to take a false oath of allegiance in order to preserve their property. Maggie's parents were surely in this category.

The text of the *Daily Times and True Union* article, courtesy of the Tennessee State Library & Archives, follows as it appeared in the paper:

December 29th, 1864.

Why a Young Lady of Columbia Became Loyal.

We had placed in our hands some days ago, by an officer, a pack of female letters, picked up in one of the large deserted mansions in this vicinity during the great fight. The owner of the house probably left in too great a hurry to allow the ladies to gather up their correspondence. If the young lady who wrote the letter from which the following passage is extracted does not immediately change the name of "Mercer Hall," we shall prosecute her for defamation:

Mercer Hall
Near Columbia, Aug. 20, 1864

My own dear Maggie: - You have heard, ere this, of the death of Captain Erwin. We had all become much attached to him. He was one of the best and noblest of young men, and I feel certain that he is now in a better world. Willie Forrest is also dead. Is it not heart-rendering to have our noble boys butchered by these vandals and negroes? But I must not write such "treason," for next week I expect to become very "loyal." I tell you I am thinking strongly of taking the oath. You know Pa's property is to be sold on the third of October. By taking that oath I can save mine and Annie's portion of the property, which was settled on us by our mother. I feel sometimes that I would rather take it than to be poor and dependent all my life; and with what I will save perhaps I can one day help my exiled father and brother. What do you think about it? Write immediately, and if you hear that I have taken it, tell your parents my reasons for doing so.

It is reported that Player Martin is to be married very soon to a Miss Cobb of Mississippi.

I scarcely believe it, for he is a mere boy, but I suppose he thinks that as he is a soldier he deserves a wife. So think I, and hope he may get a good one.   *   *   *   We heard from Pa and Buddie a few days ago. Buddie is on Uncle Gideon's staff (General Pillow). He ranks as Captain. I tell you I am very proud of my dear Brother.

And this from a lady—whether young or bald-headed, beautiful, or ugly as sin, we cannot say—who claims to belong to the Southern aristocracy! For the sake of a few dollars, and to avoid the disgrace of working for a living, she is ready to swear to support the Government, while she secretly writes fulsome eulogies on officers of Gen. Pillow's staff.

Saturday, January 14th/65.

Up late, feeling better but still weak. Received a letter from Mollie in answer to a long one I wrote to her a few days since. In it she speaks of a letter from Queeny to me being published in the "Times" edited by Mercer, and he threatens to publish more. I now remember of having left my portfolio of old letters at home and they are now in the hands of that vile scoundrel. Kate Perkins and Cousin Lou Ewing came to see us. I am almost afraid to go to the country for so many robberies are committed. Cousin John, Mrs. Bradford and many others were visited by these marauders and as all guards have been called, it only gives license to the most shocking acts of wantonness. O! the times are terrible and no man can call his life his own. Oh! God look down in tender mercy upon our afflicted land and raise thy rod of chastisement.

Sunday, January 15th 1865.

I rose late being still unwell. Reading my Bible and was struck by the 5th chapter of Lamentations of Jeremiah.[174] Oh! It is truly applicable to our times. Clear and lovely.

Monday, January 16th/65.

A month today since we witnessed the retreat of our noble army, many of whom are never to return to their homes. Ellen received some precious keepsakes of dear Tom's sent to her by

---

[174] Reference is to the sorrow felt by the Old Testament prophet Jeremiah over the plight of Jerusalem. The city that he had tried to save was at last taken captive by the Babylonian armies under King Nebuchadnezzar.

Brother from Pulaski. O! he was a noble boy and I feel confident that he has been taken to the Saviour whom he loved so dearly. Received a long letter from Mrs. Hattie Moore in answer to one I wrote to her some time since. O! what a happy death bed dear Annie had! Her last words were, "Glory! Glory!" May I emulate her many virtues and cherish her memory unfadingly in my head. Cousin Sam came down. Clear and delightful out.

Tuesday January 17th, 1865.

I rose early. Aunt Jane and Hettie went to Triune. Went to see dear Miss Clouston. Clear and cold. Unusually sad to day. It is reported that Ft. Fisher[175] which commands the entrance to Wilmington has fallen. O! That his horrid war would cease!

Wednesday, January 18th, 1865.

Dear Cousin Jane came and assisted on my going out. Clear, but cold.

A month goes by; Maggie has returned from Hedge Lawn and is now with the family in Nashville. It has been three years since the surrender and ensuing occupation of Nashville. Maggie records the third anniversary of the "Great Panic."

Nashville, February 7th, 1865.

Again in the city after an absence of three weeks, which were pleasantly spent at "Hedge Lawn." During that time we have had very severe weather, the thermometer being several degrees below zero. Frank put up splendid ice. I hope he may enjoy it. Last night we had a heavy fall of snow.

February 8th, 1865. (Wed)

Up late. Busy knitting Nannie Perkins stockings and hope to finish them soon.

Thursday, February 9th, 1865.

Up late. Finished Nannie's stockings. Cousin Ann Carter and Laura Holloway came to see us. Cold and clear. Mr. James Woods is living at our place as [the] government has taken possession of his brothers. When will these lawless times end!

---

[175] Fort Fisher was the last Confederate port whereby supplies could be brought in to aid Lee's beleaguered army at Petersburg.

February 10th, 1865.

Up late. Busy making my neck-tie. Delightful out. Nothing of any interest.

Saturday, February 11th, 1865.

Up early. Nothing, nothing to write. Clear!

Sunday, February 12th, 1865.

Up late. Reading my precious Bible and finding so much comfort in its pages. Pa is very gloomy on account of hearing of the severe illness of his old friend Mr. Correy. They have long been devoted friends, but I hope their friendship is in Christ. Clear.

Monday, February 13th, 1865.

Up late. After getting through our household affairs, Sister and I paid a visit to Mollie. Three months since we had seen each other. Very unhappy today on account of displaying my temper. Clear.

Tuesday, Feb. 14th.

I rose late. Invited to a party to night. O! who can engage in such heartless gayety during such times as these! O! it is almost heart rending to witness the want of feeling shown by some of our people. Cloudy.

Wednesday, Feb. 15th.

Up late. Helping Aunt Jane in making her gowns.

Thursday, Feb. 16th/65.

Rose early. The third anniversary of the "Panic". It is a clear day. I feel very small today.

Chapter Fifteen
War's End

"O! our noble heroic band have fought most valiantly for four years and have at last to submit to the superiority of numbers!"

William Tecumseh Sherman

On February 17, 1865 Columbia, South Carolina was captured and Charleston, thus threatened in the rear, was evacuated the next day. In this emergency, Johnston was again called to the command of the Confederate forces. He gathered their scattered armies and vigorously opposed Sherman's advance. After fierce engagements at Averysboro on March 15 Bentonville on March 18, he was driven back, and Raleigh was captured on April 13.

The Federal siege of Richmond began in late March. General Lee's position was fast becoming desperate. His only hope lay in getting out of Richmond and joining with Johnston. Their united armies might prolong the struggle. Grant was determined to prevent this, and compel Lee to surrender, as he had forced Pemberton[176] to do. Lee determined to attack Grant's right, in order to hide his plan of retreat, and especially in the hope that Grant would send troops from the left to succor the threatened point. In that case, he would slip out, with the main body of his army, by the nearest road southward, which ran close by the Union left. The assault was made on Fort Steadman, but it was a signal failure. Three thousand out of five thousand engaged in the attempt were lost. To make matters worse, a Union assault followed directly afterward, and a portion of the Confederate outer defenses was captured. Thus Grant's grip was only tightened. He had made no change in the position of his troops, and this sortie neither hastened nor delayed the grand, final attack. This movement began Wednesday

---

[176] This reference is to the earlier Fall of Vicksburg. Confederate General John C. Pemberton surrendered the Rebels' Mississippi River stronghold to Grant in July 1863. With the surrender, the Confederate areas east and west of the river were sealed off from each other. The Union's divide-and-conquer policy was falling into place.

morning, March 29. Sheridan with his cavalry of nine thousand sabers and heavy columns of infantry, pushed out from Grant's left wing to get around in Lee's rear. Cloaking his plan by a thick screen of cavalry, to conceal the movements of his infantry, he threw a heavy force behind the Confederate position at Five Forks Assailed in front and rear, the garrison was overwhelmed, and five thousand men were taken prisoners. The effect of this brilliant affair was at once to render Lee's position untenable. His right was turned, and his rear threatened. The next morning at four o'clock, the Union army advanced in an overwhelming assault along the whole front. By noon, the rebel line of entrenchments before which the Army of the Potomac had lain so long, was broken, and thousands of prisoners were captured. That night Petersburg and Richmond were evacuated. The next morning the Union troops took possession of the Confederate capital, the coveted goal of the Army of the Potomac for four long bloody years. Meanwhile, Lee, having only the wreck of that proud array with which he had dealt the Union army so many crushing blows, hurried west, seeking some avenue of escape. Grant urged the pursuit with untiring energy. Sheridan, "with a terrible daring which knew no pause, no rest," hung on his flanks. Food now failed the Confederates and they could get only the young shoots of trees to eat. If they sought a moment's repose, they were awakened by the clatter of pursuing cavalry. Lee, like a hunted fox, turned hither and thither; but at last Sheridan planted himself squarely across the front. Lee ordered a charge. His half-starved troops, with a rallying of their old courage, obeyed. But the cavalry moving aside, as a curtain is drawn, revealed dense bodies of infantry in battle line. The Civil War was about to end in one of its bloodiest tragedies, when the Confederate advance was stopped. General Grant had already sent in a note demanding the surrender of the army. Lee accepted the terms; and, April 9th, eight thousand men, the remains of the Army of Virginia laid down their arms near Appomattox Court House, and then turned homeward, no longer Confederate soldiers, but American citizens. The officers and men were allowed to go home on their paroles not to take up arms against the United States until exchanged, and the former to retain their private baggage and horses. After the surrender had been concluded, General Lee said that he had forgotten to mention that many of his soldiers rode their own horses. Grant at once replied that such should keep their horses to aid them in their future work at home and that the two armies so fiercely opposed for four years could have parted with no words but those of sympathy and respect was an assured presage of a day when all the wounds of the restored Union should be fully healed.

General Ulysses S. Grant

This closed the war. The other Confederate armies, Johnston's, Dick Taylor's, and Kirby Smith's all promptly surrendered. Jefferson Davis fled southward, hoping to escape, but was overtaken near Irwinsville, Georgia on May 11, and sent a prisoner to Fortress Monroe.[177]

Friday, Feby 17th, 1865.

I rose early. Practiced two hours to day. I have sadly neglected this duty for some time. Rained very hard last night, and about six o'clock this morning we were visited by a severe hail storm. Much cooler and I think will clear off. Busy assisting Aunt Jane in various ways. Pa is sick in bed.

Saturday. Feby 18th/65.

Up late. Clear and a delightful day although very muddy. Little Nannie Perkins came to see us today. Pa is much better.

Sunday, Feby 19th/65.

I rose early this morning. Ellen and I attended the Episcopal Church. Clear and delightful out. O! how I enjoyed such a day as this at my dear, dear home. I feel at times almost weary of life, but I hope these severe lessons may prove beneficial to me.

Monday, Feby 20th 1865.

I rose early. Busy all day cleaning, &c. perfectly delightful out; such weather dissipates all gloom. Received a long letter from my dear brother of a very old date, Nov 19th. It was read and reread with much interest O! I am truly blessed in having such a noble brother. Cousin Sam came down.

Tuesday, Feby 21st/65.

I rose early and dusted our room. Cousin Sam returned to day. Had a visit from Miss Minnie Rutledge and other friends. Finished the skirt of my dress. Mattie started to school today for the first time in her life. I hope she may learn to love her books and advance rapidly in all her studies. She has a good mind and application will soon render her studies

---

[177] Barnes, *A Brief History of the United States*, Epoch V, pages 272-275.

comparatively a pleasure. Sister and Hettie started to Mrs. Meig's. Busy today making clothes for my self and Aunt Jane. Cloudy and looks very much like rain!

Wednesday, February 22nd.

I rose very early this morning and dusted our room. Uncle William started for Memphis this morning. Cloudy and raining at times. Very <u>gloomy</u> and <u>low spirited</u>, <u>Charleston</u> has <u>fallen</u> and every rumor concerts that it was burned by the Confederates. I trust it is so, for our enemies would have wreck all their vengeance on the people. These are <u>gloomy</u>, <u>gloomy</u> times but we <u>must</u> succeed, being engaged in such a <u>noble cause</u>. God rules and reigns and I leave the issue in his hands!

Thursday, Feb 23rd 1865.

Up late. Finished my apron. Mattie returned from school to day in much distress at having so <u>many</u> lessons, but I took her off to herself and she soon surmounted all her difficulties. Cloudy and raining.

On February 24, 1865, Maggie can find some good even with the enemy.[178] She records that General Steadman came to see Aunt Jane.

Feb. 24th 1865.

I rose late. Nothing, nothing to write. Assisted Hettie and Aunt Jane in their sewing. Genl. Steadman came to see Aunt Jane, I left the room. He was very kind to Cousin Sam when encamped at Triune and it is well to remember his kindness, as it is <u>so</u> seldom met with the Federal army. Cloudy.

On Saturday, February 25, 1865, a Colonel LeDuc[179] comes to occupy an upstairs room at Aunt Janes. Maggie records some concerns over such arrangements but also shows some scheming in getting the house released from Federal control.

Saturday, Feb. 25th/65.

Up late. Cloudy and raining. Colonel LeDuc came to get a room upstairs for forty days and I fear forever for it seems when they once "get a foothold anywhere, they can never be

---

[178] Refer to journal entry from January 4, 1865.
[179] In 1863, Colonel William LeDuc and his Quartermaster Corp built the USS Chattanooga, a steamboat used to carry supplies to General Grant's besieged army at Chattanooga, TN.

dislodged." He expects to be ordered to Huntsville soon and I hope by treating him politely, to get the whole house released. Feel very unwell.

Sunday, Feby 26th 1865.
I rose late. Sick all day with a sore throat and aching pains all over me.

Monday, Feby 27th.
I rose late. Still feel uncomfortable. Heard Mattie's lessons and am glad to see the interest she is taking in her studies and hope it may continue. Cloudy, but cool.

Tuesday, Feby 28th 1865.
I rose early feeling better having taken some medicine. Assisted Aunt Jane in cleaning up down stairs. Practiced my instrumental music, but cannot yet summon up moral courage to resume my vocal. Why can't I overcome my diffidence and sensitiveness? Clear and a lovely day. Sallie Read and Addie Sealy came to see me today. What happy days we have all spent together!

Wednesday, March 1st.
Up late. Nothing of any consequence. Another lovely day. "M. B." [Montgomery Baxter] came to see me. I was really glad to see him.

Thurs. March 2nd 1865.
I rose early. Busy doing little jobs for Aunt Jane. Very much pleased with Mattie's account of her success in her lessons. Cloudy and raining now very steadily.

Friday, March 3rd.
Up late. Very gloomy. O! how I long for the pleasures of my home. Rain! Rain! This weather doesn't tend to enliven the spirits, but "some days must be dark and dreary."

Saturday, March 4th/65.
Up late. Had a visit from my own dear Mollie. How many happy hours we have spent together, roaming in the wild woods, wading in creeks and indulging in other childish amusements, little dreaming of the sad future in store for us, but I hope we look for eternal happiness in Christ. Very much surprised to see Cousin Sam and Ella and the baby. Cloudy, but cooler.

Sunday, March 5th/65.

Up late. Attended Sunday school at Mrs. Fall's church. Her class is rather large and she has kindly offered to divide it with me. O! I gladly accept the offer and hope to do the work faithfully. Clear. Mattie is quite sick.

Monday, March 6th/65.

Up early. Busy sewing. Mattie is much better. Clear and delightful out.

Tuesday, March 7th/65.

I rose early. Ellen and I have been busy shopping for Cousin Ella who expects to return tomorrow. Clear and a lovely day.

Wednesday, March 8th/65.

Up late. Cousin Sam returned today. Rained hard all morning but cleared off and very warm. Feel sad. O! I wish I could hear from my dear brother.

Thursday, March 9th.

Very much surprised to find it pouring down rain and about 10 o'clock it commenced sleeting. Helping Aunt Jane to make Hettie's dress.

Friday, March 10th/65.

Very cold and clear today. Heard that Ida Johnson intended on leaving for the South, and wrote a note requesting her to take a letter to dear brother, but judging from the time of her reply, she would prefer not being troubled.

Saturday, March 11th/65.

Up late. Showed Mattie her lessons and then took my bath. Clear. Nothing of any interest to day.

Sunday, March 12th/65.

Up late with a headache. Ellen and I went to Sunday school. However, I assisted her in her class and hope to have one myself next Sunday. Clear and delightful out.

Monday, March 13th/65.

Rose early. Busy writing letters and hearing Mattie's lessons. Clear and a lovely day.

Tuesday, March 14th/65.

Up early and assisted Ellen in dusting. Aunt Jane invited Col LeDuc[180] to tea. O! what consummate hypocrites we are. I was compelled by Ma and gave my feeble assistance in entertaining him. Cloudy and warm.

The Tea Party

Wednesday, March 15th/65.

Up late on account of our last night's dissipations! I spent the morning pleasantly visiting friends, Lizzie Fall, Anna Mayson, Laura Woodfolk and Miss Allison. Clear and very warm.

---

[180] During the post-war years, Colonel William LeDuc served as Secretary of Agriculture under President William B. Hayes. He helped developed the tea industry in Georgia and South Carolina. We're left to wonder whether Aunt Jane's tea party may have influenced his taste for tea.

Thursday, March 16th/65.

Up late. Had a severe thunder-storm and a hard rain. Cousin Sam came down. Snowing at times but is now clear. Gave way to my vile temper on hearing Mattie's lessons. Why can't I possess a little patience! Took cold and feel unwell. Cousin Sam returned.

Friday, March 17th/65.

Up late. Clear. Ellen and I spent the evening at Aunt Sallie's. Cousin Sam returned.

Saturday, March 18th.

Rose early. Ma and Pa went out to our dear home. All were getting on well. Went to see Mrs. Hill and Irene Watkins. Clear and lovely out.

Sunday, March 19th.

I rose late. Attended church. Cloudy and very warm.

Monday March 20th 1865.

Up late. Anna Mayson and Mollie Berry came to ask me to spend the week this morning. Commenced a letter to Queeny. Heard Mattie's lessons before I went. Cloudy and warm.

Friday, March 24th 1865.

Spent a delightful week with Mrs. Fall's family. Went to have our photographs taken and hope they will be good. Took a long walk with Miss Clouston and Mary Miller. O! I have learned to love dear Anna Mayson so dearly. She is truly a noble girl, and the many trials she has been called upon to bear, has only made her Christian character shine more brightly.

Saturday, March 25th.

Up late and I feel considerably wasted by my week's dissipations. Kate Perkins came to see us and staid some time. Clear and cool.

Sunday, March 26th 1865.

Up late. Attended Sunday school and church. Spent ther day very profitably reading an interesting and instructive work, "The Family at Heatherdale." It is full of instructions and I hope the leading characters may make a firm impression on my mind.

Monday, March 27th.

Up late. Spent the morning sewing and the evening hearing Mattie's lessons. Very warm and cloudy. Mollie came to show me her photographs which were very good.

Tuesday, March 28th 1865.

I rose early. Aunt Jane went to Triune for Cousin Ella. Misses Hewitt and Brown, the latter is a relation of Aunt Jane's, came to see us today. Cloudy and raining.

Wednesday, March 29th.

Up late. Cousin Ella arrived this morning worn out with her ride. Yoder Brown and Colonel LeDuc spent the evening with us. Rain and warm. Very unhappy to day.

Thursday, March 30th/65.

I rose quite late. Learned a new piece of work, Coronation Braid. O! I wish that I could be more useful to myself and others. I lack self _confidence_ and _perseverance_. Sadly, I fear I can never acquire either trait.

Good news arrives on March 31, 1865. Aunt Jane's house is released. It's tea time again.

Friday, March 31st.

I rose early. A lovely day. Busy hearing Mattie's lessons and attending to other duties. Aunt Sarah and Mamie came down. Colonel LeDuc got the whole house released and in order to show him we appreciated _his kindness,_ Aunt Jane invited him to tea. He expects to leave for Knoxville Tuesday and I trust he will _never_ cross my path again.

Saturday, April 1st 1865.

Up late. Nothing of any consequence.

Sunday, April 2nd 1865.

Up late. Attended Sunday school and have now five little girls in my class. O! I hope to be the means of bringing them to Christ! Aunt Sallie and Dellie spent the evening with us. Very cloudy and I think will be raining. Commenced the "The Two Families" by the author of Rose Douglass. I found the latter full of interest and religious instruction and I hope the one I am now reading may prove equally so.

The journal entry for April 3, 1865 shows a day of sadness, with news coming of the fall of Richmond and Petersburg.

Monday, April 3rd/65.

Oh! this has indeed been a day of sadness. Richmond, Petersburg <u>has fallen</u>, and I fear many precious lives have been lost. Great excitement has prevailed throughout the city; flags are suspended across every street, and everything wears on an air of triumph.

Wednesday, April 5th/65.

Colonel LeDuc left today. I am anxious to hear of anything from Virginia. Clear and warm.

Saturday, April 8th/65

Genl. Lee and his noble army has surrendered being outnumbered by the foe. O! our noble heroic band have fought most valiantly for four years and have at last to submit to the superiority of numbers! O! it is heart-rending in the extreme, so many precious lives are lost and for naught. I shall ever entertain a feeling of enmity towards a Northern man, and I hope to live and die a <u>bitter rebel</u>. Cousin Sam came down yesterday.

Sunday, April 9th/65.

A gloomy, gloomy day, the rain is pouring in torrents. Reading my precious Bible and find it a source of inexhaustible comfort.

Monday, April 10th/65

Up late. The Saturday news is all confirmed. Genl. Lee and his gallant army have surrendered on the following terms. The officers and men are to be paroled, (the former retaining their sidearms) and allowed to return home until exchanged. There is a rumor that the same terms have been offered to Genl. Jos E. Johnston by Sherman, and I trust that they will be accepted as further resistance is useless. Too much precious blood has been shed and I want to see my friends and relatives return and make an attempt to get the reins of power out of the hands of these Northern fanatics.

General Robert E. Lee

Wednesday, April 12th/65.

Up late, cleared off at last. The papers assert that Forrest and his whole command have surrendered. Nothing else left them.

Thursday, April 13th/65.

Up late, clear and a lovely day. Glad to hear that Cousin Dan and Cal being taken prisoner at Petersburg. They are now at Fort Delaware.[181]

Friday, April 14th/65.

I rose early. It is expected that the paroled taken at Petersburg are to be here tomorrow. The Federals are preparing for a grand celebration tomorrow. Cloudy and it is now raining steadily.

---

[181] A prisoner-of-war camp used to house Confederate soldiers, political prisoners, and hardened criminals. The most noteworthy soldier detained was Confederate General Joe Wheeler.

Chapter Sixteen
Lincoln

"Everything is excitement about the bloody affair at Washington and many predict the most horrible results."

In the midst of the universal rejoicings over the advent of peace, on the evening of April 14 the intelligence was flashed over the country that Lincoln had been assassinated. While seated with his wife and friends in his box at Ford's Theatre, he was shot by John Wilkes Booth who insanely imagined he was riding his country of a tyrant. Booth stealthily entered the box, fastened the door, that he might not be followed, shot the President, then waving his pistol shouted "Sic Semper Tyrannis" (so be it always to tyrants), and leaped to the stage in front. As he jumped, the American flag draped before the presidential box caught his spur causing him to break his leg as he hit the stage floor. The assassin, however escaped from the house in the confusion, mounted a horse which was waiting for him, and fled into Maryland. He was at length overtaken in a barn, here he stood at bay. The building was fired to drive him out, but, being determined to defend himself against arrest, he was shot by one of the soldiers. The accomplices of Booth were arrested, tried and convicted. A nearly fatal attempt was also made at the same time upon William H Seward, the Secretary of State, who was lying sick in his bed at home.

About the unconscious body of the President gathered the most prominent men of the nation, who mourned and watched, waiting in vain for some sign of recognition until the next morning, when he died. The funeral was held on the 19th. It was a day of mourning throughout the land. In most of the cities and towns funeral orations were pronounced. The body was borne to Springfield over the same route along which Lincoln had come as President elect to Washington. The procession may be said to have extended the entire distance. The churches, principal buildings, and even the engines and cars were draped in black. Almost every citizen wore the badge of mourning.[182]

---

[182] Barnes, *A Brief History of the United States*, Epoch V, pages 275-277.

Maggie records on April 14, 1865 that Nashville was preparing for a grand Federal celebration for the next day. Much excitement existed throughout the city, but April 14, 1865 forever changed the entire country. Telegraphic dispatches brought the news of Lincoln's assassination. The grand celebration quickly gave way to all flags being placed at half-mast and heavily draped, with minute guns being fired all day.

Saturday, April 15th/65.

This has indeed been an eventful day! Cousin Ella gave birth to a fine baby boy this morning about 7 o'clock. Both are doing well. About 9 A.M., a telegraphic dispatch reached this place containing the startling intelligence of the assassination of President Lincoln and Secretary Seward! Everything pertaining to the military was in readiness for a grand celebration, but it soon gave place to gloom. All flags were at half mast and heavily draped. Minute guns were fired all day. It must have been a horrible affair. The deed was committed by Booth, the tragedian, at Ford's Theater on Friday night. No particulars are yet given. Cousin Sam came down. Clear and delightful out.

Sunday, April 16th/65.

I rose early. Attended church and Sunday school. Everything is excitement about the bloody affair at Washington and many predict the most horrible results. Several were arrested and among them Dr. Martin.

Monday, April 17th/65.

Up late. Tillie and Irene Watkins came to see us. Clear. Cousin Sam returned this morning.

Wednesday, April 19th.

Nothing happened yesterday of any interest. Dr. Martin is still in the Penitentiary but Col. Parkhurst promised to release him on parole provided his daughter Mollie takes the oath. What horrible state of affairs. Kate Perkins came to see me today. She hears [from] Cousins Dan and Cal often and I hope [they] may be prevailed to come home. Cousin Ella is doing well notwithstanding the confusion that reigned throughout the city. President Lincoln's funeral took place today. Hand bills were passed throughout the town by the infuriated soldiers compelling all citizens to make some demonstration. Of course we obeyed!

Thursday, April 20th.

Up late. Mrs. Claire came to see us today. Mrs. Porter and Mrs. Genl Ewell called also. Clear and warm.

Friday, April 21st/65.

Up late. Cousin Sam came down. Commenced another band.

Saturday, April 22nd/65.

Up late. Busy all day hearing Mattie's lessons. Clear and very cool.

Sunday, April 23/65.

Up very late. Attended Sunday school and [taught] my class. Clear and very cool. Passed the day very profitably.

Monday, April 24th/65.

Heard Mattie's lessons and displayed my temper. O! can I ever, ever be free from this sin! At times I feel disgusted with myself, and am almost tempted to give up trying to become one of the fold of Christ, for my wanderings are long and often!

April 26th/65.

Such a lovely day I could not stay indoors so I paid a long visit to Ida Johnston and Sue Booker an old schoolmate of mine. Heard Mattie's lessons with more success.

Thursday, April 27th.

Have felt uncommonly low spirited today. An extra was out today containing the news of the capture of Booth. Poor fellow! I was in hopes he would escape, as his conscience would be sufficient punishment. Little Nannie Perkins came to see us and kept the house alive with her joyous prattle. Cloudy and very warm. My friend, M.B. came to see me tonight and I was glad to learn of his success in his profession.

Friday, April 28th/65.

Up very late. Busy working on my bands. Raining all day. Unhappy about my queer self.

Chapter Seventeen
The Homecoming

"Dear Brother came home to day!"

In 1865, the Senate provided a study of the war and came up with the following information. On the Union side approximately 2,324,516 men enlisted with about 360,000 deaths. The Southern Confederacy had approximately 1,000,000 enlisting with 135,000 killed. Within six months nearly all surviving soldiers had returned home. Thus the mightiest host ever called to the field by a Republic went back without disturbance to the tranquil pursuits of civil life. In short time, there was nothing to distinguish the soldier from the citizen, except the recollection of his bravery. Other nations prophesied that such a vast army could not be disbanded peacefully. The Republic, by this final triumph of law and order, proved itself the most stable government in the world. The dollar cost of the war on the Union side was $6,189,908 with the Confederate side hard to determine. It is thought to have been about half the cost of the Union. Moreover, the larger cost to the country was the loss of a generation of young men. It would be 30 years before the nation would recover from this great loss.[183]

Springtime 1865 finds a great many paroled Confederates in town. Maggie records frequent visits of friends and relatives, many of whom have been away in Rebel service. Maggie seems to lose track of time. The original journal entries show a date of April 31st but are then corrected to show the 29th being wrongly dated. Maggie had started a new journal page, which may have been the source of the error. What is the gain of one day during this time of guarded happiness yet nervous tension?

Saturday, April 30th 1865.

Up late. Cloudy at times. There seem to be a great many paroled Confederates in town. Genl. Jos. E. Johnston has certainly surrendered upon the same terms as Lee. O! how

---

[183] Barnes, *A Brief History of the United States*, Epoch VI, pages 281-282.

fervently I hope my prayers have been heard and my dear brother and other relatives and friends have been spared. Cleared off in the evening. Busy mending.

Sunday, April 31st.

Very much surprised to see it cloudy and very cool. Attended Sunday school but not church. Wrote a long letter to my dear Queeny and entreated her to turn her attention to religion. I love her most devotedly and of course pray for her spiritual as well as her earthly welfare. Cloudy and very cool.

Maggie keeps a watchful eye open every day waiting for Brother to be among the hundreds of soldiers pouring into town.

Monday, May 1st

What a cold, cold day this has been for the commencement of the flowery month. Busy all day. It's rumored to day that before the surrender of Genl. Johnston, Genl. Cheatham and many of his division had gone to California. I trust Brother is not among the number.

Tuesday, May 2nd/65

Up late. Have been so unhappy to-day on account of my vile temper. O! I get completely discouraged, but still I must battle with all opposition and every defeat only make me more determined to conquer.

Wednesday, May 3rd/65.

What a lovely day this has been, but still too cool for Spring. Ellen and I walked out to see Mrs. Fall. Laura Woodfolk and Lizzie Fall have gone north. Why can't Southern girls overcome such bad habits? Pa says Mrs. Martin told him Mrs. Crutcher had received news from Genl. Maney saying Brother would soon be home. What a happy thought! Bless his precious heart, a truer soldier never fought!

Thursday, May 4th/65.

Up late, feeling weak. Sissie and I spent the morning shopping. Clear but getting much warmer. Heard Mattie's lessons very patiently. Charlie told me four hundred of Johnston's men came in this evening and eight hundred were expected tomorrow. O! I hope my dear brother is among them.

Friday, May 5th 1865.

Very much disappointed at Brother not coming but I hope [he] will come when we least expect him. Cloudy and warm!

Saturday, May 6th/65.

I rose early. So very warm. I was compelled to put on my summer clothes. Heard Mat's lessons. Cloudy but I think cooler than it has been.

Sunday, May 7th/65.

Up quite early. Went to Sunday School. Very cloudy and warm. Spent the day reading my Bible and sleeping.

Monday, May 8th 1865.

Up early. A rainy day. Mat is quite unwell. Finished my everlasting band. Why don't Brother come? I feel at times almost afraid to look for him.

Tuesday, May 9th 1865.

Done nothing in the world this morning, but look out [the] window and watch the "ragged rebels." Bless their hearts! I love every rag on them! Ellen and I went out with Aunt Jane after dinner. Clear and quite pleasant.

Wednesday, May 10th/65.

Had another visit from Irene Watkins. Mrs. Elliston came to see me; she is quite sociable. Cloudy. Hemming Mattie's dress! Another rumor is afloat that Genl. Cheatham and Staff have sailed from Savannah for New York. It is hard to believe everything we hear! Had a long chat with two Confederate soldiers who were resting on our steps. They were refused transportation to their homes by the military authorities and were compelled to foot it. Both belonged to Cheatham's Division. Poor fellows! I wish I could have helped them, but I would soon have found myself transported to the Penitentiary. What freedom under the old flag! Cloudy and I think will rain. O' I have been so unhappy to-day. Everybody misunderstands me.

Thursday, May 11th/65.

Up late. Raining the whole day, but so cool will certainly clear off.

Friday, May 12th 65.

Up late. Clear and cool. Ellen and I took a walk and had a chat with some rebels on High Street. They belonged to Loring's Division.[184]

Saturday, May 13th/65.

I rose late. Busy hearing Mattie's lessons. Ed Saunders got in this morning. Everybody is coming but my dear Brother. Took a walk.

Sunday, May 14th/65.

I rose rather late feeling very unwell. Attended Sunday school. Ellen had a visit this evening from a Confederate officer, Capt Helm of Mississippi. He and Capt Sydney Rodgers took supper as they both expect to leave tomorrow. O' how we enjoyed their society! Jeff Davis is caught! What will the wretches do with him! Clear.

Monday, May 15th 1865

Owning to our setting up late, we were lazy rising. Jeff Davis will pass through tomorrow. Busy sewing and entertaining friends, among them Capt. Helm who did not get off as he expected. He knew Brother well and saw him at Augusta about four weeks ago. Very warm.

Tuesday, May 16th/65.

Up late. Cousin Ella expected to get off to day, but on account of the baby's being <u>quite sick</u>, she has postponed going. Aunt Jane too is very unwell. Brad Nichol got in this evening. Cloudy and warm.

Wednesday, May 17th/65.

Up late. Dear Mollie came to see me at last. She is so springhalt and full of life. I wish that I could look on the bright side of things as she does. Warm with frequent showers! Great numbers of Confederate troops are coming, mostly cavalry. I do wish Bul would surprise us. I think his arrival would cure Aunt Jane.

Thursday, May 18th/65.

Up about 5 o'clock to see Cousin Ella off. I hope the baby will improve. Aunt Jane is still very unwell owing entirely I think to her uneasiness about Bul and the baby. I pray her heart may be

---

[184] Confederate General William Loring, a veteran of the Mexican War. During the Civil War, he saw service starting in western Virginia and ending in the Carolina campaign.

gladdened by a happy account of them both. Had a long visit from an old friend, Sam McCall. O! it is such a treat to entertain them, but oh! how sadly we miss <u>the</u> <u>lost</u> ones, who have nobly defended their cause and have done <u>all</u>, the least that man can do. Showery all day.

Friday, May 19th/65.

Up unusually early. Cousin Sophy Nichol spent the day with us. Busy sewing on my band. Heard Col. Snowden[185] had gotten in. Had a very hard rain. Aunt Jane still very unwell.

Saturday, May 20th/65.

What a happy, happy day this has been! Dear Bul came about four o'clock bringing some friends. O! how deeply I rejoice with dear Aunt Jane. Clear and very warm.

Sunday, May 21st/65.

Attended Sunday School and then went to the Catholic Church as we heard there was to be fine music. Cloudy and warm with several heavy showers.

Monday, May 22nd/65.

I rose early. Joe Percy came last night. Busy sewing. Joe Mayson came to see me. O! I am so glad to see old friends. Ellen and I walked out to see Mrs. Fall.

Tuesday, May 23rd/65.

I rose very early. Dr. Gale and Joe came to see me tonight. Busy sewing.

Wednesday, May 24th.

Up late. Dr. Rice from Memphis took dinner with us. Heard of several of my friends coming in. Colonel Snowden called.

Thursday, May 25th.

Up very late. Busy sewing and hearing Mattie's lessons. Col. Bradshaw and Dr. Bruist took tea with us. I <u>do</u> wish Brother would come! He must have some very <u>important</u> <u>business</u> in Augusta. Raining all day.

---

185 Colonel Robert B. Snowden, a close friend of Brother Joe Vaulx and a member of the Rock City Guard unit.

Friday, May 26th.

Up late. Busy sewing all day. Nat Baxter[186] came to see me: he has improved so much and it is the case with all the boys. Hettie and Sister went to the Opera to night with Charlie. Very cool out to day.

Saturday, May 27th 1865.

Up quite late. Ellen and I went out to visit Ellen Fall. Orville Ewing and Willie Watkins called. Clear and very cool. The girls attended the Matinee.

Sunday, May 28th 1865.

Up late. Attended Sunday school. Ma has been very unwell with a severe chill. I hope she will soon be well. Had a very hard rain. Six Confederate officers were quartered on us.

Monday, May 29th 1865.

Up early. Our Confederates took the oath and left for their homes in Kentucky. Ellen Fall and Laura Woodfolk came to see us, also Letha Allison and her Brother.

Tuesday, May 30th/65.

I rose very late. Busy sewing and shopping.

Wednesday, May 31st/65.

Up late. Sewing all morning. Three Confederate officers called. Ellen and I took a walk. Clear and warm.

Thursday, June 1st.

I rose very late. Busy sewing. Very warm. Unhappy to day. O! I have so little self confidence!

On June 2, 1865, the Vaulx family finally has good news. Brother Major Joseph Vaulx returns safely home!

---

[186] Nathanael Baxter, a war veteran having served as a Lieutenant in the artillery. He was full-brother of Montgomery Baxter and half-brother of CSA Captain Edmund Baxter.

Friday, June 2nd.

Dear Brother came to day! Looking as fat and well. O! how I love him. He is everything I could wish in an own brother. Have done no work at all. Harry Martin called; it really seems like old times again. Poor Tom Percy, how sad it is to think of his fate, yet he died a noble death.

The Homecoming

The June 2, 1865 journal entry states, *"Poor Tom Percy, how sad it is to think of his fate, yet he died a noble death."* Now may be an appropriate time to note Maggie's relatives and friends who did not survive the war. The relatives are: Uncle James Armstrong, killed in action at Stones River. Cousin Berry W. Morgan at Shelbyville, Cousin Frank McNairy during a skirmish near Fort Donelson, and Cousins Tom Percy and Joe Nichol, both at the battles around Atlanta. The friends include: Albert Fall, a childhood friend who fell mortally wounded at Fort Donelson and later died, Jimmie May[187] who was killed in action at the Battle of Shiloh, Capt. W. G. Erwin and Willie Forrest who lost their lives in the Battle of Atlanta. Family friend Bob Bradford perished while being held as a prisoner-of-war at Camp Chase, Ohio, Tom Wilson who died

---

[187] Friend Jimmie May will not be found within the text of the journals. He is identified only on the inside back cover of Volume One.

during a skirmish in West Tennessee, and a close family friend, Mr. Taylor died from injuries received during the Battle of Stones River. An unknown friend with initials of H. S.[188] also died at the Battle of Stones River. Maggie would note others who survived but were still deeply affected by the war.

Saturday, June 3rd 1865.

Up late. Brother went out to Mr. John Harding to rest from his "overland route." Joe Mayson called this evening. Five more Confederates were quartered on us. Very warm!

Sunday, June 4th/1865.

Very lazy rising. Attended Sunday school. Joe Percy left for Mississippi this evening. I hope he may change so as to be the pride and comfort of his sisters. Ellen and I went up to see Mrs. Massengale. She speaks so highly of Brother.

Monday, June 5th.

Sick all day. Very warm. Brother returned.

Tuesday, June 6th 1865.

Still feel unwell. Nat Baxter and Frank Porterfield came to see me.

Wednesday, June 7th

Rose early feeling better. Sewing all day. Capt's Ed Saunders and W. G. Ewing called. Also Joe Mayson, Harry Martin and Pillow Humphreys.

Thursday, June 8th

I rose early. Miss Kittie McEwing came to see me this morning and insisted upon my attending a party at Mrs. Wilkins. I don't attend going as I hear it is to be a mixed affair. Dr Foster[189] called to see us. He is looking so well!

Friday, June 9th 1865.

I rose very late. Aunt Jane went to Triune as Cousin Ella is very sick. Pa, Mat, Brother Joe and I went out home. The place is looking beautiful.[190] O' I wish Ma [was with us]. On our

---

[188] Unknown friend H. S. will also not be found within the text of the journals. He is identified on the inside front cover of Volume Two as the presenter of a pressed fern collected at the Asylum and given to Maggie.

[189] Dr. R. Foster, another surviving member of the Rock City Guard unit.

way out we stopped at Dr Foster's. A great fire occurred today. Half of the Taylor Depot (Government) burned; loss is estimated from $12,000,000 to $15,000,000.

Saturday, June 10th 1865.

A note from Aunt Jane reached us containing the sad news of Cousin Ella's severe illness; something like a congestive chill. She requested us to send Dr. Martin immediately. He and Charlie left about 9 o'clock this morning. May God in His Infinite mercy spare her is my fervent prayer. Amy Bradford, Willie Martin and Capt. Coleman called. Very warm. Dear Brother staid all night with us.

Sunday, June 11th 1865.

I scarcely slept a wink last night thinking of Cousin Ella. Charlie and Dr. Martin got down about 2 o'clock. He thought Cousin Ella was entirely out of danger and on the whole a false alarm. Brother went out to Genl. Harding's.

Monday, June 12th 1865.

Up late. Brother returned and went out to Mr. McGavock's in order to avoid going to three parties. I don't blame him! Little Charlie Thompson came to invite me to go out and attend a little "sociable" at Dr. Foster's. I declare I feel too gloomy for such gayety.

Tuesday, June 13th.

Up late. Bessie came and insisted upon my going out. I truly appreciate such kindness and hope they will take no offence at my refusing so flatly. Sewing all day.

Wednesday, June 14th.

I rose late. Dr. Quintard[191] came to see Ellen. What a noble name he gave dear Tom Percy. Poor boy! He has been taken to a world better suited to his disposition. Joe Mayson[192] called this evening to insist upon Ellen and myself going out and spending the day at Mrs. Fall's. Heard from Cousin Ella. She is very ill with typhoid fever.

---

[190] Even though the war had heavily damaged her beloved home, Maggie can still find beauty.
[191] Dr. Charles T. Quintard, a CSA chaplain and surviving member of the Rock City Guard unit.
[192] Joe Mayson, another surviving member of the Rock City Guard unit.

Thursday, June 15th/65.
I rose early. Busy sewing. Nothing of any interest.

Friday, June 16th.
Heard Cousin Ella was better though very weak and reduced. Ellen and I attended the Ice Cream saloon. Very warm.

Saturday, June 17th/65.
Three more Confederates quartered on us. We receive them with greatest pleasure and gave them the best we have. Very warm with no prospect of rain. Miss Clouston came to see me.

Sunday, June 18th/65.
Up late. Attended Sunday school. In the evening Ellen and I went to the Episcopal Church and heard a most excellent sermon from Dr. Quintard. Had two hard rains.

Monday, June 19th/65.
Up early. Doing nothing all day. Bul Brown came down from Triune. Cousin Ella is slowly recovering. Capt. Joe Gale and Amy Bradford came to see me this evening. Mrs. Holcombe's Commencement takes place tonight.

Tuesday, June 20th/65.
I rose quite early. Went to see Miss Clouston who expects to leave tomorrow. Paid a visit to Irene Watkins and Mrs. Frank Nichol. Clear and delightful out.

Wednesday, June 21st/65.
Very late getting up. Busy sewing all day. Ellen received a note from Aunt Jane saying Cousin Ella was rather worse. O! I wish she was well. Clear and warm.

Thursday, June 22nd/65.
I rose early. Sewing all day.

Friday, June 23rd.
Had a visit from Ellen Fall and Miss Brock Correy called. Willie Goodwin came also. He is a noble little fellow! I wish I could see Mollie. I feel like having a good long talk with her. I

wonder if she has strayed from "the narrow path" as often as I. I trust not for I feel as if I were sadly straying from God. O! how many difficulties a Christian has to encounter in this vain world, but oh! what precious promises we have of everlasting happiness in the kingdom of Christ, when the temptations of this life are over.

Saturday, June 24th/65.

Up late as we sat up until twelve o'clock talking over dear old times spent at Mount Alban. Sometimes I feel as if my heart would break when thinking of the past, it is filled with so many sad memories. Our country subjugated, overpowered and the flower of the land forever gone! Very warm and dusty! O! how I miss the pleasures of my dear home! Brother went out to Farmer Fosters to spend some days.

Sunday, June 25th/65.

Up quite early. Went to Sunday school and church. Had a pleasant chat with dear Anna Mayson before service. She is truly a noble girl. So Christian like and patient under the trial she is laboring under, casting her burden on the Lord. I love her most devotedly and shall ever sympathize with her in her grief. Heard a joyful piece of news which I hope may be true. Charlie told me there was to be preaching in our church next Sunday by a minister from Texas. Had a hard rain.

Monday, June 26th/65.

Up early. Clear and delightful out. Mrs. Nicholas took dinner. How sadly she has changed! She has indeed been taken through the fiery furnace, and I hope she is made a better Christian by it. Capt. Joe Gale and Dr. M. Baxter came to see me. The latter is looking in wretched health. Went out late in the evening and attended to some business for Ma.

Tuesday, June 27th/65.

Up late. Glad to see John Brown. Cousin Ella is still improving. Harry Martin came to invite me to go to the supper tonight at the Masonic Temple given for the benefit of Dr. Quintard and his church. I hope it will succeed without my humble appearance. Clear and warm.

Wednesday, June 28th.

Up early. Went out to see my dear Mollie. She has certainly become quite a fashionable young lady, but I <u>trust she is not neglecting her God for momentary happiness</u>. Ellen and I called on Mrs. Todd and Mary McGavock, but not finding her at home, we paid a visit to the Ice Cream Saloon, <u>which was far more preferable!</u> Dr. Bruist[193] and Brother spent the evening with us.

Thursday, June 29th.

Lazy! lazy! lazy!! Can I ever overcome this misfortune? Passed the morning shopping with Cousin Sophy Nichol. Pillow Humphreys and Charlie Martin called while we were out. Cousin Joe left for Arkansas. We have been very much exercised about Charlie, who has been as taciturn as he is usually talkative. Something disagreeable has happened, and yet I dare to hope that it is owning to a change of heart. That he has come to the sense of his lost condition and has now determined to follow in the narrow but pleasant path that leads to life everlasting. God grant that it is so! I love Charlie as a brother and would be too happy to see him possess the pearl of great price, and I shall ever pray for him. O! I wish I possessed the gift of influence, to know that I by my humble endeavors am the means of bringing others to Christ. What a happy thought! That me by the grace of God, are the chosen instruments of working out His noble plan of redemption; and if we neglect those means what a fearful responsibility is ours! Let me pray most fervently for that gracious gift and ever be conscientious in the performance of it.

Friday, June 30th.

I rose late. Practiced my instrumental and a little of my vocal music! Cousin Sam came down and gave us a cheering account from Cousin Ella. Raining steadily at times. Ellen and I went out to attend to some business of Aunt Jane. Charlie and I had a long talk this evening and during the conservation, I approached the subject upper most in my mind but my effort was a faint one and I fear will be attended with no success. I must trust in God for success. Dr. Preston Scott from Kentucky spent the evening with us.

---

[193] Dr. J. R. Bruist, another surviving member of the Rock City Guard unit.

Saturday, July 1st.

I rose late. Mamie Nichol spent the day with us. She intends going north soon. Nat Baxter and Willie Ewing called. A lovely day.

Sunday, July 2nd 1865.

Up early. Another lovely day. Had preaching at our church by the Rev. McNealy of this state formerly chaplain of the C.S.A. O! how I enjoyed it. Attended church at night.

Monday, July 3rd/65.

Aunt Jane and dear little Nannie came down. Bless her little heart! She is so sweet and interesting. Busy sewing on my bands. It seems as if I am never to get through with them!

Tuesday, July 4th 1865.

What a noisy disagreeable day this has been! Sissie and Hettie left for Triune this morning, expecting to stay all summer. I hope they will as they need a change. Dr. Bruist and Col. Snowden took dinner with Brother. Had a magnificent display of fire works to night. I must confess I feel anything but patriotic.

Wednesday, July 5th/65.

Had a most charming visit from my dear Mollie. I trust she is not changed, but hope most fervently she is more devoted to the service of her Maker. O! I wish I possessed the blessed gift of leading others to their Redeemer. Oh! I feel as if my life is without an aim, that I am truly an unprofitable fugitive! Very warm.

Thursday, July 6th

Out visiting with Mollie. Displayed my vile temper on account of being disappointed about going to a little entertainment at Mr. James Wood's. What little self-control I possess!

Friday, July 7th

Ellen and I have been busy shopping for Aunt Jane and it was truly a warm business. Nothing of any interest. Practiced my singing.

Saturday, July 8th

Busy mending my clothes. Cousin's Dan Perkins and Cal at last condescended to come to see us. They both gave me pressing invitations to come out. I shall certainly accept it soon. The warmest day we have had. Went out to see Ellen Fall and the other girls.

Sunday, July 9th

Attended Sunday school and now have five in my class. O! may I act a conscientious part towards them. Had a fine sermon from Rev. McBrantley from Texas. Attended church at night. Had a rain. Willie Goodwin walked home with us.

Monday, July 10th

Up late! Tried to work but it has been so warm, I made a complete failure. Had several rains. Mrs. Nicholas and Mrs. Hickman came to see us. They have indeed been terribly visited by this war.

Tuesday, July 11th 1865

I rose early. Ellen Fall spent the morning with us and of course no work progressed. I declare I am getting very lazy. Dr. Felix Robertson[194] died yesterday. He was the oldest inhabitant of this place. Very warm and cloudy!

Wednesday, July 12th/65

Ellen and I went to see cousin Dorcie Nichol. Had a delightful walk, the day being cloudy and cool. Brother went out to Dr. Gale's to a party. Busy working my bands. I wish I never felt lazy.

Thursday, July 13th 1865

Up late with a headache and a dull pain in my stomach. Out shopping, however for Aunt Jane. Very warm and I think will rain soon. Unhappy! O! I do think I am a queer, queer

---

[194] DEATH NOTICE FROM THE *NASHVILLE DAILY PRESS AND TIMES* FOR 1865: This widely known and highly respected citizen of Nashville died on Sunday night. He was the first male child born in this city and the sixth child of Col. James Robertson. His birth dates back to the 11th of January, 1781, making him eighty-four and a half years old, lacking a couple of days, at the time of his decease. The old gentleman has long lived on Cherry Street "ripe in years and full of honors," esteemed and beloved by more than thirty thousand of his immediate fellow citizens.

girl. I feel a perfect contempt for myself at times. What am I living for? Would that I could look back upon each day and feel confident that I had spent it to the glory of God. Ah! I fear I shall never overcome the many obstacles that are constantly besetting me. Sometimes I feel very buoyant in spirits, but the least little stumbling-block throws me back in my material state of despondency.

Friday, July 14th

Up early and cleaned our room. Had a visit from Capt. Ewin. Cousin Sam came down. Cousin Ella still improves. Ellen and I spent the evening at Mrs. Fall's. Very warm again.

Saturday, July 15th

Up early and cleaned our room. O! I feel so much better when I stir around. Ellen Fall and Mrs. Hickman spent the morning with us. Busy doing some work for Ma. Charlie and I had a long chat. O! I wish I could succeed! Very warm!

Sunday, July 16th/65

Raining hard all day. Employed the day reading my Bible and looking over my diary.[195] Wrote a long letter to Queeny.

Monday, July 17th/65.

Up early. Ellen and I gave our room a good cleaning. Busy all morning practicing and sewing. Cleared off delightfully. Ellen and I paid a visit to Mary and Dellie Nichol. What inconsistent girls they are!

Tuesday, July 18th 1865

Up early and surprised to find it raining. Busy all day sewing, trying to make up for lost time.

Wednesday, July 19th

Very gloomy today on account of hearing such sad news from dear Queeny. She has had a severe spell of sickness, which has terminated in consumption. O! I do hope she is a Lamb of

---

[195] With Maggie reflecting back, perhaps this is when she added statements to the January 27 and February 16, 1862 journal entries. Those entries noted very sad times in her young life.

God. Raining. Busy all day sewing and practicing. Mr. Bunting, our minister came to see us. Two more Confederates were quartered on us!

Thursday, July 20th
Up early. Busy sewing and practicing, sang all my pieces [took] two hours! What is to happen! Very warm again.

Friday, July 21st
Up early and cleaned our room thoroughly before breakfast. Practiced two hours. Very warm.

Saturday July 22nd
Lazy! Busy mending my clothes. Cousin Sam and Uncle James came down. He looks much better. Nate Baxter and Trim Brown came to see me. Ellen and I frequented the Ice Cream Saloon.

Sunday, July 23rd 1865
Up very early. Cousin Sam returned. Attended Sunday school and church and heard an excellent sermon from Mr. Bunting, the text being the VI chapter of Romans, 23rd verse: "For the wages of sin is death but the gift of God is eternal life through Jesus Christ our Lord." Willie Goodman went with me at night. O! I hope to be a true friend to him and shall ever pray for him. Warm.

Monday, July 24th/65
Up early. Busy sewing and practicing. Jimmie Woods came to see me. He is looking wretchedly, the result of prison life. There is to be a little entertainment at "West Wood" given to Roberta Armistead who is now here on a visit from Wheeling where they now reside. Ellen and I went to see Cousin Lil Rancks. While we were gone Henry Martin and Henry Yeatman came to see us. Very warm.

Tuesday, July 25th 1865
Up early. Irene Watkins and Orville Ewing were married this morning at 5 o'clock. Busy sewing. Col. Reese and brother took supper with us.

Wednesday, July 26th

Busy shopping all morning. Mollie came and insisted upon my going out to Dr. Foster's with her. Enjoyed it very much.

Sunday, July 30th

Up early. Attended Sunday school and church. The Sacrament of our Lord's Supper is to be administered to the members of the church this day [and the next] two weeks. I hope to become a member. Have spent the last few days with Mollie. Mrs. Knox came this morning.

Monday, July 31st

Up early. Busy sewing for Aunt Jane. Very warm.

Tuesday, Aug 1st

Up early. Busy shopping. Joe Mayson called.

Wednesday, Aug 2nd

Aunt Jane and Ellen left for Louisville this evening expecting to be gone several weeks. O! how I miss them. Practiced my singing. Clear. Mrs. Knox went to Mrs. Hill's to stay.

Thursday, Aug 3rd

Up late as I feel completely worn out! Willie Goodman came to see me. What a good boy he is and I trust he may direct Charlie in the way he should go. O! for the gift of influence. Jimmie Woods came to see me.

Friday, Aug 4th

Busy sewing and practicing. Nannie and Janie Eakin called. Very warm.

Saturday, Aug 5th 65

Up late and cleaned my room. Busy sewing and practicing. Joe Mayson came to see me tonight.

Sunday, Aug 6th 65

Up early. Attended Sunday school and church. Harry Martin went with me at night. O! I wish I could exert a good influence over my friend. Rained a little.

Monday, Aug 7th

Up early. Gave my room a thorough cleaning and then sat myself to darning old clothes. Received a letter from Ellen from Frankfurt. Glad to hear of her pleasant trip and to know that she is enjoying herself. Willie Goodwin paid me one of his delightful visits. Very pleasant.

Tuesday, Aug 8th/65

Up late as I was up late writing to Ellen. Charlie went to Triune to spend a few days. Charlie Thompson called. Very warm.

Wednesday, Aug 9th/65

I rose early and cleaned my room before breakfast. Busy all morning practicing and sewing. In the evening, I spent the time reading an interesting religious work entitled, "The Minister's Family." Very warm and sultry. Wrote to Aunt Jane.

Thursday, Aug 10th/65

I rose early, sewing all morning. After dinner, I passed the time reading my dear Bible.

Friday, Aug 11th/65

Up late, but cleaned my room before breakfast. Willie Goodwin and Mr. Rainey called. Attended church and have now acknowledged my Redeemer before men and how fervently do I pray to be a faithful servant in the kingdom of Christ. Mr. Bunting preached a melting sermon from the text: 22 chap. Matt. 11 and 14th verse. "And when the king came in to see the guests, he saw there a man which had not a wedding garment: For many are called but [few] are chosen." O! I was so glad to see many of my friends choose the better part which shall never be taken away. O' may we be disciples of Christ, not <u>only</u> in <u>name</u> but in <u>deed</u> and <u>truth</u>. Gracious Father, endow us with the gift of influence and may we use it to the glory and the advancement of thy kingdom.

Saturday, Aug 12th

Passed the day reading my Bible and praying for a closer walk with God. Mr. Bunting called and set my heart to rest on many undecided points. Willie Goodwin went to church with me at night. O! he expressed such a delight at my joining the church. May we be <u>firm</u> friends in Christ.

Sunday, 13th/65

Up early. Attended Sunday school. What a happy day this has been to me. Yes! I am baptized in the name of the Father, Son and Holy Ghost and have declared myself a disciple of my blessed Lord and Master, by partaking of His body which was broken for our sins. I feel as if a new life had begun, and now that I have declared my Redeemer before men, I shall ever try to imitate his example to us when on earth. "Pray for one another" shall ever be my motto in my intercourse through life. O'! that I had more the spirit of prayer! I do at times "roll my burdens on the Lord" and find peace in doing so; but too often I turn and take it up again. Yet my wayward heart is in the school of Christ, and will be disciplined at last.

Monday, Aug 14th 1865

I cleaned my room thoroughly before breakfast. Mollie and Willie Goodwin spent the morning with me. I feel certain they are my friends in Christ, and may we grow in grace daily. O! I do so long to become entirely God's own! Had a visit from Irene Carter. I was shocked at a remark she made. We were speaking of the different churches and I expressed my delight at seeing them again filled with their respective congregations. She agreed with me, but remarked she took no interest in church going. O! what a dreadful state of mind! Attended church at night and heard a fine sermon from Dr. Langley from the text, 3rd chap. John 7th verse. "Marvel not that I say unto thee, ye must be born again." Charlie returned from Triune to night. O! may he soon be brought to Christ, and "be born again." Clear and warm.

Tuesday, Aug 15th 1865

I rose early and cleaned my room and then wrote a short note to Sister. Passed the morning reading my dear "MLD." O! May I ever strive to imitate her example. Passed the evening at Mrs. Fall's. Had a quiet chat with Lizzie during the latter part of my visit. I know she is a sister to me in Christ. Went to church at night and heard a soul stirring address from the text, 3rd chapter Revelation, 20th verse. "Beloved I stand at the door and knock; if any man hears my voice, and open the door, I will come in to him and will sup with him, and he with me." O! why have I rejected this earnest plea so long! May dear Charlie "be born again" and may he remember that now is the accepted time.

Wednesday, Aug 16th 1865

I rose early. Passed the morning sewing and reading "Bickersteth on Prayer". It is full of instruction and I trust that God may make it instrumental in bringing me nearer to my long neglected Saviour. Help me gracious Father to overcome this vain world and may it be my steady aim to love the Lord. Pa and I attended church and heard a fine sermon from dear Mr. Bunting from the 26th chapter of Acts 28th verse. "Then Agrippa said unto Paul, Almost thou persuadest me to be a Christian." O! how many Agrippa's are among us?

While residing at Aunt Jane's house, Maggie records the last entry of Volume Two on Thursday, Aug. 17, 1865. This last journal entry will include one of her daily weather reports.

Thursday, August 17th 1865.

I rose early. Had a visit from Sallie Buckner. Spent the morning cleaning the house and practicing and the evening in quiet meditation. Received a letter from dear Ellen. She too is a disciple of the Lord. Clear and quite cool.

Chapter Eighteen
Volumes Five and Six

THE PRIVATE JOURNALS OF MAGGIE N. VAULX, 1868-1875
(The original journals as remembered by Ross E. Hudgins)

Volumes Five and Six covered the years 1868 through 1875. They were given to Maggie's descendents in 1977. Ordinary journal books from that era, they were probably purchased from one of the stationary stores of downtown Nashville. The book covers were red leather and they had lined pages. The inside covers were of heavy paper embossed with a marbled multi-color design. I believe one of them may have had a stringed page marker. The pages were gilt-edged. Both books were approximately 8"x6" and about ¾" thick. The University of Tennessee researched the books in 1965 and accidentally tore off the back cover of Volume Six.

Volume Five opened sometime during the year 1868 or 1869. Mt. Alban was still the family home. In later years, it would be called Breeze Hill. It survived the war and over 100 years later it was bulldozed over for a Kroger store. It was located on the present day corner of Kirkwood and Franklin Road, with Gale and Thompson Lanes just to the Southwest. Nashville's Civil War monument would be located nearby with its land being donated by the Vaulx descendants around 1902. Those living in the home included Joseph Vaulx, Sr., his wife Eleanor Ryburn Armstrong Vaulx, and daughters Margaret, Catherine and Martha. The son Joseph was also a member of the household but was frequently away on business. All of these were spoken of with regularity. The 1870 federal census listed two domestic servants by the surname Edwards in the household. Outside friends included the Ewing's, Van Leer's, Baxter's, Harris's and Edwin and Percy Warner. There was also an entry of a family visit to Mrs. James K. Polk's residence in Nashville.

Several things came to my attention about the differences between the first two volumes and the last two. The first two frequently mentioned spiritual things. The last two had far fewer of these, with the exception of going to church and revivals. Maggie mentioned the health and well being of her aging parents quite often in the last two volumes. Maggie still struggled with her temper and her relationships to others.

Some of the national events which I recall being recorded included references to President Grant's administration, the "Great Chicago Fire", the death of Gen. Robert E. Lee and some local news. In reference to the fire, Maggie records her mother's concerns that due to the construction of Nashville, it could happen there. In Volume Five, a gentleman identified as Mr. George Bell Crockett came into Maggie's life.

The last volume began around 1870. It had a lot of skipped dates and ran through the year 1875. Interestingly, it ended with half of the book being unused. The most memorable event contained in the last volume was the courtship of Maggie and George Bell Crockett of Williamson County. From what was recorded, George Bell must have been some type of businessman or store owner. Maggie referred to him as Mr. Crockett during their courtship and even after he proposed marriage. Maggie wrote of being torn between her emotions and wanting Pa's approval. She was no longer reserved towards her mother, and consulted with Ma over the matter. Unlike with Montgomery Baxter in 1864, this time the answer was yes. It was recorded that Ma went to Pa and prepared him for the upcoming marriage request and blessing. Maggie at the time was 26 and George Bell Crockett about 38 years of age.

The wedding took place at the First Presbyterian Church on August 29, 1871. She recorded the person performing the ceremony and to the best of my memory it may have been either Dr. Bunting or Dr. Fall. The happy couple spent the night at the newly reopened Maxwell House Hotel and left by train the next day for Buffalo, NY. While there, she recorded visiting Niagara Falls. From Buffalo, the couple went to New York City where George Bell completed some scheduled business and Maggie went shopping. While in New York, it was recorded that wedding pictures were made. From New York, the couple went to Washington City and then home to Nashville.

In the last journal, Maggie went for long spells without recording journal entries and then at other times wrote quite regularly. The family's first child, Joseph Vaulx Crockett, was born on September 3, 1873. His full name never appeared in the journals, only being affectionately known as darling little Vaulx. A souvenir envelope in the last volume contained a little lock of blond hair which may have been little Vaulx's. A similar souvenir found in Volume One may have been one of Maggie's departed siblings.[196] The journal's last two years found Maggie consumed with tending to little Vaulx who was often sick. The very last entry will always be in my mind because Maggie recorded it this way; she wrote, "very busy attending to dear little Vaulx who is quite ill today." The journal ended with that entry and up until 1977, I had always assumed the child had died.

---

[196] Newspaper notice for November 8, 1856 - Died on Friday morning the 7th inst, Bolling, infant son of Mr. Joseph Vaulx of this vicinity. The friends and acquaintances of the family are invited to attend the funeral from the residence of Mr. Vaulx on the Franklin Turnpike. Burial in the Nashville City cemetery.

Epilogue

In conclusion, on the inside covers of the first two volumes, Maggie wrote the following Bible verse: *"Remember now thy Creator in the days of thy youth."* Margaret Nichol Vaulx grew up when the daily life of a young girl should have been simple and carefree. Yet due to troubles well beyond her control, Maggie's world was filled with struggles. Maggie endured many family hardships including separation, fear of harm, and death. She had responsibilities placed upon her and she persevered. Through all this, Maggie remained faithful to her Lord. One of the last recorded entries within this narrative will find Maggie being baptized into her Savior. This narrative shows clearly that Maggie was indeed an "ornament to Society and a delight to her dear parents." May readers both young and old look to Maggie and learn to make the most out of life.

Accounts of the latter years of some of the principle characters within this work are as follows.

Margaret Nichol Vaulx, the source of this narrative, was born at Hedge Lawn, the Vaulx homestead, in the area of Donelson, TN on December 17, 1844. On October 25, 1895, Maggie died at the relatively young age of 51. At the time she was residing with her mother on High Street, Nashville, TN. Maggie is buried at Nashville's Mt. Olivet Cemetery alongside her husband and oldest daughter Catherine Bell Crockett.

Joseph Vaulx, Sr., the beloved father of Maggie, was born on January 3, 1799 in North Carolina. His father Daniel moved the family to Nashville around 1809. Joseph was a successful Nashville businessman. He had local ties to General Andrew Jackson, General Robert Armstrong, George Washington Campbell, and Josiah Nichol. His wartime Nashville ties played an important role in the ability of his daughter Maggie to record such entries in her journals. Joseph Vaulx died October 22, 1878 and is buried across from Maggie in Mt. Olivet Cemetery.

Eleanor Ryburn Nichol Vaulx, the beloved mother of Maggie and wife of Joseph Vaulx, was born at the Hermitage on January 27, 1816. She was the daughter of General Robert Armstrong and Margaret Dysart Nichol. She was a devoted wife, mother, and grandmother. She died in Nashville on December 21, 1895. Eleanor is buried alongside her husband in Mt. Olivet Cemetery.

Major Joseph Vaulx, Jr., the dear brother of Maggie, was one of the most respected and well-known members of the family. He was the son of Joseph Vaulx, Sr. His mother was Susan Hobson, the first wife of Joseph Vaulx, Sr. He never knew his mother who died only one month after his birth. He was born at Hedge Lawn on September 13, 1835 and lived to see the new century. He passed from this life on February 25, 1908.

The following eulogy was taken from the *Confederate Veteran* magazine regarding his death:

> On the evening of the 23rd of February last Major Vaulx went out in a carriage to visit an old man slave, once his own servant, who had been reported to him to be in a state of destitution. Death came to him before finding the object of his search, but it will always comfort his friends to know that he died on a mission of mercy.

Joseph was educated at the Western Military Academy and was one of the original members of the Rock City Guards. He possessed a natural aptitude for military affairs; a Southern man, he early espoused the cause of the country and was made captain of Company A, 1st Tennessee Regiment of Infantry. He shared the fortunes of that distinguished regiment until its reorganization in 1862. With the reorganization, General Benjamin Franklin Cheatham sought him out, and he was commissioned an officer in the Inspector General Department and assigned to the division of Major General Cheatham and shared its fortunes to the end. He possessed the full confidence of his chief and of his associates and comrades of all ranks. Major Vaulx was always ready for duty; no man was assigned to more delicate or perilous ones, and no man performed them with more cheerfulness or sagacity. When Cheatham's Division was in action, he could be found on the front line of fire. The men were familiar with Major Vaulx, and his presence was encouraging to both officers and soldiers. He was an active participant in the great battles fought by the Army of Tennessee. These battles included Perryville, Murfreesboro, Chickamauga, the Georgia campaign, Franklin, Nashville, and Carolina. It was reported that he was the only member of Cheatham's staff not to suffer being wounded during the war. Much more could be written concerning this brave man and one only has to go to the *Confederate Veteran* publication to learn of his gallantry during the early hours of the Battle of Franklin. After the war, Joseph was in business in New York City and later Tennessee businessman. He was a prominent figure in the iron industry of Dickson, Montgomery, and Stewart Counties. His business associates included Nashville natives Edwin and Percy Warner and the Van Leers of Dickson County. Joseph never married, and was buried in the old Nashville City Cemetery alongside his mother Susan and his paternal grandparents Daniel and Catherine Vaulx.

Catherine Clement Vaulx was the younger sister of Maggie. She was known as Sister, Kate, Kattie, or Kat. She was a close companion to Maggie during those long months in 1862 and 1863. She shared in the same lonely hardships of family absence and concern over the war. She was born at Mount Alban on November 7, 1847 and lived to the age of 84. She never married, and died in 1931. Catherine is buried next to her father and mother in Mt. Olivet Cemetery.

Martha Vaulx, the youngest sister of Maggie and known as Little Mattie or Mat, was born September 3, 1852 at Mount Alban and died on January 28, 1919. She shared in some of the family separations but always had her two older sisters to lean upon. In 1883, Martha married Robert S. Cowan and later became the mother of J. Vaulx Cowan.

George Bell Crockett, the husband of Maggie was born of a distinguished Williamson County family on July 13, 1832. He was a veteran of the war and a local Nashville businessman. He passed from this life on January 2, 1888.

Joseph Vaulx Crockett, the darling love life of Maggie was known as "dear little Vaulx" in the last volume of Maggie's journals. He was born in 1873 and died in 1943. Joseph was a well known businessman of Nashville. He was in the Fire Insurance Business which served the Nashville area well. Joseph Vaulx Crockett married Mary Weakley Thomas in 1898. Joseph and wife Mary was the parents of five children and to this day have descendents living in the Nashville area. They are both buried at Mt. Olivet within the Vaulx plot.

Catherine Clement Crockett, the oldest daughter of Maggie and George Bell Crockett was born in 1875 and died of thyroiditis in 1909. She is buried in Mt. Olivet with her parents at her side.

Eleanor Armstrong Crockett, the youngest daughter of Maggie and George Bell Crockett was born in 1877. She married Eugene Crockett, a cousin. According to the 1900 Federal census, the young couple was living in Washington, DC. Eleanor later became a successful Philadelphia magazine column writer.

Appendix One

The following information can be found within the opening pages of Volume Two.

Rules for Regulating my Conduct

No 1. That the salvation of my soul shall be my first and great concern.

No 2. That I will always speak the truth and nothing but the truth; never indulge in the very least equivocal terms, but always be both verbally and substantially correct; and to this oh God set me carefully watch every word I utter.

No 3. That I shall always be ready to confess a fault or ask forgiveness for it, no matter the character or position of the person against whom I have offended.

No 4. That I will <u>daily</u> and <u>carefully</u> study the word of God.

No 5. That I will encourage meditation upon death and eternity.

No 6. That I will give my whole life to God. That I will strive never to engage in anything which I should shun if assured I was living the last hours of my life.

No 7. That upon all occasions I will discountenance improper levity and conversation in what ever company I am in.

No 8. That I will carefully guard my temper and never show the least symptoms of impatient emotion; not even by an altered look or tone of my voice.

No 9. That I will never speak impatiently to my little sisters or any of my family: on the contrary I will be kind, gentle and affectionate which will gain my desires all the sooner.

No 10. That my conversation be of love and as far as possible adapted to the tone of feeling in those with whom I converse. That I will not talk of failings and defects of others.

No 11. That I will never waste a moment of time unnecessarily.

No 12. That I will be temperate in eating, drinking &c.

No 13. That I will strictly guard against pride in dress, and every other of its manifestations; against envy, jealousy, vanity and self conceit.

No 14. That I will live only to serve God and for the good of those whom I lover. Never to seek my own pleasure or gratifications at the expense of every one else; but as far as possible forget there is self.

No 15. That I will love my dear parents and do all in my power to promote their <u>spiritual</u> and temporal happiness.

With the help of my Heavenly Father I hope to be enabled to carry into effect my resolutions.

Adopted March 16th, 1862

Tis sweet to know we have an earthly friend who will pity while witnessing our struggles to do right; and to whose face we can lift our tearful eyes in loving confidence as much as to say: "See how I hear it," and be sure of pity and sympathy. But it is sweeter far to have a heavenly Friend to whom we may lift our hearts at all times and in all places secure not only of sympathy but of aid and strength.

Nashville, June 21st/62

The 1861 epic poem "My Maryland," was destined to become a battle standard for the Confederate cause. Maggie copied it into Volume Two during the month of April 1862. In 1939, it would be officially adopted as the state song of Maryland.

My Maryland

The despot's heel is on thy shore.
Maryland, my Maryland!
His torch is at thy temple door.
Maryland, my Maryland!

Avenge the patriotic gore
That wept over gallant Baltimore.
And be the battle queen of yore
Maryland, my Maryland!

Hark to a wandering son's appeal
Maryland, my Maryland!
My mother state to thee I kneel
Maryland, my Maryland!
For life and death, for woe and weal
Thy peerless chivalries reveal.
And gird thy beauteous limbs with steel
Maryland, my Maryland!

Thou wilt not cower in the dust,
Maryland, my Maryland!
Thy beaming sword shall never rust
Maryland, my Maryland!
Remember Carroll's sacred trust
Remember Howard's warlike thrust
And all thy slumberers with the just,
Maryland, my Maryland!

Cover 'tis the red dawn of the day,
Maryland, my Maryland!
Come with thy panoplied array,
Maryland, my Maryland!
With Ringgold's spirit for the fray,
With Watson's blood at Monterey,
With fearless Lowe and dashing May
Maryland, my Maryland!

Dear Mother burst the tyrant's chain
Maryland, my Maryland!
Virginia should not call in vain
Maryland, my Maryland!
She meets her sisters on the plain
Sic simper tis the proud refrain
That baffles minions back again
Arise in majesty again
Maryland, my Maryland!

Come! For thy shield is bright and strong,
Maryland, my Maryland!
Come for thy dalliance does thee wrong
Maryland, my Maryland!
Come to thine own heroic throng
That stalks with liberty along
And give a new key to thy song
Maryland, my Maryland!

I see the blush upon thy cheek,
Maryland, my Maryland!
But thou wast ever bravely meek
Maryland, my Maryland!
But lo! There surges forth a shriek
From hill to hill from creek to creek
Potomac calls to Chesapeake
Maryland, my Maryland!

Thou wilt not yield the Vandal toll
Maryland, my Maryland!
Thou wilt not crook to his control
Maryland, my Maryland!
Better the fire upon thee roll
Better the shot, the blade, the bowl,
Then crucifixion of the soul,
Maryland, my Maryland!

I hear the distant thunder hum
Maryland, my Maryland!
For Old Line's bugle, fife and drum
Maryland, my Maryland!
She is not dead nor deaf nor dumb-
Hazza! She spurn's the Northern scum!
She breathes! She'll burn! She'll come,
she'll come.
Maryland, my Maryland

Contained within Volume Two opening pages, Maggie lists four pages of what she deems important war events. These are titled "War for Southern Independence."

<u>War for Southern Independence</u>
<u>Important Events</u>

South Carolina seceded.................................Dec 20th 1860
Texas Seceded .... Feby 1st 1861
Fort Sumpter occupied by Major Anderson...............Dec 25th 1860
Congress of S. Confederacy at Montgomery Ala.......... Feby 4th 1861
Jefferson Davis elected President of S. C. .... Feby 9th 1861
Jefferson Davis inaugurated................................ Feby 19th 1861
Lincoln inaugurated.. March 4th 1861
Arkansas seceded...March 20th 1861
Attack on Fort Sumpter..................................... April 12th 1861
Surrender of Fort Sumpter .... April 13th 1861
Lincoln issues his proclamation .... April 15th 1861
Massachusetts regiment at Baltimore .... April 19th 1861
Virginia seceded .... April 25th 1861
Charleston blockaded.. May 11th 1861
Battle of Phillips, Va... June 3rd 1861
Battle of Roming Va .... June 11th 1861
Battle of Brownsville Mo....................................June 18th 1861
Defeat of Pegram at Rock Mountain Va ....July 12th/61
Battle at Carrack Ford, Genl. Barnet killed................July 14th/61
Battle at Bull Run... July 21st/61
Genl. Polk takes command of Columbus, Ky................Sep 4th/61
Genl. Grant takes command of Paducah......................Sep 6th/61
Battle of Ganley Bridge Va................................... Sep 10th/61
Battle of Cheat Mountain Va .... Sep 12th/61
Surrender of Col. Mulligan Lexington Mo .... Sep 20th/61
Attack on Santa Rosa Island................................Oct 8th/61
Battle of Ball's Bluff..Oct 21st 1861

Battle of Springfield .... Oct 24th/61
Genl. Scott resigned .... Oct 31st
Battle of Belmont .... Nov 6th/61
Port Royal captured .... Nov 7th/61
Mason and Slidell captured .... Nov 8th/61
Occupation of Beaufort .... Dec 6th 1861
Great fire at Charleston .... Dec 11th 1861
Battle of Cheat Mountain .... Dec 13th 1861
Battle of Munfordville .... Dec 17th 1861
[South's] fleet sunk at Charleston harbor .... Dec 21st 1861
Mason and Slidell surrendered .... Dec 27th 1861
Battle of Dranesville Va .... Dec 30th 1861
Florida seceded .... Jan 18th 1861
Alabama seceded .... Jan 11th 1861
Georgia seceded .... Jan 19th 1861
Louisiana seceded .... Jan 25th 1861
Florida seceded .... Jan 18th 1861
Tennessee seceded .... Jun 8th 1861
Captured of Port Royal .... Jan 1st 1862
Attack on Huntersville Va .... Jan 5th 1862
Battle of Paintsville Ky .... Jan 6th 1862
Battle at Romney Va .... Jan 7th 1862
Battle at Roanoke Island .... Feby 7th 1862
Battle of Springfield Mo .... Feby 13th 1862
Bowling Green evacuated .... Feby 14th 1862
Surrender of Fort Donelson .... Feby 16th 1862
Battle at Sugar Creek Ark .... Feby 18th/62
Nashville occupied .... Feby 23rd/62
Columbus Ky evacuated .... Mar 3rd/62
Battle of Pea Ridge .... Mar 7th/62
Naval engagement between Merrimac and Monitor .... Mar 8th/62
Surrender of Pulaski .... Mar 11th/62
Battle of Newbern SC .... Mar 16th/62
Battle of Winchester .... Mar 23rd/62

Battle of Pittsburg Landing .... Apr 6th/62
Battle of Shiloh .... Apr 7th/62
Island No. 10 surrendered .... Apr 8th/62
Huntsville occupied... Apr 10th/62
New Orleans taken... Apr 24th/62
Fort Macon NC surrendered................................... Apr 26th/62
Yorktown evacuated .... May 4th/62
Battle of Williamsburg .... May 6th/62
Norfolk occupied .... May 10th/62
Another engagement between Merrimac and Monitor ..... May 15th/62
Battle at Front Royal .... May 23rd/62
Retreat of Banks .... May 25th/62
Battle at Hanover Court house .... May 27th/62
Corinth evacuated .... May 29th/62
Naval engagement at Memphis................................ June 6th/62
Memphis occupied .... June 7th/62
Battle of Curso Keys Va .... June 8th/62
Steamer Merrimac burnt... June 12th/62
Battle before Richmond.. June 25th/62
Battle of Mechanicville... June 26th/62
Battle of Garne's Hill .... June 27th/62
Battle of the Chickahomey .... June 28th/62
Battle of the Peach Orchard.................................... June 29th/62
Battle of White Oak Swamp.................................... June 30th/62
Battle of Turkey Bend .... July 1st/62
Battle of Dug Spring Mo... Aug 1st/62
Battle of Commerce Mo .... Aug 19th/62
Battle of Perryville .... Oct 7th/62
Victory of the Abolitionist at La Vergne Tenn .... Oct 6th/62
Victory of the "rebels" at Fredericksburg Va .... Dec 13th/62
Battle of Stones River .... Dec 31st/62

Our enemies may strip us of external distinctions and ornaments; but wisdom and grace cannot be taken from us; they may banish us from friends, relations and country; but they cannot deprive us of the presence of the Lord; they may exclude us from the benefits of common providences, rob us of Liberty and confine us in dungeons; but they cannot shut us out from the throne of grace, or bereave us of the blessings of salvation.

Hedge Lawn, August 21st, 1862

Self Examination
Copied from the book of Private Devotion Aug 8th 1862 and Recopied at Hedge Lawn, April 14th, 1863

I must remember each day that I have:

"A God to glorify– A Soul to save– Repentance to seek and perform– A body to mortify through the spirit– Graces and virtues to implore by prayer– Sins to weep over and forsake– Mercies and deliverances to remember– A hell to avoid– A paradise to gain– An eternity to meditate on– Time to redeem– A neighbor to edify– Works of charity to perform– A world to fear and yet to conquer– Devils to combat– Passions to subdue– And perhaps Death to suffer– And Judgment to undergo– And all these must be met and performed in the Graces of Jesus Christ and not in my own strengths which is perfect weakness: Phil.IV and 13th verse.

Questions for "Self Examinations"

Morning

1st. Have I this morning sought of the Lord his spiritual and protection for the day?
2nd. Am I going forth in my own strength, or simply looking to God alone to help and deliver?
3rd. Am I so sensible of my own weakness as ever to watch and pray?

4th. Am I living by faith in a daily and simple dependence on God?

5th. Do I constantly remember that I am accountable to God for the right improvement of the talents entrusted to me?

6th. Have I determined this day to lay my self out for the glory of God?

7th. Are all the faculties of my soul engaged to render affectionate, intelligent encore and us unto service?

8th. Have I resolved, in the strength of God to forsake all sin, however dear to me, and whether it be pride, temper, malice [and all] other sins?

9th. Is it my constant desire to abstain from the every appearance of evil and to keep my self unspotted from the world?

Evening

1st. Did I this morning make my resolutions to walk closely with God in dependence in his gracious assistance?

2nd. Have I this day put up my petitions against my besetting sins?

3rd. What have I committed and what have I omitted to-day?

4th. What mercies have I received this day — answers to prayers — deliverances from evils — common remarkable blessings?

5th. What have I done this day for the glory of God or the good of my fellow creature; or what opportunities have I neglected for so doing?

6th. Have I been enabled willingly to take up my cross?

7th. Have I been watching to-day against the first rising of pride, worldly mindedness? Have I guarded against the appearance of evil?

8th. Have I kept up an hourly dependence upon Divine Providence, in the duties of the day?

9th. With what success have I encountered the many sins which my circumstances or constitution inclined me?

10th. Have I been looking to Jesus as my righteousness, my strength and my example?

11th. How have I improved my time this day? Have I made my forgiveness in religion? Have I thought on Death and Judgment? Have I walked with God?

12th. Have I this day tried to mortify sin?

13th. Have I prayed and how? Have I said the Scriptures and how?

General Questions

1st. Do I think much and frequently of God and am I zealous for his glory?
2nd. Do I enjoy communion with God when I pray to Him or do I desire this?
3rd. Do I strive to become like Him?
4th. Am I actively desiring and seeking the good all around me, even as to my own?
5th. Is my love to others like that of Christ to me?
6th. Have the miseries of others called forth compassion and efforts to relieve them?
7th. Am I seeking the salvation of my fellow creatures?
8th. Is sin hateful to me? Do I loathe it as the worst of evils?
9th. Have I an habitual mourning for sin?
10th. Have I deeply felt my corruption and guilt?
11th. Do I believe that the Gospel is the appointed and only complete way of salvation?
12th. Do I believe thoroughly the only hope of forgiveness is in the blood of Christ?
13th. Am I so believing in Jesus and rely upon Him as my saviour?
14th. Am I truly grateful to God for his great salvation?
15th. Am I humble and lowly in mind, affection, and conversation?
16th. Does the suffering of Christ for sin affect my heart with godly sorrow?
17th. Do I hunger and thirst after righteousness?
18th. Do I earnestly desire to obtain that righteousness which is through Christ?
19th. Do I seek to know God myself and to diffuse his knowledge through the world?
20th. Am I laboring to spread the Gospel of Peace?
21st. Have I resigned myself to the will of God?
22nd. How do I spend my Sabbaths? Do I not in too many instances employ those opportunities in unprofitable and sinful conversation; or in doing many unnecessary works? Am I promoting the glory of God?

To be read thoughtfully and with much prayer. O! God let them sink deep into my heart and ever be practiced in me with my fellow creatures.

Rules for "Domestic Happiness"
Copied April 26th, 1862

1st. Every day let your eye be fixed on God through the Lord Jesus Christ that by the influence of his Holy Spirit you may receive your mercies from him and that you may use them to his glory.

2nd. Never suffer your regard for each other's society to rob God of your heart or of the time which you owe to God and to your own soul.

3rd. Be careful that custom and habit does not lessen your attention to each other or the pleasing satisfaction with which they were once shown and received.

4th. Whenever you perceive a languor in your affections, always make it a rule to inspect yourself. The object that once inspired regard may perhaps be still the same and the blame only attached to yourself.

5th. Be sure to avoid unkind and irritating language. Always conciliate. It is your interest and duty. Remember what God has borne with in you.

6th. Study your partner's character and disposition. Both must accommodate or you will both be unhappy.

7th. Do not expect too much. You are not always the same, no more as your partner. Sensibility must be watched over or it will become its own tormentor.

8th. When you discover feelings which you did not suspect, and this you may be sure will be the case, make it your prayer that your regard be not diminished. If you are the heirs of the grace of life, your feelings will be shortly over; you will hereafter be perfect in the divine wage. Esteem and love each other. Forbearance is the trial of this life only.

9th. Forget not that one of you must die first. One of you must feel the pang and chasm of separation. A thousand little arrows will then wound the survivor's heart.

10th. Pray constantly. You need much prayer. Prayer will engage God in your behalf. His blessings can make the bitterness of life wonderfully sweet. He can suspend all of our joys. Blessed be His holy name! He can and often does suspend our sorrows. Never pass a day without praising Him for all that is past, glorifying Him for your mercies and trust Him for all that is to come.

Mount Alban –

"God leads some of His children gently, and over a smooth and comparatively easy path; and to others He appoints the [winding] way both dark and dreary. And while the same hand leads alike over plains and through the intricate way, the favored pilgrim will not boast himself; neither will the weary one repine".

July 26, 1863

Mount Alban–

Good Nature!

"Good Nature is one of the sweetest gifts of Providence. Like the pure sunshine it gladdens, enlivens and cheers. In the midst of hate, revenge, sorrow and despair, how glorious are its effects!"

Religion

Religion! Pure and Heavenly guest. Possessed of thee, I feel I am blessed! Though every other hope depart. Still may I clasp thee to my head. And when sickness, sorrow, pain or dread. Had gathered thickly o'er my head. Ye bade the waves of sorrow cease. And pointed to the paths of peace. When hopes o'er my spirit threw, A radiant light like evening dew. Had faded from earth away, Swift as a meteor's passing ray. An angel form still lingered near, With joy my wounded heart to cheer. One angel friend mercy came. Religion was her heavenly name!

May 8th, 1864

Important to Remember!

In the Old Testament there are 39 books; 929 chapters; 23,214 verses; 592,493 words; 2,728,100 letters. In the New Testament there are 27 books; 260 chapters; 7,959 verses; 181,253 lines; 828,380 words. The middle chapter is the 117th Psalm which is also the smallest. The middle verse is the middle of the 118th Psalm. The middle line is the 15th verse of the 4th chapter of the Second Book of Chronicles. The 19th chapter of the Second Book of Kings and the 37th of Isaiah are alike.

July 31st, 1864

Appendix Two
The Jackson Building

The Jackson Building, where some person or persons unknown abandoned Maggie's journals decades after she finished Volume Six, was built in Nashville during the early 1890's. The building was located on the corner of 5th and Church, just across from the First Presbyterian Church. It consisted of seven floors, not including the basement area. The building provided leases to assorted businesses which served the downtown area. The upper three floors were rented out to patrons as personal residences. The building was razed in 1950 to make room for the Cain-Sloan Department store expansion. This following announcement appeared on May 20th, 1949 on the front page of the evening paper, the *Nashville Banner*. The May 21st, 1949, *Nashville Tennessean* newspaper article is on the next page.

Building Opposite Present Site Announced

By MILTON RANDOLPH

Announcement was made today by John Sloan, president of Cain-Sloan Company, that the firm will construct a new modern department store building to cost in excess of a million dollars, on the south side of Fifth Avenue and Church Street, the site now occupied by the Jackson Building and the Lusk Building.

JOHN SLOAN

The Cain-Sloan Company acquired this property in 1915 for the purpose of expanding its department store.

At the time the property was taken over by the Cain-Sloan Company there were leases existing which have expired or will by the end of this year.

All tenants on the upper floors (Continued on Page 6, Column 7)

Building
(Continued From Page One)

have expired and these tenants have been notified to vacate in 90 days so that the wrecking of the buildings may be started at that time.

It was explained by Sloan that considerable time can be saved by starting the wrecking and removing all the interior partitions, plumbing and electrical work from the second floor up, so that by the first of the year when the ground floor leases terminate, the buildings can be demolished in a minimum time, thereby greatly expediting the construction.

When work is started on construction of the new Cain-Sloan building shortly after January 1, 1950, it will mean the elimination of the present lobby to the Princess Theater.

Kermit C. Stengel, executive vice-president of the Crescent Amusement Company, said the lobby will be moved to its old site on Fifth Avenue, which is now occupied by a barber shop. Stengel said a thoroughly modern lobby containing innovations in panel boards, lighting and a streamlined concession stand will be installed along with an elaborate marquee with animated lighting.

This new lobby will probably be completed around the first of the year, Stengel said, adding that the theater will be completely refurbished and renovated.

The Cain-Sloan Company plans to continue to occupy its present building having extended their lease on this property for a long period. The firm plans to expand its operations greatly to include many departments which it does not now have. The present store building will be renovated to accommodate a number of these departments.

John H. Dubuisson, director of store planning, will supervise the planning and construction of the new building and the remodeling of their present quarters. Dubuisson said studies are now being made of other stores throughout the country so that the latest features of department store design and merchandising can be incorporated in the plans for the new structure. It is the intention of the firm to erect a building containing all the facilities necessary to render the best possible service and presentation of merchandise to its customers.

The new building, which will be directly across the street from the present store, will face 165 feet on Church Street and extend 120 feet south. Work on the plans will start immediately and will be completed during the time the present buildings on the property are being razed.

Cain-Sloan and Company was organized on November, 1903, by Paul Sloan, J. E. Cain, and T. H. Cain. These three men purchased Comback's Beehive, a dry goods and notion store located at 223 Fifth Avenue, North, opposite the Fifth Avenue entrance of the Arcade.

Three years later, in January, 1907, they incorporated, forming the Cain-Sloan Company with M. J. Cain, J. J. Bevington, and B. W. Landstreet as incorporators along with the three first named partners. The firm then moved to a larger building at 209 Fifth Avenue, North, which is the sixth story section of the present store.

In 1915, the company expanded further, taking in the corner of Fifth Avenue and Church with 69 feet of frontage on Fifth Avenue and 25 feet on Church with an entrance on the corner.

The main floor was completely remodeled in 1930, replacing the old wooden floor with a modern terrazzo floor. New fixtures were installed along with three modern elevators to replace the two then in use.

In 1936 the company acquired 55 additional feet of frontage on Church Street and added a fourth elevator. A new floor was added to the corner building in 1940, and air conditioning was installed through the entire building.

At the time the property was taken over by the Cain-Sloan Company there were leases existing which have since expired or will by the end of this year... tenants have been notified to vacate in 90 days so that the wrecking of the buildings may be started at that time.

Nashville Banner

May 20, 1949

Firms doing business in the lower floors of the two buildings will vacate by the close of the year... tenants [on the upper floors] have been notified to vacate in 90 days so that the wrecking of the present building may be started at that time.

Nashville Tennessean

May 21, 1949

Cain-Sloan To Erect New $1,000,000 Store

New Structure Slated at Fifth, Church; Jackson, Luck Buildings To Be Razed

Long-range plans of Cain-Sloan Co. to expand its downtown facilities, were nearing fruition yesterday with announcement that work will begin soon on a new $1,000,000 department store.

The building will be located at the southwest corner of Fifth ave. N., and Church st. directly across the street from the firm's present store. Razing of the Jackson and Luck buildings, located on the property where the new structure will stand is scheduled to begin in 90 days, according to John Sloan, Cain-Sloan president.

Long Term Leased

The company will continue to occupy its present building, having recently negotiated a long-term lease on the property. A 99-year lease on the Jackson and Luck property was obtained by Cain-Sloan in 1945.

A provision of the lease is that at some time during the term of the lease, Cain-Sloan Co. must erect a new building on the site costing not less than $400,000, which will extend to adjoining property, and which will become the property of the owners of the land.

Firms doing business in the lower floors of the two buildings will vacate by the close of the year, at which time the leases expire, Sloan said. These include Shacklett's cafeteria, Candy's shop and the Youth shop in the Jackson building; and Skeets May's Costume studio. Nashville Trunk & Bag Co., Kay's jewelry store and Florsheim shoe shop in the Luck building.

Princess to Move Entrance

The entrance to Princess theater will be moved from the Luck building to Fifth ave., according to Kermit C. Stengel, executive vice president of Crescent Amusement Co.

Thirty-nine residential tenants and 51 commercial leases, including doctors, beauty operators, lawyers, tailors and insurance men, have space in the upper floors of the Jackson building.

"All leases on the upper floors have expired and these tenants have been notified to vacate in 90 days so the wrecking of the present building may be started at that time," Sloan said.

The wrecking and removing of all interior partitions, plumbing and electrical work from the second floor up so that the first of the year when the ground floor leases terminate, the building can be demolished in a minimum time, thereby greatly expediting the beginning of construction," he said.

Annual Rent Scale

Annual rent scale to be paid by Cain-Sloan Co. for the Davidson county register at $30,000 a year for the first 20 years, $35,000 for the next 25 years, $40,000 for the next 40 years, and $45,000 a year for the remaining period.

Sloan said the firm plans to expand their operation to include a number of additional departments. The present store building will be remodeled, he said.

Planning and construction of the new building and remodeling of the present store will be supervised by John H. Dubuisson. The director said yesterday studies are being made of other department stores throughout the country "so that the latest features of store design and merchandising can be incorporated in plans for the new structure." He said it is the intention of the firm to erect a building containing all the facilities necessary "to render the best possible service and presentation of merchandise to the customers."

Work to Begin Immediately

The new building will face 166 feet on Church st. and 170 feet on Fifth ave., Sloan said. Work on the plans will begin immediately and will be completed by the time the building site is cleared, he said.

Cain-Sloan Co. was organized as a partnership in 1902 in store space at 223 Fifth ave. N. opposite the Arcade entrance. Three years later the firm was incorporated. The new company moved to larger quarters at 209 Fifth ave. N. which is the six story section of the present store. In 1915 additional frontage of 59 feet on Fifth ave. and 25 feet on Church st. were added.

Remodeled in 1930

The main floor was completely remodeled in 1930 and six years later an additional 55 feet on Church st. were acquired. The present building is leased from the Jackson estate, which has no connection with the Jackson heirs who own the Jackson building property.

Sam Shacklett of Shacklett's cafeteria said yesterday he is considering three sites for relocation, one of which is between Eighth and Twelfth avenues on Broadway. Kay's Jewelry shop has announced plans to move to the space now occupied by National Shirt Shop at 600 Church st., and Florsheim Shoe shop will be moved to 215 Sixth ave. N. Managers of other stores affected in the expansion said yesterday their relocation plans have not been completed.

Appendix Three

Index

Page Numbers in **Bold** refer to Maps, Pictures and Sketches

A

Abington, Washington (county) Va., 216, 230
Abolition, 117, 127, 288
Adams, John (CSA General), 226
Alabama, 4, 165, 287
Alford, Robert, 228
Alford, Mrs. Robert, 229
Altoona, Ala., 206
Allison, Letha (1840-1917), 246, 262
Anderson, Robert (USA Major), 4-5, 96, 286
Anaconda Plan, x11
Appomattox Court House, 242, 221, 242
Arkansas, 5, 172, 205, 268, 286
Armistead, Birda, 180
Armistead, Bob (friend), 182, 185, 203
Armistead, Mrs. Robina (family neighbor), 154
Armistead, Roberta (friend), 136, 139, 154, 177, 180, 185, 198, 272
Armistead, William Blair (family neighbor), 85, 204
Armstrong, Dr. (Vaulx family relative), 8
Armstrong, Margaret Dysart, 215
Armstrong, General Robert, 215, 279
Armstrong, James (CSA Captain), 32, 34, 39, 49, 55, 82, 114, 121, 263
Asylum, 89, 91, 98, 103, 113, 184, 199, 203, 213, 223, 264
Atlanta Campaign, 183, 184, 194, 195, 199, 206, 263
Atlanta, Ga, x11, 179, 202, 263, 179, 184, 186, 190, 200, 202, 203, 205, 209, 221, 263
Augusta, Ga, 260, 261
Aunt Amelia, (a Nichol family servant), 60

B

Baltimore, MD, 88, 227, 286
Bardwell, Mr., 45

Barnes, A. S, 1x, x, 5, 6, 24, 31, 35, 45, 54, 68, 73, 83-84, 90, 95, 109, 111, 134, 138, 144-45, 147-48, 165, 172, 179, 184, 209, 221, 232, 233, 243, 253, 257
Barrow, General George, 39
Battle of Antietam, 111
Battle of Belmont, 287
Battle of Ball's Bluff, 31, 286
Battle of Brownsville, 286
Battle of Bull Run (1st Manassas), 24, 30, 45, 151, 221, 286
Battle of Bull Run (2nd Manassas), 83, 88
Battle of Carrack Ford, 286
Battle of the Chickahomey, 288
Battle of Chickamauga, 133, 172, 280
Battle of Chancellorsville, 138, 144, 172
Battle of the Crater, 189
Battle of Cheat Mountain, 286-87
Battle of Commerce, Mo, 288
Battle of Curso Keys, Va, 288
Battle of Dallas (Ga.), 186
Battle of Dranesville, 287
Battle of Fort Donelson, x11, 35, **36**, 39, 51, 65, 92, 111, 151, 263, 287
Battle of Dug Spring, Mo, 288
Battle of Fort Sumpter, 4, 106, 151, 286
Battle of 1st Franklin, 142
Battle of 2nd Franklin, 209, 221, 224, 226, 233, 280
Battle of Front Royal, 288
Battle of Fredericksburg, 90, 109, 111, 114, 138, 151, 288
Battle of Hanover Court house, 288
Battle of Ganley Bridge, Va, 286
Battle of Garne's Hill, 288
Battle of Gettysburg, 144, 172
Battle of Iuka, 111
Battle of Lookout Mountain, 163

Battle of Marietta, 187
Battle of Mechanicville, 288
Battle of Missionary Ridge, 163
Battle of Munfordville, 287
Battle of Nashville, 209, 221, **222**, **223**, 226, 227, 233, 280
Battle of Newbern, SC, 287
Battle of New Hope Church, 186
Battle of Paintsville, 287
Battle of Pea Ridge, 45, 111, 287
Battle of Peach Orchard, 288
Battle of Perryville, 84, 96, 100, 280, 288
Battle of Phillips, Va, 286
Battle of Pickett's Mill, 186
Battle of Pittsburg Landing, 288
Battle of Resaca, 61, 186, 202
Battle of Roming, 286
Battle of Romney, Va, 287
Battle of Springfield, Mo, 287
Battle of Seven Days, 68
Battle of Shiloh, 35, 53-54, 151, 263, 288
Battle of Stones River (Murfreesboro), 34, 73, 102, 104-05, 107, 109, 111, 114, 200, 264, 280, 288
Battle at Sugar Creek, Ark, 287
Battle of Turkey Bend, 288
Battle of White Oak Swamp, 288
Battle of Williamsburg, 288
Battle of Winchester, 287
Bauch (USA General), 143
Baxter, Montgomery (a friend), 171, 176-78, 180, 182, 183, 184, 186, 191, 192, 195, 196, 245, 255, 278
Baxter, M. Dr, 267
Baxter, Nathaniel (Judge), 171
Baxter, Nate (CSA sergeant, officer), 262, 264, 268, 272
Baxter, Edmund (CSA Captain), 171, 262
Beauregard, Peter (CSA General), 5, 53, 54, 73
Beauty and Piety, 173
Bee, Bernard (CSA General), 24
BelAir Estate, 231
Belgium, 42
Berry, Mollie J. (friend and classmate), 8, 17, 23, 88, 90, 118, 121, 131, 134-40, 142, 144, 146, 149-51, 153-159, 162, 169, 172-78, 180-81, 185, 190-99, 203-04, 207, 211-12, 219, 237, 239, 245, 248, 249, 260, 266, 268, 269, 273
Berry, William W, 8, 84, 135-136, 140, 157, 186, 189, 206, 211, 217

Berry, Mrs., 136, 174, 185, 196, 197, 203, 205
Bilious fever (liver dysfunction), 154, 175
Billet doux, 192, **193**
Blackburn, Dr, 216
Blunkhall, Mr. William (a family tenant), 126, 198, 226
Blunkhall, Mrs. Susan, 136, 141, 214
Bonaparte, Napoleon, 46, 135
Booker, Sue (schoolmate), 255
Booth, John Wilkes, 253-255
Bowling, Dr. (Nashville doctor), 175, 199, 218
Bowling Green, Ky., 34-35, 287
Bradford, Amy, 226, 265, 266
Bradford, Bob, 194, 263
Bradford, Evy, 232
Bradford, Mrs. Virginia, 237
Bradshaw, (CSA Colonel). 261
Bragg, Braxton (CSA General), 73, 84- 5, 87, 96, 97-8, 100-111, 133, 200
Branch, Liza (friend), 148, 157, 171, 172, 178, 180, 181, 191, 196, 198
Branch, Sallie (friend), 148, 157-158, 180, 191, 196, 198
Branch, Theora (friend), 232
Breckenridge, John C (CSA General), 88, 91
Breeze Hill (later day name for Mt. Alban), 277
Brentwood, Tn., 104, 127, 156
Bridgeport, Ala., 163
Brown, Jane Ramsey Nichol (aunt), 28, 42, 58, 61, 81, 98, 105, 126, 190, 200, 202, 204, 207, 210, 218, 224, 230, 231, 232, 238, 239, 243, 244, 245, 246, 247, 249, 259, 261, 264, 265, 266, 268, 269, 270, 273, 274, 276
Brown, Bob (friend), 226
Brown, John (abolitionist), 3
Brown, John P. W (cousin), 61- 63, 105, 107, 200, 202, 260, 261, 266, 267
Brown, Miss (South Side Institute Student), 102, 249
Brown, Mrs. (a Morgan family neighbor), 107, 180
Brown, Trim, 272
Brown, Yoder (Nashville Unionist), 249
Brownlow, William aka Parson, 197
Bruist, Dr. (CSA physician), 261, 268, 269
Brunston, Alice (friend), 93
Brunston, Sallie (friend), 93
Buchanan, Mrs. John H. (a Morgan family neighbor), 115
Buchanan, President James, 4

Buckner, Sallie, 276
Buckner, Simon (CSA General), 35
Buell, Don Carlos (USA General), 35, 42, 54, 84, 88, 95-96
Buffalo, NY, 278
Bunting, Robert Franklin (CSA Presbyterian Chaplain), 272, 274, 276, 278
Burnside, Ambrose (USA General), 115, 189
Bushwhacking, 190

C

Caldwell, Mr. James E. (a Vaulx family friend), 101
Caldwell, Mrs. James E., 127
Calhoun, John C, 4
California, 3, 258
Camp Chase, Ohio, 194, 263
Camp Robinson, 101
Campbell, George Washington, 2, 279
Campbell, General William Boren, 75-6
Campbell Mr., (Unknown neighbor), 85
Canada, 140
Cantrell, Mrs. (Unknown neighbor), 139, 176, 195
Carney, Joe, 128
Carter, Ann (cousin), 238
Carter, Irene, 275
Carter, John (CSA General), 226
Catholic Church, 261
Charleston, SC, 4-5, 148, 154, 172, 241, 244, 286-87
Charlton, Dr, 116
Chattahoochee River, 195, 206
Chattanooga, Tn, 55, 65, 81, 155, 109, 133, 163, 172, 183, 184, 206, 244
Cheatham, Benjamin F. (CSA General), 14, 21, 85, 100, 109, 186, 225, **228**, 229, 258, 259, 280
Cheatham's Retreat, 228
Cherry Street, Nashville, 42, 270
Christian Church, 51
Christon, Miss., 162
Church Street, Nashville, 295
Cincinnati, OH. 84
City of Rocks (Nashville), 97
Clare, William (CSA Major), 227
Clare, Mary Hadley, 107, 227, 255
Hadley, Mary, 107, 227
Clay, Henry, 3
Cleburne, Patrick (CSA General), 226
Closton, Miss, 181, 187, 207, 238, 266
Coleman Capt. (CSA Officer), 265

College Street (Nashville), 117
Colored Troops (Union), 156, 229
Columbia, SC, 241
Columbia, Tn., 23, 88, 140, 156, 210, 217, 224, 236
Columbus, Ky, 286-87
Confederate States of America, 4, 42, 84, 87-88, 184
Confederate Veteran Magazine, 21, 280
Congestive chills, 205
Consumption (tuberculosis), 20, 271
Contrabands, 117
Corinth, MS, 35, 55, 88, 111, 288
Correy, Mr. (Joseph Vaulx friend), 239
Correy, Miss Brock, 266
Covington, KY, 84
Cowan, Robert S., 281
Cowan, Joseph Vaulx, 281
Cramp colic, 218
Crittenden, Thomas (Union General), 110
Crockett, Mr. George Bell, 278, 281
Crockett, Joseph Vaulx, 278, 281
Crockett, Catherine Bell, 279, 281
Crockett, Eleanor Armstrong, 281
Crockett, Eugene, 281
Crutcher, Mrs., 258
CSA, 81, 171, 175, 197, 209, 224, 257, 258, 262, 269
Cumberland Gap, 98
Cumberland River, x11, 14, 36, 97, 140

D

Daily Times and True Union, 235, 236, 237
Dalton, Ga., 179
Daniel the Prophet, 12
Davis, Jefferson, x1, **4**, 73, 88, 179, 286
Davis, Jeff (USA General), 106
Davis, Sam, 21
Declaration of War, 151
Dixie (South), 84, 138, 140, 143, 175, 177, 182, 211, 232
Dixie (song), 109
Donaldson, Colonel (USA officer), 197
Donelson, Tn, 89, 279
Dresser, (USA Major), 107
Durham, Walter, 40, 61, 95, 101, 104, 111, 140, 201
Duncan, Mary Lundie, 8, 215, 217, 275
Duncan, Mattie, 196
Duncan, Mr. (a Vaulx family friend), 205
Dunn, Ann (Cousin), 205

E

Eakin, Janie, 273
Eakin, Nannie, 273
Early Piety (Literary work), 215
Edgefield, TN, 14, 101
Edmunson, Mr. (a Morgan family friend), 92, 94, 110
Edmunson, Lena, 102, 103
Edmunson, Mary, 123-1255
Edmunson, Mrs. (a Morgan family friend), 104
Edmunson, Sallie, 102, 103, 116
Eliza, (Cousin John Lea's cook), 230
Elliot, Dr. (unknown doctor), 227
Elliston, Mrs, 259
Elm Wood Estate, 8, 88, 174, 189, 197, 198, 206
Episcopal Church, 235, 243
Emancipation Proclamation, 111
England, 4, 42
Episcopal Church, 98, 266
Erwin, W. G. (Confederate officer), 195, 236, 263
Ewell, Mrs. Lazinka Campbell (Confederate General Richard S. Ewell's wife (un-named), 255
Ewing, Cousin Lou, 86, 91, 237
Ewing, J. H. (a Vaulx family neighbor), 197
Ewing, Orville (CSA Captain), 225, 262, 272
Ewing, Mrs. Orville, 205
Ewing, W.G. (Confederate officer), 264
Ewing, Willie, 269
Exiles, 73, 88, 119-120, 134

F

Fairview, Tn, x, 301
Fall, Albert, 51, 263
Fall, Carrie Miss., 51, 199
Fall, Ellen, 51, 148, 177, 262, 266, 270, 271
Fall, James, 51
Fall, Lizzie (friend), 148, 172, 181, 199, 247, 258, 275
Fall, Phillip S. (church of Christ Minister), 51, 144, 147-148, 199, 278
Fall, Mrs., 246, 258, 261, 265, 271, 275
Falmouth, Va., 138
Farmer, Squire (a Morgan family friend), 203
First Presbyterian Church, 17, 204, 210, 215, 216, 278, 295
First Tennessee Infantry Regiment, 21, 83, 89, 97, 200, 280
Flag, 4, 54, 82, 87, 90,107, 202, 250, 253, 254

Florida, 4, 287
Floyd, John (Confederate General), 35
Flux, 195, 205
Food prices, 85
Foot, Commodore A. H, 35, 54
Foot, Dr. (unknown preacher), 146, 178, 180, 213
Ford, Dr. (Presbyterian Minister), 178, 180
Ford's Theatre, 253-54
Forrest, General Nathan B., 35, 80, 85, 89, 90, 92, 94, 100, 144, 185, 205, 206, 209, 251210, 211, 219
Forrest, Willie, 236, 263
Fort Fisher, 238
Fort Delaware, 251
Fort Henry, 35, 111
Fort Mackinac, 40
Fort Macon, NC, 288
Fort Monroe, 173, 197, 202, 203, 205
Fort Moultrie, 4
Fort Pillow, 54
Foster, R. Dr. (Confederate Physician), 84, 264, 265, 273
Foster, Mrs. Julia (neighbor), 175, 176, 217, 219
Fosters, Farmer, 267
Fosterville, Tn., 113
Foust, Stephan, 1x
France, 4, 42
Frank Ann, 1x
Frankfurt, Ky., 84, 274
Franklin, Tn., 84, 91, 122, 135, 142, 158, 219, 221, 224, 225, 226
Fugitive Slave Law, 3

G

Gale, Dr. (unknown physician), 261, 270
Gale, Ed (friend), 189, 191, 204
Gale, Joe (Confederate Officer), 226, 266, 267
Gallatin, Tn., 101
Galveston, 172
General Questions, life –291
Georgia, 4, 163, 165, 183, 184, 185, 186, 209, 247, 287
Gist, States Right (Confederate General), 226
Glen Leven, 106, 223
Goff, Mrs. (unknown lady), 92, 122
Goodwin, Willie (friend), 177, 266, 270, 272, 273, 274, 275
Gout, 66, 154
Granbury, Hiram (Confederate General), 226
Grant, General Ulysses S., 35, 53-54, 148,

163, 178, **179**, 209, 221, 233, 241, **242**, 244, 286
Great Chicago Fire, 277
Great Panic, x11, 35-36, 119, 144, 238, 239
Greenfield Estate, 174, 225
Greeneville, Tn., 150
Guerrillas, 190
Gurley, Capt., 190, 199
Gurley, Mrs. (family friend), 91

H

H. L. (unknown rebel soldier), 264
Hadley, Fenton (unknown man), 102
Hale, Nathan, 105
Hamilton, Ida, 166
Hamilton, Martha, 201
Hammond, Union General, 228, 229
Hardcastle, Yeatman, 177, 180, 190
Hardee, General, 195
Harding, John, 264, 265
Harper Ferry, MD, 5, 30, 90
Harris, Cassie Miss (unknown lady), 102
Harris, Unknown Dr, 86, 98
Harris, Mrs. Dr. Harris (wife), 87, 91
Harris, Isham, x1, 14, 39
Hayes, President William B., 247
Hays, Anna (a family friend), 105
Hedge Lawn Estate, 73-131, 75, 96, 98, 102, 279, 109, 117, 184, 235, 238, 279, 280, 289
Helm, (Confederate Officer), 260
Hendrick, Dr., 45, 62, 64
Hickman, Mammie, 198, 219, 270
Hickman, Mrs., 270, 271
High Street, Nashville, 279
Hills, Mrs., 273
Hillsborough, Tn., 135, 141
Hindman, General, 55
Hobson, Susan, 280
Holcombe, Emma, 15, 25, 59, 60, 92, 134, 154, 159, 160, 187, 207, 213, 214, 266
Holcombe, Fannie, 92, 214
Holloway, Laura, 238
Hood, John Bell (Confederate General), 179, 183, 184, 209, 217, 221, 224, 226, 227, 228, 233
Hooker, Joseph (Union General), 138, 144, 163
Hopper, Confederate Capt., 89
House, Sallie (1844-1932), 37, 177
Howard, William (Union Colonel), 107, 109
Howell, Dr., 216
Hudgins, Charles E., 301

Hudgins, Claudia Jones, 301
Hudgins, Brayton, v
Hudgins, Joseph, v
Hudgins, Katie, v
Hudgins, Marsha D, v, 301
Hudgins, Ross E, x, 277, **301**
Hudgins, Rosha, v
Hudgins, Stacy, v
Hudson, John (rebel sympathizer), 105
Humphrey, Annie, 23, 236
Humphrey, Buddie, 237
Humphrey, Judge, 135, 226
Humphrey, Pillow, 140, 219, 264, 268
Humphrey, Queeny, 23, 83, 137, 180, 181, 210, 235, 236, 237, 258, 271
Huntsville, Ala., 209, 245, 288

I

29th Indiana Volunteers, 106
5th Iowa Cavalry, 217
Intermittent fever, 210
Irving, Washington, 48
Irwinsville, GA., 243
Island Number Ten, 54, 111, 288

J

Jackson Building, x, 295, **296**, **297**
Jackson, General Andrew, x, 279
Jackson, General Thomas "Stonewall", **24**, 87-88, 90, 111, 138, 194, 206
Jackson, MS, 140
Jaundice, 218
Jefferson, Thomas, x1
Jeremiah (Old Testament Prophet), 237
Johnson, Andrew, 51, **80**, 91, 94-95, 134, 215, 218
Johnson, General Bushrod, 21
Johnson, Ida, 246, 255
Johnson Island, 199
Johnson, Mrs. Eliza, **94**
Johnston, General Albert Sidney, 31, 35, 53-55
Johnston, General Joseph E, **105**, 172, 178, 179, 183, 190, 233, 241, 250, 257, 258
Johnston, Ida, 255
Jones, Mrs. (a Morgan family neighbor), 112
Jones, Mrs. (family friend), 154, 157

K

Kansas, 3
Kelly, Dr. (unknown doctor), 174, 204
Kentucky, 202, 213, 215, 224, 262

Kentucky Campaign, 84, 87, 96, 109
King, Mollie (unknown friend), 92
Kingsley, Mrs. (unknown lady), 128
Kirkman, John, 61, 105, 107
Knight, Union General, 228, 229
Knox, Mrs., 273
Knoxville, Tn., 100-101, 155, 197, 216, 249

L

Langley, Dr. (Presbyterian Minister), 275
La Vergne, Tn., 86-88, 91-93, 100, 102, 110, 156, 200, 288
Lea, Cousin John, 223, 224, 225, 226, 227, 228, 229, 237
Lea, Cousin Lizzie, 46, 230
Lealand Estate, 225-30
Lebanon, Tn., 85
LeDuc, William (Union Colonel), 244, **247**, 249, 250
Lee, General Robert E, 105, 111, 138, 144, 172, 178, 189, 233, 241, **250**, 257, 278
Lexington, Ky, 84
Lexington, Mo, 286
Lincoln, Abraham, 1x, x1, 3, **5**, 80, 106, 211, 214, 215, 218, 253, 254, 286
Loring, William (Confederate General), 260
Louisiana, 4, 172, 287
Louisville, KY., 273
Luter, Mrs. Matilda, 92, 95, 102, 213, 214

M

Mack, (Cousin John Lea's foreman), 229
Manassas, Va, 221
Maney, George (Confederate General), 65, 97, 258
Maney, Mr. (a Judge and family friend), 209
Maney, Judge Mrs. (a Vaulx family friend), 205
Marietta, Ga., 190,
March to the Sea, 184, 206, 207, 209
Marshall, Earl W., 1x
Maryland, 144, 253
Martin, Charlie, 268
Martin, Dr., 28, 254, 265
Martin, Harry, 263, 264, 267
Martin, Henry, 272
Martin, Molly, 254
Martin, Player, 200, 236
Martin, Terry, 23
Martin, Willie, 265
Masonic Temple, 267
Massachusetts Regiment, 5, 286

Massengale, Mrs., 264
Mason, J. M., 42, 287
Maury County, Tn., 139
Maxwell House Hotel, 278
May, Jimmie, 263
May, Miss., 134
Mayson, Anna, 199, 248, 267
Mayson, Joe (CSA soldier), 261, 264, 265, 273
McBrantly, Rev. (minister), 270
McCall, Sam, 261
McClellan, Geo. B. (Union General), 83, 90, 215, 218
McCook, Robert (Union General), 81, 190
McEwing, Kittie, 264
McGavock, Mr., 265
McGavock, Mary, 268
McKee, John Miller, x11, 144
McLean, Wilmer, 221
McNairy, C. (a female cousin), 186
McNairy, Frank (Confederate Colonel), 65, 263
McNealy, Rev. (Army chaplain), 269
McPherson, James (Union General), 194
Meade, George C. (Union General), 144
Meigs, Fielding (Union Captain), 229,
Meigs, Mrs., 244
Melrose Park, 184
Memphis, Tn., 111, 205, 244, 261, 288
Mercer, Samuel C (Newspaper Editor), 235, 236, 237
Merrimac, 111, 287-88
Micaria (Southern literary work), 231
Mississippi, 4, 113, 172, 264,
Mississippi River, 54, 111, 148, 170
Military Draft, 203
Military Order, 210
Military Pass, 86, 91, 115, 117, **118**, 205, 206
Miles, Captain (Union Officer), 210
Miller, John (Union General), 106, 231
Miller, Mr. (unknown man), 213
Mississippi, 260
Missouri Compromise, 3
Mississippi River, x, 11
Mitchell, (Union General), 84, 117
Mobile Ala, 82
Montgomery, Ala, x1, 286
Montgomery, Mrs. (a Vaulx neighbor), 156
Monitor, 287-88
Mooney, Josie (Sister Kate's friend), 122
Mooney, Mrs. (a Morgan family neighbor), 93, 122
Moore, Annie (school mate), 171, 173, 177,

178, 199, 213, 238
Moore, Miss Hattie, 214, 238
Morgan, Berry (cousin), 75, 100, 112, 126, 128, 263
Morgan, Calvin (cousin), 75, 87, 100-101, 103, 112, 126, 128, 251, 254, 270
Morgan, Frank (cousin) ,74, 79-80, 84-85, 92-95, 97-98, 103, 109-110, 123, 174, 203, 212, 234, 235
Morgan, Jane L. Williams ,73-74, 80, 83, 86-87, 89-91, 93-94, 97-98, 101, 103-104, 107, 110, 112-116, 120, 123, 126, 129, 135, 149, 184, 186, 190, 195, 238
Morgan, John Hunt (Confederate General), 101, 133, 150, 203
Morgan, (Confederate Colonel), 93, 97
Morton, Captain James St. Clair, 81, 106
Mount Alban (home), **2**, 36, 38, 56, 61, 67, 75-78, 86-89, 96, 98, 100, 106-107, 109, 119, 121, 134, 153, 161,162,165, 166, 167,168, 170, 173, 177, 178, 180, 181, 189, 218, 223, 224,225, 226, 230, 231, 233, 237, 248, 265, 267, 277, 281, 289
Mt. Olivet Cemetery, 106, 231, 279, 281
Murfreesboro, Tn., 88, 91, 95, 97-98, 100-104, 109-110, 112-113, 121, 126, 133, 146
Murmuring in the Trees (piano work), 170
My Maryland (epic poem), 153, 284

N

Nashville Banner, 295, 296
Nashville City Directory, 171, 175
Nashville City Hospital, 171
Nashville Daily Press, 160
Nashville Press and Times, 270
Nashville Daily Times and True Union, 299
Nashville Old City Cemetery, 215, 278, 280
Nashville Tennessean, 295, 297
Nashville Union and American, x11, 31
Nashville, Tn., 1x, x, x11, 17, 31, 35-36, 39, **40**, 43, 86, 90-92, 94-95, 97-98, 100, 103, 109, 127, 134, 140, 151, 159, 169, 184, 197, 199, 200, 209, 210, 215, 216, 221, 223, 224, 228, 230, 231, 232, 233, 234, 238, 254, 270, 277, 278, 279, 284, 301, 287, 301
Nashville University, 21
Nebuchadnezzar (King of Babylon), 237
Negley, James (Union General), 81, 84, 90-91, 93
Negroes, 191, 197, 203, 218, 219, 224, 229, 236
Nelson, William (USA General), 84, 106

Neuralgia, 185
New Jersey, 215
New Orleans, La., x1, 111, 145, 288
New York, 259, 278, 280
Niagara Falls, 278
Nichol, Uncle Alex Ramsey, 42, 83,
Nichol, Brad, 260
Nichol, Ben McCulluch (cousin), 33
Nichol, Dorcie (cousin), 270
Nichol, Dellie, 271
Nichol, Edgar, 129
Nichol, Eleanor Rayburn (Grandma), 28, 43, 62, 64, 68, 111, 117, 126, 137, 200, 215, 216, 217, 230
Nichol, Mrs. Frank, 266
Nichol, James (uncle), 272
Nichol, Josiah, 28, 215, 230, 279
Nichol, Josiah (cousin), 200, 263
Nichol, Aunt Julia, 90
Nichol, Leslie, 232
Nichol, Mamie, 269
Nichol, Margaret Dysart, 279
Nichol, Mary, 271
Nichol, Sarah, 29, 249
Nichol, Sophy (cousin), 261, 268
Nichol, William (maternal great uncle), 230, 244
Nicholas, Mrs., 267, 270
Nicholas, Mary, 145
Nolensville, Tn., 110
Norfolk, 5, 111, 288
North Carolina, 5, 165, 279

O

Oath of allegiance, 105, 137, 236, 254
Ohio, 150, 199
51st Ohio Infantry Regiment, 40
59th Ohio Infantry Regiment, 107
Overton, John, 46, 227, 230
Overton, Mrs. John, 104

P

Paducah, Ky., 45
Paine, Thomas, 3
Panelle, Elise Miss., 160
Parkhurst, Union Colonel, 254
Paul the Apostle, 9
Pemberton, John (Confederate General), 148, 241
Penitentiary, 62, 63, 68, 92, 105, 107, 190, 199, 254, 259
Pennsylvania, 144

Percy, Charlie, 27, 39, 45, 137, 145, 171, 181, 186, 189, 190, 210, 231, 258, 262, 265, 267, 268, 271, 273, 275
Percy, Ellen, 28, 41, 50, 53, 70, 117, 200, 201, 202, 204, 205, 212, 231, 234, 235, 237, 243, 246, 247, 258, 259, 260, 261, 264, 265, 266, 268, 269, 271, 272, 273, 274, 276
Percy, Hettie, 70, 143, 154, 204-05, 212, 231, 232, 238, 244, 246, 262, 269
Percy, Joe (cousin), 226, 261, 264, 268
Percy, Thomas (cousin), 199, 237, 263, 265
Perkins, Daniel Price, 76, 100-02, 109, 112, 116, 251, 254, 270
Perkins, Ella Brown (cousin), 38, 52, 61, 81, 104, 147, 175, 176, 211, 217, 231, 245, 246, 249, 254, 260, 264, 265, 266, 267, 268, 271
Perkins, John Preston (baby boy), 260
Perkins, Morgan, 205, 208
Perkins, Samuel Fearn, 38, 41, 52, 147, 175, 194, 200, 213, 217, 231, 238, 243, 244, 245, 248, 250, 254-255, 268, 271, 272
Perkins, Nannie, 186, 203, 210, 231, 238, 243, 255, 269
Perkins, Kate Morgan (cousin), 76, 78, 80, 102, 104, 123, 126, 134, 149, 195, 203, 209, 212, 235, 237, 248, 254
Perkins, Mary (cousin), 76, 80-81, 100, 104, 113, 116, 122
Perkins, Nancy (cousin), 127
Peters, James Dr., 139
Petersburg, Va., 189, 233, 238, 250, 251
Philadelphia, PA., 199
Pickets, 41, 42, 43, 79, 85, 86, 88, 89, 90, 91, 96, 100, 113, 135, 159, 224
Pillow, Gideon (Confederate General), 23, 35, 237
Pneumonia, 171
Plague, 197
Polk, Mrs. James K., 277
Polk, Leonidas (Confederate General), 35, 286
Pope, General, 54, 83
Port Hudson, 172
Porterfield, Frank, 264
Price, General, 35, 45, 85, 96, 101
Provine, Dr., 79, 82
Provisional Army of Tennessee, 14
Provost Marshal, 117
Pulaski, Tn., 205, 217, 238, 287

Q

Quartering of Troops, 207

Quintard, Dr. Charles T. (Confederate Chaplin), 265, 266, 267

R

Rains, Lizzie, 6
Rainey, Mr., 274
Rancks, Lil (cousin), 272
Read, Sallie, 181, 212, 218, 245
Reese (CSA Colonel), 272
Rice, Dr. (Memphis physician), 261
Richmond, Va., x1, 5, 88, 233, 241, 250, 288
Robertson, James (early Nashville settler), 270
Robertson, Dr. Felix, 270
Rock City Guard Unit, 14, 21, 261, 264, 265, 268, 280
Rock Mountain, Va, 286
Rogers, Miss (friend), 187
Rodgers, Captain Sydney, 260
Rome, Ga., 184
Rosecrans, William (USA General), 106, 107, 133, 155, 163
Rosseau, Lovell H (USA General), 84, 88, 106, 110
Rules and Regulation, 136, 292, 283, 289
Rutledge, Minnie Miss, 243

S

Sacrament, 210
Safeguard Order, 85, 106-07, 136, 230, 237
Santa Rosa Island, 286
Saunders, Ed (CSA officer), 260, 264
Savannah, Ga., 233, 259
Schofield, John (USA General), 209, 221, 224
Scott, Preston Dr., 268
Scott, Winfield (USA General), x11, 5, 214, 287
Sealy, Allie, 177-78, 181, 186, 245
Self Examinations, 78, 85, 87, 136, 289
Servant, 210
Seward, William H., 42, 253-254
Sharp, Mrs. (a Morgan family neighbor), 115, 116
Sharpe, Sallie (friend), 113
Shelbyville, Tn., 126, 128, 138, 141, 149, 203, 263
Sheridan, Philip (USA General), 233
Sherman, William (USA General), 163, 172, 178-179, 183-184, 194-195, 203, 206-**207**, 209, 221, 233, **241**
Sidell, W.H. (Union gunboat), 140
Sill, Joshua (USA General), 104, 110
Sion, Mrs. (friend), 153

Slidell, John, 42, 287
Smiley, Mrs. (a Morgan family neighbor), 105
Smith, Kirby (CSA General), 84
Smith, Tom Mrs., 114
Smuggling, **201**, 204,
Snowden, Robert B. (CSA Colonel), 261, 269
South Carolina, x1, 3, 4, 148, 165, 241, 247, 286
South Side Institute, 15, 17, 134, 159-163, 165-170, 177-178, 180-181, 189, 214
South Side Institute classes, 29, 160, 162, 166
Sparta, Tn., 89
Spencer, Kayla, v
Spencer, Richard, v
Spring Hill, Tn., 139, 207
Springfield, Ill., 253
Statistics, War, 257
Storm Party, 173-76
St. Cloud Hill, 81,101
Steadman, (Union General), 244
Stephens, Alexander H., 4
Stoneman, George (General), 233
Stowe, Harriet B, 9
Strahl, Otho (CSA General), 226
Sue Bettie W. (a friend of Brother Joe), 211
Summer Street (Nashville), 178
Synder, Mrs. (unknown Yankee lady), 122

T

Tableaux (vivid display), 154
Tatting, 199, 205-07, 210, 212
Taylor, Mr. (Confederate soldier, spy), 91-92, 94-95, 97-98, 100, 102, 112, 264
Taylor, Mrs. (a Morgan family friend), 93
Taylor Depot, 265
Tennessee, x1, 5, 36, 102, 105, 111, 172, 184, 197, 209, 287
Tennessee Iron Industry, 280
Tennessee River, x11, 221,
Tennessee State Library and Archives, 236
Tennessee Valley Authority, 301
Texas, 3, 4, 172, 267, 270, 286
Thanksgiving Day, 88
The American Crisis, 3
The Hermitage, 279
The Official Records of the War of Rebellion, 21
The Prophet Daniel, 12
The Sacra Privata, 77
The Tariff of 1828, 3
Thomas, George (USA General), 133, 163, 209, 221, 233

Thomas, Mary Weakley, 281
Thompson, Bessie (unknown), 187
Thompson, Charlie, 265, 274
Thompson, John, 223, 224
Thompson, John Mrs., 106,147
Thompson Lane, 219, 223-24
Thompson, Sallie, 147
Total Destruction, 206
Todd, Mrs., 268
Trabue, Mr. (a Morgan family friend), 97, 112
Traveller's Rest, 227
Trent Affair, 42
Trimble, Les, 23
Triune, Tn., 36, 45, 48, 134, 147, 194, 200, 202, 205, 207, 213, 238, 244, 249, 264, 266, 269, 274
Trunsdale, Col William, (Union chief of Police), 117
Tullahoma, Tn., 112
Typhoid fever, 116

U

Umbra (head-dress), 175, 209-212, 217
Uncle Tom's Cabin, 10
USS Chattanooga, 244
University of Tennessee, 277

V

Vallandigham, Clement, 140
Van Dorn, Earl (CSA General), 127, 139
Van Dorn William (USA Lieutenant), 140
Vaulx, Andrew, 224, 230
Vaulx, Bolling (brother), 278
Vaulx, Catherine Clement (grandmother), 280
Vaulx, Catherine Clement (sister, Kate), 30, 40, 49, 59, 67, 84, 90-92, 98, 109, 115-118, 129, 134, 138-139, 143, 148, 158-159, 162, 174-176, 178, 182, 194, 198-199, 204-205, 206, 210-213, 214, 215, 224, 234, 239, 244, 258, 262, 269, 275, 277, 281
Vaulx, Daniel, 279, 280
Vaulx, Eleanor Ryburn Armstrong (Ma), 38, 45, 53, 57, 63, 83, 86, 89-90, 92, 95, 97-98, 102, 104, 109, 114-117, 119-120, 122, 127, 129-131, 134, 137- 140, 142-143, 145-146, 150, 155, 158, 162, 165-166, 168, 170, 171, 175, 177, 182, 183, 184, 185, 190, 194, 195, 199, 200, 202, 203, 204, 205, 206, 211, 212, 214, 215, 216, 217, 228, 229, 230, 248, 262, 264, 267, 271, 277, 278, 279
Vaulx, Harry (family servant), 65
Vaulx, Henry (family servant), 175

Vaulx, Joseph (Pa), 2, 14-**15**, 38, 57, 59, 63, 68, 88-89, 91, 103-104, 106, 109, 114-115, 117, 119-121, 134-136, 162, 166, 168, 170, 174, 175, 183, 186, 193, 195, 196, 199, 200, 205, 206, 208, 209, 210, 212, 214, 215, 216, 218, 223, 224, 225, 229, 230, 231, 233, 234, 235, 239, 243, 248, 258, 264, 276, 277, 278, 279, 280

Vaulx, Joe Major (Brother), 14, 21, 39, 46, 49, 55, 57, 82, 87, 90, 100-102, 104, 106, 110, 112-114, 116, 121, 128-129, 134, 138-141, 143, 163, 173, 176, 177, 186, 189, 190, 197, 199, 200, 201, 203, 204, 205, 207, 208, 209, 211, 224, 225, **227**, 228, 234, 237, 243, 246, 257, 258, 259, 260, 261, 262, **263**, 264, 265, 267, 268, 269, 270, 272, 277, 280

Vaulx, Margaret Nichol, 1x, x, **x111,** 115, 271, 277, 279

Vaulx, Mattie (sister, Mattie, Mat), 40, 42, 46, 49, 57, 66, 89, 103, 109, 114, 119, 134-137, 142-143, 145-147, 150, 154-159, 176, 185, 186, 193, 195, 203, 204, 205, 206, 210, 212, 213, 214, 215, 224, 226, **227**, 243, 244, 245, 246, 248, 249, 255, 258, 259, 260, 261, 264, 277, 281

Vaulx, Uncle William, 244

Vicksburg, 31, 111, 141, 148, 172, 241

Virginia, 5, 90, 139, 165, 172, 209, 250, 286

W

Wallace, William Vincent (composer), 170

War for Southern Independence, 111, 153, 286

Washington D.C., x11, 5, 87, 253, 254, 278, 281

Watkins, Irene, 47, 177, 248, 259, 266, 272

Watkins, Willie, 262

Weaver, Dempsey ,77, 80, 83, 84, 85, 88, 89, 91, 92, 97, 98, 103, 112, 114-115, 117, 129, 203, 212, 217

Weaver, Mrs., 80, 84, 86, 100, 110

Weber, Mr. (music teacher), 162, 167-170, 183, 187

Western Military Institute, 21, 280

West View Plantation, 36, 38-43

West Wood estate, 272

Wharton, Dr. (Church of Christ Minister), 150, 153-154, 157-159, 162-163,166, 171, 174, 177, 178, 180, 181, 185, 187, 189, 190, 192, 194, 195, 199, 202, 203, 206

Wheeler, Joseph (Confederate General), 195, 203, 251

Whelan, Bishop, 126, 128

Wheeling, WV, 272

White, Nannie (friend), 172, 205, 212,

Wilkes, Captain Charles, 42

Wilkins, Mrs., 264

Wilmot Proviso, 3

Wilson, Eugene (a CSA soldier), 128

Wilson, Fannie, 76, 84, 90, 95, 115, 130,

Wilson, Lucy, 84, 90, 95, 103, 115, 130, 209

Wilson, Thomas, 89, 263

Williamson County, Tn., 123

Wilmington, VA., 238

Winchester, Va., 46, 115

Woodfolk, Laura, 258, 262

Wood, Thomas J. (USA General), 224

Woods, Albert Lee, 214

Woods, James Mr. (a Vaulx neighbor), 138, 225, 226, 227, 230, 231, 234, 238, 269

Woods, James Mrs., 138, 175, 176, 191

Woods, Jimmy, (CSA POW soldier), 272, 273

Woods, Joe (a Vaulx neighbor), 139, 227

X

Y

Yankee (Northern slang name), 185, 189, 190, 193, 196, 199, 203, 206, 225, 226, 229, 230, 234,

Yeatman, Henry, 272

Yorktown, 288

Z

Zollicoffer House, 117

Bibliography

The Private Journals of Maggie N. Vaulx, 1861-1865

Barnes, *A Brief History of the United States* by Joel Dorman Steel, P.H.D, F.G.S and Esther Baker Steele, Lit.D., published by the American Book Company, New York, NY, copyright 1885

Walter T. Durham, *Nashville, the Occupied City 1862-63*, (Knoxville, the University of Tennessee Press)

War of Rebellion, A Compilation of the Official Records of the Union and Confederate Armies, 1880-1901

John Miller McKee, *The Great Panic*. Nashville: Johnson and Whiting, Publishers, 1862

The Confederate Veteran Magazine
Southern Bivouac, August 1885
Harper's Weekly
The Nashville Times
Nashville *Daily Times and True Union*
Nashville *Union and American*
Nashville *Daily Press*

Davidson County Tennessee Archives
Tennessee State Library and Archives, Nashville
The Ohio Historical Society

Sketches provided by Pepper Mayfield

About the Author

I consider it an honor to be able to present this historical biography to my generation of readers. It has been a labor of love for over 35 years.

I was born in Nashville, Tennessee on August 2, 1950 to Charles and Claudia Jones Hudgins. At that time, my family was living at the Separation Center located between Radnor Yard and Franklin Pike. My family moved to East Nashville in the early 1950s and subsequently to Williamson County, TN in 1958. There at Old New Hope School while in the second grade, I met Miss Marsha D. Hughes. We were close friends throughout our school years. We dated after graduation and married in 1970. The marriage produced five wonderful children and six beautiful grandchildren. Except for a six-year military service and several years out of the area with the Tennessee Valley Authority, Fairview has been my family home since 1973.

www.ingramcontent.com/pod-product-compliance
Lightning Source LLC
Chambersburg PA
CBHW052012070526
44584CB00016B/1721